The Eclectic Trainer

EDITED BY

Robert E. Lee
Shirley Emerson

Geist & Russell Companies
Limited
Galena, Illinois
Iowa City, Iowa

First Printed September 1998

10 9 8 7 6 5 4 3 2 1

Manufactured in the United States of America

ISBN 1-884228-28-3

Library of Congress Catalog Card Number:
98-74054

Geist & Russell Companies, Ltd. Editorial Offices:
833 N. Johnson Street
Iowa City, Iowa 52245
Tel./Fax: (319) 337-4874

About the Editors

ROBERT E. LEE, Ph.D., is clinical director of the doctoral marital and family therapy specialization at Michigan State University. He has been in the clinical practice of marital and family therapy for 30 years and, for at least two decades, has provided supervision to clinicians in private and agency practice. He is an Approved Supervisor of the American Association for Marital and Family Therapy and a Diplomate in Clinical Psychology, American Board of Professional Psychology.

Dr. Lee has published extensively with regard to professional training, marriage and family life, divorce, and individual and family assessment. In recent years he has helped develop and administer the national examination program in marital and family therapy. On a more personal level, he is married to a physician and has two daughters. He believes that being the father of daughters is the greatest thing that has ever happened to him. That, and being the husband of a physician, have also raised his consciousness about attitudes and behaviors with regard to women. Any insensitivities in this regard are solely his responsibility and should not be blamed on his family—who have done their best.

SHIRLEY EMERSON is a Professor of Counseling and a licensed Marriage and Family Therapist. She has been in clinical practice for 20 years. Her research and writing reflects her eclectic interests—from the results of abuse in families and relationships, to the use of novels and stories in teaching about families, to the healing power of groups. She was the first Approved Marriage and Family Supervisor in Nevada, and is now actively training other supervisors. She has served on the state licensing board for 10 years, and worked with Bob Lee, her co-editor, on the Board of the Association of Marital and Therapy Regulatory Boards. Her pet "peeve" is abuse in any form, and led to endeavors to reduce abusive practices between therapists and clients, teachers and students, and supervisors and interns.

On the personal side, she is happily married for 44 years to a research chemist, also a professor. They have two sons, one a chemical engineer and the other a computer specialist, and one daughter, a clinical psychologist. They also have six grandchildren who are beautiful, brilliant, challenging, and subjects of many stories—if you show the slightest willingness to listen to their grandparents. Marriage and family are central interests in her life!

Contributors

Julie Brownell
Department of Family and Child Ecology
Michigan State University
East Lansing, Michigan

Marsha T. Carolan
Department of Family and Child Ecology
Michigan State University
East Lansing, Michigan

Heidi J. Dombeck
Marriage, Family, and Child Counseling
  Program
School of Education
University of San Diego
San Diego, California

Timothy F. Dwyer
Department of Psychiatry
Louisiana State University School of Medicine
New Orleans, Louisiana

Shirley Emerson
Department of Counseling
University of Nevada, Las Vegas
Las Vegas, Nevada

Deborah Kloosterman
Department of Family and Child Ecology
Michigan State University
East Lansing, Michigan

Patricia B. Kochka
Department of Family and Child Ecology
Michigan State University
East Lansing, Michigan

Marjorie J. Kostelnik
Department of Family and Child Ecology
Michigan State University
East Lansing, Michigan

Robert E. Lee
Department of Family and Child Ecology
Michigan State University
East Lansing, Michigan

Patricia A. Markos
Department of Counseling
University of Nevada, Las Vegas
Las Vegas, Nevada

Eric E. McCollum
Department of Family and Child
Development
Virginia Polytechnic and State University
NOVA Graduate Center
Falls Church, Virginia

Chandra Nagirreddy
Profile Employee Assistance Program
Centura Health
Colorado Springs, Colorado

William C. Nichols
The Nichols Group, Inc.
Watkinsville, Georgia

Esther E. Onaga
Department of Family and Child Ecology
Michigan State University
East Lansing, Michigan

William H. Quinn
Marriage and Family Therapy Program
University of Georgia
Athens, Georgia

Judith VanderWal
Department of Family and Child Ecology
Michigan State University
East Lansing, Michigan

Timothy R. Waskerwitz
Department of Family and Child Ecology
Michigan State University
East Lansing, Michigan

Joseph L. Wetchler
Department of Behavioral Sciences
Purdue University Calumet
Hammond, Indiana

Lee M. Williams
Marriage, Family, and Child Counseling
Program
School of Education
University of San Diego
San Diego, California

Contents

Part One
A CLIMATE SUPPORTIVE OF LEARNING

Part Two
INTEGRATIVE AND ECLECTIC SUPERVISION

Part Three
ENLISTING THE VOICE OF THE CLIENT

Part Four
ATTENDING TO CONTEXTUAL INFLUENCES

Preface

Why another book on supervision? We have put together contributions from a variety of marital and family therapy trainers and we would like to tell you why.

Our collaboration began several years ago. Because of our involvement in state licensure and the national examination program for marital and family therapists, we had an opportunity for long discussions. Because we both were trainers, supervision—and our mutual self-doubt—was a frequent topic. It seemed a natural subject for joint research and writing.

There already were excellent definitive textbooks on the models and methods of supervision. However, we wanted to add to these a book of supplementary readings that therapists just beginning to venture into the supervision field might find interesting, helpful in the most practical way, stimulating, and even buoyant. We wanted something that captured the life and joy of supervision, on the one hand, and kept things simple, on the other. We wanted to capture the essentials, offer minimalist presentations that were logical and easy to implement, and get people started into their supervisory careers with a sense of ease, conviction, hope, and joy. We knew that becoming a supervisor, like becoming a therapist, is a lifelong process. We wanted to offer a base and some innovative ideas with which training careers could be started, and on which complexity, nuances, and esoterica could be added over time.

There probably is an optimal level of gravity and arousal in most pursuits. It often is problematic if one is not worried enough, or if one is too worried. We wanted to strike a balance in this book. Supervision should not appear to be too grim, worrisome, or esoteric. Nor should it be taken too lightly. There is, in our personal opinions, too much fear in all of the persons involved in the therapy process—from the clients, to the therapists (especially students and interns), to the supervisors. We wanted to acknowledge fear and trepidation as normal to the supervision process, but also to "lighten things up." Accordingly, we decided to invite fellow trainers to contribute something from their perspective that a learning (and aren't we all always learning?) supervisor might find useful. This volume is the result.

A cynic once said, "There is a difference between being an eclectic and a Renaissance man." The implication is that eclecticism involves breadth while lacking conceptual connections, depth and, in some cases, investment. In contrast to this cynical statement, we do have a conceptual framework and driving values. The conceptual framework is provided by an integrative approach that takes into account the many ways of thinking about and approaching training and therapy challenges—moving from the simple and obvious to the complex and esoteric—and the developmental level of the supervisor as well as the therapist. We believe that an eclectic approach is best suited to helping therapists develop their own unique treatment personality and resources while equipping them to deal most adequately, in terms of skills and outlook, with their future clinical lives. We believe that good training is collaborative, strengths-focused, and developmental.

Accordingly, we attempt in this book to stimulate conversation, raise consciousness, and provide strategies and innovative techniques in four areas: (1) establishing a climate supportive of learning; (2) undertaking integrative and eclectic supervision; (3) taking advantage of collaborations possible throughout the training system; and (4) appreciating the wider context that influences what we perceive and therefore think, feel, say, and do.

When people are afraid, learning is inhibited. In too many disturbed families, institutional settings, rigid organizations, and some supervision groups, a feeling of emotional safety is missing. The first step in teaching, supervising, or therapy is the necessity to provide a safe environment. In Chapter 1 a group model is applied to the relationship between family therapy interns and supervisors, and ways are suggested to enhance growth by minimizing fear. In Chapter 2 we look at the positive and negative nature of power and how power flows up and down the training system. Chapter 3 considers the importance of self-disclosure by supervisors. It describes a recent qualitative study and discusses types of self-disclosure, the potential benefits and risks, and factors indicating and contraindicating its use.

Part 2 addresses the process of integrative and eclectic supervision and provides some basic and innovative approaches. In Chapter 4 we present a minimalist model that beginning supervisors can use to get started. Chapters 5 and 6 give an appreciative look at live, videotape, and case presentation approaches to supervision and explore their respective uses and limitations. Chapter 7 then describes the use of sand play in supervision, Chapter 8 looks at parallel processes and blind spots at all levels of the training system, and Chapter 9 explores the metaphors that govern training.

In Part 3, the contributors emphasize the importance of collaboration to training. Collaboration needs to occur between supervisors and trainees, but also between these two parties and clients. Several techniques are offered that make explicit the clients' role in training by giving them a voice in supervision.

Finally, Part 4 deals with human diversity and the biases, values, judgments, assumptions, and comfort zones involved in therapy and training. Perhaps the initial, and even the best, approach to appreciating diversity is to become aware of one's own culture. Chapter 13 suggests ways in which supervisors and therapists in training can be introduced to their own culture. Chapter 14 explores the implications of gender role at all levels of the training system and describes how awareness of gender can be integrated into training. Chapter 15 raises some of the salient issues faced when working with gay, lesbian, or bisexual trainees or clients. It also describes some likely perspectives of gay, lesbian, or bisexual supervisors. In Chapter 16, a senior-level college professor gives a personal narrative that illustrates how unquestioned assumptions and cultural values can turn what is needed to be a cooperative, therapeutic relationship into a destructive one. Finally, Chapter 17 describes a formal model designed to facilitate teaching of an integrative ecosystemic approach to supervision.

Robert E. Lee
Shirley Emerson

PART ONE

A Climate Supportive of Learning

CHAPTER 1

Creating a Safe Place for Growth in Supervision

Shirley Emerson

When people are afraid, learning is inhibited. In too many disturbed families, institutional settings, rigid organizations, and some supervision groups, a feeling of emotional safety is missing. The first step in teaching, supervising, or therapy is the necessity to provide a safe environment. The author suggests a model applicable to any supervision group, work group, organization, classroom, or family. A group model, specifically applied to the relationship between family therapy students or interns and supervisors, suggests ways to enhance growth by minimizing fear.

Supervision of family counseling-therapy students and interns has been studied extensively (Borders, 1992; Mead, 1990; Mueller & Kell, 1972; Rosenblatt & Mayer, 1975). The intent of this article is to stimulate thinking and discussion among supervisors about some of the less tangible aspects of supervision. A group supervision model is suggested. The model encourages students' own growth as they learn ways to encourage parallel growth in their clients. The model, adaptable to any supervision situation, formal or informal, is presented here in the context of family therapists' supervision during graduate training and internship.

PROBLEMS IN SUPERVISION SESSIONS

In the supervision of students and interns in the helping professions, one theme too often prevails: fear. Beginning students are fearful that they will be found deficient by their supervisors, especially when their performance is observed live or on videotape in which mistakes cannot be

Source: This chapter originally appeared in *Contemporary Family Therapy,* 1996, 18, 393–403. Reprinted by permission of Plenum Publishing Corporation.

hidden (Salvendy, 1993; Sappington, 1984; Taibbi, 1993). "Neurosis-bound" is the descriptor used by Stoltenberg and Delworth (1987) when referring to anxiety about evaluation. Kottler and Blau (1989) described most therapists in graduate school as "insecure, confused, and terrified of failure" (p. 22) because of ever-present evaluation of their professional adequacy. In academic classes, not mastering material or failing a test is perceived as a deficiency that may be temporarily uncomfortable, but is correctable. In the experience of practicum or internship, being found wanting is not only a block to graduation or licensure, but often interpreted as personal inadequacy, a criticism of one's essence rather than one's behavior, thus beyond redemption. One perceives that more of one's "self" is on the line.

The dynamics of power between supervisor and supervisee are clear in any situation in which one person has an evaluative role. Similar dynamics apply in the less formal, but nonetheless potentially inhibits the dynamic of a colleague or consultant whose approval is highly sought.

This author has observed sessions in which students worked positively with client families, modeling acceptance and respect for all the family, providing a place where members felt safe to explore and grow, but in the supervision session immediately afterward, the rules were changed. Feedback seemed based on a different set of standards, with students under attack. Although students are taught that it is the process that is important, feedback sessions often seem to bog down in criticism of content. When review of sessions becomes personal criticism of the students, they understandably feel less open and willing to risk. When they are anxious about evaluation of their performance, they become less effective with their clients. Fear of failure or inadequacy interferes with both learning and performance. In live supervision it is natural and relatively unavoidable for students to be worried about how they are appearing to the trainer or training group (Schwartz, 1988). Paradoxically, however, as students concentrate on performing for the supervisor, they become less and less congruent, behavior antithetical to therapy; students learn spurious compliance (Rosenblatt & Mayer, 1975). For example, when a client makes a statement, the therapist may experience a feeling response; but rather than respond in a natural way, the therapist delays, processes questions of safety, often followed by feelings of fear, thinking of what the supervisor expects. The internal process of the therapist modifies the response into what the supervisor will deem "correct." The therapist learns to be less trusting of self and more concerned with not making mistakes. Ultimately two unacceptable outcomes occur. The therapist hesitates to take risks, focuses on the supervisor's evaluation, unable to feel and behave naturally. Then the client, who often learns from therapist behavior, is denied a model of genuineness and spontaneity. The client is faced by an anxious, inhibited therapist. When supervisors seem more intent upon skewering the student for mistakes, valuable modeling in how to be personally congruent is lost. Are we teaching one set of values and modeling something entirely different?

Just as punishment does not help in the training and discipline of children, "punishment" does not help, and, in fact, impairs students. When one is expecting punishment, one naturally feels fear. When one is afraid, the learning process is greatly inhibited. As children learn from parents' actions much more than from words, so students learn from experience rather than criticism. The greater the fear, the less the learning (Sappington, 1984; Taibbi, 1993).

In a situation in which students are attacked, punished, degraded for mistakes, and threatened, not only does fear develop and learning stop, but also we may be modeling the abuse of power. Helping professionals often see families in which one member misuses power over another—abusing spouse and children, physically, sexually, and emotionally. We recognize this as gross abuse of power, but perhaps we are blind to the only slightly less obvious abuse of power when, as supervisors clearly in a power position, we attack or threaten, no matter how subtly, the self-esteem of our students. We teach our students about pathogenic families in which victims are taught by example to become perpetrators. The abuse literature is replete with statistics on rapists and perpetrators, nearly all of whom were abused themselves (Finkelhor, 1986; Finkelhor, Gelles, Hotaling, & Straus, 1983; Groth, 1979). Abusive behavior is learned. If an abusive model of supervision is used, are not students being given covert permission to abuse their clients? And, perhaps even more obvious, if therapists exercise their power over some members of the family (usually quite out of awareness), are we not modeling exactly the power dynamic that we may, on a more conscious level, be attempting to change in the couple or family? The parallel process is usually at work in supervision; should we not use that process to support learning, growth, and change, with students who, in turn, may follow our example when working with clients? Abuse of power by a supervisor is filling the supervisor's needs, not the students'. Although supervisors don't set out to foster unhappy outcomes, perhaps concern over teaching students to "do it the right way" should be tempered to avoid even unintentional self-aggrandizing at the expense of others' self-esteem.

A basic human need is for safety and trust. This is not meant to advocate a supervisor's "doing therapy" with students (Whiston & Emerson, 1989), but to suggest the necessity for creation of an atmosphere in which students feel safe enough to take a risk, and trusting enough to know that they will not be personally attacked. This is not doing therapy with students or "being nice," but modeling unconditional positive regard and basic respect. We train therapists to "reframe" clients' problems into positive terms with which they can cope, in order to make changes.

Perhaps negative comments about students' work would profit from reframing into terms they can hear without needing to be defensive. That is, if there is no "offense" launched by the supervisor, no "defense" is needed. Ideas for changing behavior that isn't working can usually be heard as just what they are: ideas. One is seldom on the defensive when a supervisor has an "idea." If we cannot accept students as worthy of that minimum respect, perhaps we should consider a career change.

A MODEL "SAFE PLACE" FOR SUPERVISION

Suggested here is an approach to supervision that can be incorporated into any basic supervision theory or model already in use. The approach is based on "TRIBES," (Gibbs, 1987), a group process stressing cooperation, responsibility, relatedness, and respect. This process was originally developed for classroom use, is applicable to any helper training, to family therapy, and to family relationships, because all have similar goals: cooperative learning for personal and social development. The TRIBES model starts with a set of norms which, when agreed to by members of a group, lead to development of a safe atmosphere, allowing participants autonomous growth and development.

Norms for Supervision Sessions

1. Attentive Listening. Paying close attention to another's words, and the feelings behind those words, respecting and accepting the individual. Listening is a complex intentional behavior, central to relationship, the bedrock of communication. Most families presenting themselves for therapy indicate they don't "communicate" well. How much happier most family members might be if they were truly listened to, actively and attentively, by other family members. Supervisors expect students to demonstrate listening skills; supervisors must listen too, really listen. Supervision parallels therapy, and therapy parallels supervision, whether we like it or not.

2. No Put-Downs. No hurtful negative remarks, which never improve the other's behavior. We live in a society where put-downs are the rule. This is a form of violence in which someone is victimized. Observers of violence are also the victims of violence (Bradshaw, 1988).

Because humor is an essential ingredient in effective relationships, and therapy would seem bland without some humor, it is important to differentiate humor from put-downs. Humor does not have a victim. It is not for the aggrandizement of one at the expense of another. Teaching families to resist the "put-down" of members, even in the guise of teasing, can go a long way toward more harmonious family relations.

One also needs to be aware of self put-downs. We can pick away at our own self-esteem even more effectively than others can. A parent's saying to a child, "That sounds like a put-down of yourself when you say . . . I think you are better than that," can encourage development of personal strength. Supervisors might effectively use the same sentence with students. Stated appreciation for others' unique qualities, values, and contributions encourages growth.

3. Right to Pass. "Choosing when and to what extent you will participate in group activities, recognizing that each person has the right to control her/himself though within a group setting" (Gibbs, 1987, p. 21). Therapists encourage clients to be assertive and say "no" when they feel unwilling or unable to do something. One of the most frequent problems needing amelioration in families is a lack of personal boundaries between members, yet students' boundaries are sometimes ignored in supervision. They are expected to reveal all, to be open to any criticism, to implement every suggestion without the right to say no. This does not make thinking or acting for oneself feel safe. Some supervisors might argue that this "norm" would prevent students from experimenting with new techniques and behaviors. In this author's experience, the opposite is true. The paradox is that being free to choose not to engage also makes one free to choose to engage. The Right to Pass creates a safe place in which one is empowered to take more risks rather than fewer. When therapists allow family members the right to pass, they respect boundaries and individual autonomy. That modeling teaches parents how to strengthen children's autonomy and ability to stand up to peer pressure better than a thousand lectures. One cannot "just say no" unless one has been taught through genuine respect, which grants permission to protect oneself.

4. Confidentiality. When others' sharing is honored, a norm of trust is based on confidence that what is said in the supervision group stays there. Unfortunately, confidentiality, a condition we promise our clients for their sessions, is often not an integral part of supervision sessions. Students' comments and behaviors have been talked about in faculty meetings, at parties, and on the street. This inhibits risk-taking or openness during supervision sessions. This does not apply to consultation with a colleague about a student. Consultations are confidential; cocktail parties are not. Respect for confidentiality is essential to the creation of a "safe place." If students feel that their confidentiality is respected, they can encourage families to adopt the same norm. How many embarrassed teens might be willing to confide more in parents if they knew their confidences would not turn up at the neighborhood coffee klatch or be repeated to persons outside, or even inside, the family? Are not family therapists in a unique position to help families realize this possibility?

These norms are a foundation. Supervision groups may want to add other norms representing some of their unique concerns. Discussing the intent, and developing signals to use when someone forgets and violates a norm, can set a tone for safety and a place where we can risk being ourselves. How few such places seem to be available to us!

DEVELOPMENTAL STAGES

When the norms are lived in any group, the following stages develop (Gibbs, 1987).

Stage of Inclusion

Belonging, feeling included is a basic human need. In any organizational setting, inclusion means having adequate recognition and the opportunity to present oneself prior to tasks and agendas. Each group member is acknowledged so that his or her value and importance are validated. Alfred Adler (1964) described the concept of social interest and how encouraging the successful interaction of individuals and groups can be. He also taught that a major life task to be resolved is the task of community, building bonds and friendships with others. In every supervision session we reintroduce the concept of *inclusion.* Brief personal exchanges, validations, encouragement, and group exercises are given attention so that each person feels a sense of safe belonging.

These activities seem parallel to family rituals, which have been shown to be so important in bonding families emotionally (Imber-Black, 1989). Perhaps students who learn the good feeling that comes from being personally acknowledged and welcomed each week into the supervision "family" will introduce some such small ritual to sessions, welcoming and acknowledging each family member. Who knows, when one drops a pebble in the water, how far out the ripples will go?

Stage of Influence

To feel "of influence" is to feel of value (worth, power, individual resource to the group). The personal satisfaction gained when one feels "of influence" with others is gained when each person realizes that he or she can be a part of goal setting, tasks, and decisions of the group. His or her individuality and unique contributions are acknowledged and validated in the midst of the group. Recently in a supervision group, a student mentioned that her client attended the therapy session even though the client was ill. The student wondered if this was an example of the client's predilection toward compliance or if perhaps the client deserved reinforcement for attending even under uncomfortable circumstances. Rather than give an answer I asked the other students to respond. Five different responses, considering both content and process issues, resulted, giving the student new ideas. These perceptive responses included some ideas I had not considered. The group had reached the stage of influence in which each member felt free to contribute in a climate of cooperation. The student asking the question about her client felt free to choose the answer that seemed correct for her situation.

It was most gratifying to watch this same student, a few days later, encourage members of a client family, including the young children, to suggest ways in which the family as a whole might solve a problem that was disturbing them. All members of that family left that session looking important, listened to, and worthy of being consulted about a family situation. Parallel process seems to appear, even when not expected!

Stage of Affection

When supervision group members feel included, when they feel that they have influence in a safe and cooperative environment, a stage of affection develops. Feelings of affection result when one's thoughts and feelings are acknowledged and accepted by another. Is that not why clients often develop affection for a good therapist? In a supervision group, members develop a basic commitment to care for and support one another. This is not the same as outside social activity nor even saying that all members "like" each other. It is the warmth and satisfaction of working together well. The parallel goal for family functioning seems obvious.

Spiral of Renewal

Each time a group meets, members are different, having experienced events and emotions since the last meeting. The stages must again be passed through, so each meeting begins with an inclusion activity, honoring and valuing each member, acknowledging the influence of each. This need not be a long process, but it is vital. When members were absent from a meeting, the dynamics were different; each needs to feel welcomed back, acknowledged, and included. Some families used to do this as a ritual called the family dinner, in which each member was invited to tell about his or her day. Perhaps if we eliminate put-downs, encourage active and attentive listening, invoke confidentiality where appropriate, a family might try having dinner together and making it a positive experience.

SUPERVISION GROUP CLIMATE

"Climate" is intangible. One cannot put one's finger on it, but we all know when a situation feels comfortable and safe. Positive climate evolves from an atmosphere of trust, a sense of belonging, involvement in decision making, encouragement from supervisors and peers, authenticity, nonjudgmental attitudes, fairness, and personal congruence. A good supervision experience builds on a spirit of cooperation rather than competition. Unfortunately, much of our society is based on competition: If I win, you lose. Supervision need not be competitive. This author witnessed success through cooperation rather than competition in a supervision group a few years ago: A middle-aged man seemed especially terrified of "real, live" clients in a family practicum. His previous practicum experience, in another state, had been paperwork and teaching, not really therapy. He was also experiencing some major personal as well as career decisions, he had recently been involved in a damaging family trauma, and in general, he was in a raw emotional state. It quickly became obvious that he could not "compete" with the other students. He conducted the intake interview well, but became rigid and authoritarian when discussing the client's problem. The instructor reassured him that she understood his lack of appropriate background training. This unfortunate situation of inadequate prior training should not have occurred, but he qualified on paper to be in the practicum, so work was necessary to make up his training, while trying to extricate him from the experience intact. He needed reassurance that looking back was not helpful; one must look forward. He needed to know that by the end of the experience, however long it took, he would be competent. Admittedly, at times the staff had private doubts, but kept talking to each other about accepting him where he was, with all eyes clearly on the goal, not the deficient past. As he broke down in tears over his perceived personal inadequacies, they were reframed as training inadequacies that could be remedied. Therapy was strongly recommended to help him through the personal crises that were getting in his way. He went, and began to relax and grow before our pleased and astonished eyes. It seemed that as soon as he really trusted that his performance was not being compared with others', and that the supervisors were determined to bring him up to speed before he was finished, he was able to relax his rigid and authoritarian attitude, to really hear his clients' concerns, and to listen fully to supervision feedback. Without our explaining anything to the other students, they seemed to adopt the same supportive attitude, giving him positive strokes when he did well, and then suggesting changes to improve his skills. There was no need for them to compete, only to grow with him. He did finish, in time, at an acceptable skill level. How glad we were that we had not listened to a person in authority who, at the beginning, had told us to kick him out because of deficiencies in his schooling, over which he had no control.

The accepting attitudes suggested describe functional families and functional systems in general. The supervision group quickly becomes "family" and it can be a healthful, growth inducing family, or a dysfunctional one. Is it not the duty of supervisors to model functional family behavior, helping each member of the supervision family to grow? Abuse of power over family members in this setting is no less reprehensible than in any other setting. If we as supervisors are not secure enough within ourselves to be able to make mistakes, admit them, ask questions to which we do not have the answers, refrain from elevating ourselves at the expense of those at our mercy, allow our students to become better therapists than we are, then again, perhaps it is time for reevaluation of career positions.

CONCLUSION

It has been my personal experience, both as a student and a supervisor, that practicum can be a painful, emotionally debilitating experience. It need not be. As a supervisor I have experienced satisfaction when the model suggested here seemed to increase self-esteem, willingness to take risks, genuineness, and positive feelings that led to better work. Seeing the process transfer from supervision session to therapy session has been especially gratifying. I do not assert that this is the only way to achieve these ends, nor do I mean to imply that I always do it successfully. I invite experimentation with variations in application. After all, personal congruency can only be achieved when, taking basic principles, one creates one's own style of implementation. Whenever one has a position of authority over another, there is the possibility of abusing the power, or of assisting the growth and development of the subordinate. Did we not all become helping professionals to help alleviate pain? How inappropriate it seems to become a supervisor and then inflict unnecessary pain!

REFERENCES

ADLER, A. (1964). *Social interest.* New York: Capricorn Books.

BORDERS, L. D. (1992). Learning to think like a supervisor. *The Clinical Supervisor, 10,* 135–146.

BRADSHAW, J. (1988). *Bradshaw on the family.* PBS Video Series.

FINKELHOR, D. (1986). *Sourcebook on child sexual abuse.* Beverly Hills, CA: Sage Publications.

FINKELHOR, D., GELLES, R., HOTALING, G., & STRAUS, M. (1983). *The dark side of families.* Beverly Hills, CA: Sage Publications.

GIBBS, J. (1987). *Tribes.* Santa Rosa, CA: Center Source Publications.

GROTH, N. (1979). *Men who rape.* Beverly Hills, CA: Sage Publications.

IMBER-BLACK, E. (1989). Idiosyncratic life cycle transitions and therapeutic rituals. In B. Carter, & M. McGoldrick (Eds.), *The changing family life cycle* (2nd ed.) (pp. 149–163). Needham Heights, MA: Allyn & Bacon.

KOTTLER, J., & BLAU, D. (1989). *The imperfect therapist.* San Francisco: Jossey-Bass.

MEAD, D. E. (1990). *Effective supervision.* New York: Brunner/Mazel.

MUELLER, W., & KELL, B. (1972). *Coping with conflict.* New York: Appleton-Century-Crofts.

ROSENBLATT, A., & MAYER, J. E. (1975). Objectionable supervisory styles: Students' views. *Social Work, 20,* 184–189.

SALVENDY, J. (1993). Control and power in supervision. *International Journal of Group Psychotherapy, 43,* 363–376.

SAPPINGTON, T. (1984). Creating learning environments conducive to change: The role of FEAR/SAFETY in the adult learning process. In Innovative higher education (pp. 19–29). New York: Human Sciences Press.

SCHWARTZ, R. (1988). The trainer-trainee relationship in family therapy training. In H. Liddle, D. Breunlin, & R. Schwartz (Eds.), *Handbook of family therapy training and supervision* (pp. 172–182). New York: Guilford Press.

STOLTENBERG, C., & DELWORTH, U. (1987). *Supervising counselors and therapists: A developmental approach.* San Francisco: Jossey-Bass.

TAIBBI, R. (1993). The way of the supervisor. *The Family Therapy Networker, 17* (3), 50–55.

WHISTON, S., & EMERSON, S. (1989). Ethical implications for supervisors in counseling of trainees. *Counselor Education and Supervision, 28,* 318–325.

CHAPTER 2

Power and Pain
Unavoidable Aspects of Supervision?

SHIRLEY EMERSON

The title may sound strange to you, coming from the person who in a preceding chapter wrote about making supervision "a safe place." However, despite our desire to create such a haven in which risks may be taken and learning can occur, we cannot, and should not, eliminate power and pain. Obvious power resides in the supervisor and is an important part of that role. It also resides in the therapist. The task of the supervisory system is not to eliminate power, but to recognize it and use it constructively. I did not arrive at this position easily.

"Power is not always benign. To do good, one must sometimes be willing to inflict pain." The speaker's statement startled me. I groped for an understanding of power, its use, and its abuse. Is it really true that one must be willing to cause pain? When is it justified, and how does one know that it is acceptable in a given context? It is difficult to imagine a society functioning without the use of properly allocated power. But where does use stop and abuse begin? The omnipresent physical violence we live with is certainly abuse of power. But abuse of power need not be physical to be violent. Abuse of power can be verbal and psychological, which certainly violates its victims.

AMBIVALENCE ABOUT POWER

As a woman growing up during World War II and attending college in the lethargic 1950s, I was admonished to find a husband with good career prospects, raise a family, and do good works in the community. I did not give thought to the gaining and maintaining of power. Men, authority figures, had the overt power. Subtle, covert, manipulative power could be pursued by females, always in ladylike dress, of course. As I matured, society also was changing, although while one is busy with daily life, one does not always stop to notice. The word "power" did seem to appear more often in the newspaper, in magazines, and in social conversation. When a discussion of power arose, women, including me, usually deferred to the men present, with a comment such as "I don't need it; I don't want to control anyone."

But, did we, did I, really not want power, or was it merely the socially acceptable stance to assume? This thought plagued me. Self analysis led to the realization that having power would not necessarily be all bad. As I looked around, it seemed that not only are we as individuals ambivalent about power, but the institutions that make up our society seem equally ambivalent. Perhaps it was the "lethargic 1950s" of my college career, but when I studied anything "new" in the world, it was referred to as "modern." Now I read that we are in a "postmodern" period. Postmodern seems to indicate that no one has "the truth." This further seems to mean that we must "deconstruct" everything, including therapy, and move to "therapy as conversation." In conversation, there are generally no hierarchies. So if therapy is conversation, is there no power, no hierarchy? Is hierarchy bad, and to be avoided?

If one is on the low end of a hierarchy, it seems that one's constant struggle is to move "up" and be higher in the chain of command. Yet, if one is on top, or in charge, one has responsibility for what happens. That is power; but with power goes responsibility and demands for accountability. If total freedom were part of the picture, and one could choose the outcomes and be able to make them all happen, power could be a great thing to have. But we know that we do not have total freedom, nor can we control others' actions and therefore results. No wonder we are ambivalent about power! But no matter our ambivalence, power is necessary and must not be ignored. It is an inherent and necessary part of task-oriented and need-based relationships. Sometimes, to achieve the "good" we have to be willing to inflict pain. I'll try to illustrate what that means with some personal examples.

POWER IN LICENSING BOARD MEMBERS

Appointed by the governor, I have served for several years as president of a state board of examiners for marriage and family therapists. My first disciplinary complaint was against a man who had sexually used his female clients, breaking most of the dual relationship rules in the book. Once the board members heard the evidence, it was an easy step to revoke his license. It was sordid and seamy, but we felt justified in protecting future clients. Other somewhat minor complaints needed less severe discipline, so no one lost livelihood. We sat smugly in our power positions, ostentatiously overseeing the ethics of our profession for the state. Then came a far more complex case.

A colleague was charged with violating ethical principles, involving dual (not sexual) relationships with her clients. Her clients called in the middle of dinner, in the middle of the night, and in the middle of her life. Her social life revolved around them. One or another of her clients was constantly in crisis, and she spent whole days with them, sometimes sheltering them for weeks in her home. Even vacations were spent calling back daily to talk to whichever client claimed crisis at the time. She feared persons who, she said, were out to get her, planning to break into her office and steal her records. She described her clients as paranoid. The enmeshment seemed severe.

Board members agonized over how to treat the case. She admitted the actions, but seemed unable to understand that they constituted dual relationships, or that there was harm in what she was doing. She saw no reason to change her behavior. A licensing board is appointed by the governor to protect the public. The public is not protected when a licensee is permitted to violate ethical guidelines, no matter how benevolent or well-intentioned the behavior. To take this person's license would inflict pain; it would deprive her of livelihood. To allow her to continue her practice would be to allow harm to the public. Punishment? Rehabilitation? Harm to the therapist's financial survival or potential harm to clients? Where is the good one wants to do? Must one cause pain?

I had thought it would be easy. You sin, you get punished. But—why is there always a but?—no harm was intended, no sin contemptuously committed. The therapist did not understand that there was a problem. She just didn't get it. Her dual relationships were, at best, not helpful, and probably quite harmful. But the real problem was the therapist's delusional thinking and boundary weaknesses. To revoke her license would seem to reinforce her delusions, in this case that the board members were "out to get her," when all she intended to do was to "help" her clients. She refused therapy for herself, maintaining that she did not need it. The board members put her on probation, under supervision, which seemed only to teach her to avoid getting "caught" again. Board members attempted to avoid causing her pain; did we really prevent harm? Was there a way to protect the clients? Clear answers are often elusive.

POWER IN ADMINISTRATION

My first real position at the "top" of a clearly delineated hierarchy was that of director of a counseling agency that had been poorly managed and was in dire need of reformation and leadership. Here was my chance to really do something. I did it. The agency grew, took on a more professional staff and reputation, and kept me busy for a couple of years. We developed an identity in the community, and people came looking for jobs and services. Hiring people is pleasant; firing them is not. The first firing—a physically handicapped therapist—was done with considerable fear. It seemed obvious that a nonperforming staff member who wouldn't follow suggestions or even rules must be removed before further damage was done to the entire organization. That was not easy to do, especially for one who wants the world to love her. I wrestled for days with the fact that it had to be done. My conscience asked me whether my dislike of the individual, and awareness that I had the power to do whatever I wanted about him, might be fueling my decision to fire him. To exert the necessary power to do what was necessary was to inflict pain.

A few years ago, I was appointed chair of my department, a job I did not want, but one that had to be done. Most of my colleagues seem reasonably content and seem to trust that I just want to get the job done. But I realize that some power is real and in my control. The chair has to mediate between students and professors perceived as doing something unjust to them; the chair recommends, or doesn't recommend colleagues for tenure, promotion, and merit pay. Sometimes it is painfully necessary not to recommend. The chair has the power to carry out policy to the best of his or her ability and within personal conscience. I am aware that whatever anyone in a position of authority does, it may be perceived by some as abusive. The straight line one needs to walk must be not only guided by benevolence and caring, but also strengthened by the awareness that sometimes, to do what is right, one must inflict pain.

POWER IN THE SUPERVISOR

When I first moved to university teaching, I had not given any consideration to the concept of "power." Teaching students about working with troubled couples and families was stimulating; supervising students as they gained confidence and developed skills was exhilarating. But I soon had to learn that such a position carries power, more subtle because students look up to their professors, idealizing some, investing us with perceived expertise, which we may or may not actually have. They seem to care what we think; they react to criticism and are easily hurt sometimes by the best-intentioned suggestions. We don't want to hurt, but when students base their professional self-esteem on what we say about how "good" they are, how "talented" they are, we have power thrust upon us.

Then sometimes comes the nightmare of all supervisors: the student who cannot do it. My experience was with a young woman who was bright, wrote beautiful papers and exams, but dissociated, said inappropriate things to clients, and just did not perform in any satisfactory manner with clients. I consulted with department colleagues. She was recycled through beginning skills courses and sent to therapy. She returned to practicum, reciting theories well, but still unable to apply them. It was painfully obvious that she needed a new career focus. How could I help her to understand, to reinforce her other talents, to assure her that she was not a failure, just in the wrong career plan? I told her the faculty's decision. She was crushed and insisted she could learn, felt that I was out to get her, and that the faculty didn't understand. Unfortunately, we did. We understood that we had the power, which we had to use, to separate her from the program and her career plans. She was one of several, with varying problems, whom I have stopped in their chosen career paths. Responsible professionals must use the power of discrimination. We must ultimately decide whether it is better to allow an inept student to practice in a field for which he or she has no ability and will possibly inflict harm, or whether to exert that power, no matter how reluctantly, to stop the student, all the while knowing how much pain is involved.

POWER IN THE THERAPIST AND IN THE CLIENT

As a young person, I often wondered why old people spent so much time thinking and talking about parallels between "then" and "now." As an old person now, I catch my breath when I notice that I am continually making comparisons. A recent visit from one of my children and his family, including four little ones (two sets of twins!) brought me to sober reflection on how similar therapy is to parenting, and supervision is to grandparenting. A silly parallel, you may think, but stop to consider power in a family. We all know that the youngest member of a client family often has the most power. But, when children are little, we have absolute power over their lives. They live or die, dependent on our care or neglect. When we exert that control on such things as confining them from traffic, keeping sharp knives out of their reach, and locking cabinet doors on poisonous cleaning solutions, we sometimes notice their "pain" on receiving a "no, you can't . . .". No one argues abuse of power; it is called care. As the child matures, we no longer worry about cabinets, but shift our control to homework, curfews, and safe places to go with friends. This is still considered care and concerned use of necessary power, no matter how loudly they protest their "pain." But in case we hadn't noticed, our power is actually lessening, and responsible exertion of their growing power is to be applauded. If we are good parents, each year increases their power and lessens ours. One fine day we see healthy adult children, on their own, responsible for themselves. We have no "power over" them whatever; yet, if we have done our job well, constantly working ourselves out of a job as a parent, they come to us with questions, asking for opinions, and sometimes actually listening to the answers we so eagerly give. We have become consultants. When my son and his wife asked my advice about diminishing the tantrums of a three-year-old who was demonstrating his considerable power at earsplitting volume, I knew I had made it to the consultant stage. What struck me was not that I didn't have the perfect answer, but that we could discuss the alternative possibilities and they, the parents, would decide what to do.

Clients are developing individuals, in families, seeking guidance. Therapists cannot tell them what to do, but can suggest alternatives, new ways to look at things, ways to develop their own solutions, and to put their goals into focus. The therapist's job is similar to that of a parent, teaching and guiding, but working himself or herself out of a job. The supervisor's job is to play grandparent, if you will forgive my comparison, and to guide the "new parents," or therapists, when they are starting out, just as we do our adult children who are learning to be parents. Each must experiment with theories, methods, and techniques, some of which succeed, and some of which do not. When an experiment does not succeed, young parents or new therapists may ask for advice. We discuss other ways to do something, then send them back to try again, with our encouraging words that it will be easier the next time. Therapists return to their clients stronger, more powerful. They exert their greater power, gently we hope, with encouragement for the clients, picking them up when necessary and focusing toward the clients' chosen goals. The process is repeated and repeated. With each rerun, it is supposed to get easier, to go better. But just as a child learns a new skill, riding a bike, or reading harder words, or just toddling, there are mishaps, mistakes, and setbacks that require the therapist to pick them up once more and set their feet firmly back on level ground.

The developing therapist is, himself or herself, also like a toddler in this new role, so he or she seeks support, wanting to know, "Did I do it right?" If you have ever helped a baby learn to walk, you have experienced big delight in being held from behind, by the elbows, as he weaves and jerks his way forward. Without your firm grip, he collapses. After several tries, he walks more smoothly, and one day takes off on his own. Careful parents remove sharp objects and tippy lamps, and allow him to fall when he needs to. If we continued to hold his elbows, we would be holding him up when he is 45 years old. Supervisors need to lend that support when the novice therapist first toddles along with a client, but must step back and let the therapist fall on his or her face so that the next trip may be farther and steadier.

Is there a hierarchy here? Of course! The therapist has "power" with the clients; the supervisor has power with the therapist. But we often forget that the clients also have power. They can fire the therapist. They can take the therapist's "advice" and make it come out wrong, and blame the therapist. Clients can say "no" (with or without a tantrum) and walk away. Parallel process rules. The therapist can do exactly the same thing to the supervisor. This can all be healthy growth and part of the process. But if, from any position, one party abuses the power he or she holds over the other, growth stops and unnecessary pain may result.

NOT ALL POWER RESIDES IN THE SUPERVISOR

It will not come as a shock to you, I hope, that being a supervisor has its hazards. What I have just described could be framed as "parentification" of the "child," the therapist-in-training. As we do that, we put ourselves into a one-down position in the power equation, because as we want our "children," the therapists we supervise, to do well, we put them in charge of our own sense of well-being. When we care how they turn out, we give them power over us. When we base our satisfaction, or feelings of having done well, on someone else's behavior, we give that someone else power over our feelings. Good parents demonstrate setting appropriate boundaries; they make suggestions but encourage responsible experimentation by the children, to allow the children to develop in their own ways and at their own pace. If parents depend on the children becoming exactly what the parents think they should be, the children have the parents' happiness within their power. (How many students have you observed failing in their college classes, because they were pursuing the career path the parents wanted, rather than their own choice of direction?) In wanting our supervisees to "turn out well," it is tempting to mold them to be "more like us." We must not insist that they be our clones. We want to develop self-sufficient thinkers who can leave our training ready to move on with their own and their clients' growth.

It would be very easy, as an experienced supervisor, to "treat" the client through the therapist. It might also be easy to write your child's English essay or do his math problems but you wouldn't dream of that! We must be ever alert to the possibility, in our eagerness to have our trainees turn out well, that we do not do their math problems, or tell them how to treat the clients (just as wise grandparents do not "tell" their adult children how to discipline the grandchildren). We would fuss loudly at the therapist who made decisions for the clients. Our pedagogical goal is to help people to become self-sufficient. We insist on it for the clients; we must allow it for our trainees. Our job of protection is clear, just as suggested with the safety of children in our care, but the process of learning to be an effective therapist cannot be "taught;" it can only be learned by practice.

NECESSARY MONITORING IN USE OF POWER

Power demands constant monitoring by its holder to avoid abusive use. Abuse can be subtle and unintentional. It is the supervisor's job to be aware of his or her power and control needs, watching carefully not to abuse that power with the therapist. To work at keeping proper perspective as a supervisor, I try to remember the role of a caring grandparent. I know how the therapy process should work, and in general terms, what the therapist should do. But it is not my job to "treat" the client, any more than it is the grandparent's job to "raise" the grandchildren. The supervisor's role is to make suggestions and exert real power of prevention only when the therapist is about to "hurt" someone, himself or the client, just as we would step in when the toddler heads for the busy street. My role is to reinforce positive behavior and offer minimal suggestions, always asking first what the therapist thinks he or she should do. The therapist, in turn, needs to speak up when the clients are clearly heading for the busy street, but mostly reinforce clear thinking, positive behavior, and their work toward chosen goals.

As the process continues, the therapist "grows up" quickly (would that children might learn so quickly!) and ventures farther and farther without close supervision. The ideal development is, of course, that he or she becomes a trusted colleague, who may return with questions (as the parent may to the grandparent) not because we have "power" but because we are perceived as having some of the wisdom that comes from experience. Real collegiality is born when the supervisor asks the colleague for advice, just as grandparents ask their maturing children for suggestions. But we need to realize that there is still hierarchy. They wouldn't ask us for help if they didn't feel we knew something. We reverse the hierarchy temporarily when we ask for their expertise.

Overtly abusive behavior is obvious to most supervisors and trainees. It harms everyone by creating an unsafe place and distancing people from one another. However, I suggest that too much "caring" and molding in our way can also be abusive. As stated previously, we should not be trying to create clones, and obviously we should not be trying to make all our trainees think and behave as we do. We are the catalysts who enable them to think for themselves, develop their own style, and take more and more responsibility for their work as they move farther and farther along the path to independence. Sometimes when a supervisor experiences resistance from a trainee, he or she may need to consider whether, in an effort to make the best possible therapist of the trainee, he or she may be unintentionally abusing his power over the therapist. Just as resistance from a client often indicates that the client is not getting what he or she really wants from therapy, resistance, whether open and direct or passive and indirect, may mean that the supervisee is not getting what is needed from the supervisor. Too much "caring" and guiding of the trainee may be just as abusive as neglect of the trainee's needs. Neglect of the trainee may show up in a supervisor's canceled appointments, or as subtly as damning with faint praise, or simply ignoring therapist behaviors which should be confronted. Such behavior on the supervisor's part may be as simple as sheer laziness, but probably more often the supervisor does not want to "hurt" another's feelings. A safe place is not always the place where one receives only praise and compliments; a safe place can tolerate and must make room for constructive criticism, offered in generosity of spirit and indicating freedom to take risks and to learn from mistakes.

Both therapy and supervision include aspects of science and of art. Both are balancing acts, which include an ever-evolving mix of confrontation and support, criticism and praise, and growth and regression. There is no pat formula that one can memorize and follow to guarantee results. Therapy and supervision both include times of "trial and error," when one does not "know" what to do, but invokes the "art" portion to go with the scientific theories, sometimes just hoping for the best. It is a fine line to walk. It is exhilarating when the process goes well, and depressing when it does not. But, without mistakes, there are few triumphs. Good supervisors encourage their trainees to take risks, try new ideas and techniques, and learn by making mistakes. I recommend the same for supervisors: Take a risk, try something different, and give yourself permission to learn from mistakes. That is, in my opinion, the best modeling we can provide.

CHAPTER 3

To Speak or Not to Speak

Guidelines for Self-Disclosure in Supervision

LEE M. WILLIAMS
HEIDI J. DOMBECK

When and how should a supervisor self-disclose? The literature is silent on this matter, but it does reveal a mixture of opinions regarding the value of self-disclosure on the part of therapists. With regard to the latter, whether or not self-disclosure is good or bad depends on therapeutic orientation (Cornett, 1991; Curtis, 1981b; Edwards & Murdock, 1994). For example, a humanistic approach perceives self-disclosure as often helpful to the therapeutic relationship. In contrast, self-disclosure may be viewed as harmful from a psychodynamic perspective because it can contaminate the transference process.

The literature suggests several potential benefits to therapist self-disclosure. It can be a way to model behavior and join with clients (Curtis, 1981b; Edwards & Murdock, 1994), help therapists feel closer to clients (Palombo, 1987), and reassure clients (Hill, Mahalik, & Thompson, 1989). Self-disclosure also may be used to educate clients about the therapeutic process (Curtis, 1981b).

The use of self-disclosure by the therapist, however, also may be harmful to the therapist–client relationship. If self-disclosure is not used in an appropriate way it can cause the therapist to appear to lack empathy with the client (Cornett, 1991; Curtis, 1981a), or decrease the therapist's credibility level. Therapist self-disclosure actually may cause clients to doubt the trustworthiness and competence of therapists (Curtis, 1981a). It may also add to client resistance, cloud the therapy with the therapist's beliefs, and stop the therapist from looking at client motivation (Curtis, 1981b). Therapists from a psychodynamic perspective warn against the use of self-disclosure for two additional reasons. First, it may interfere with transference and thereby harm the therapy process (Cornett, 1991). Second, if countertransference issues exist, the therapist in turn may try to fulfill his or her own needs through self-disclosure (Goldstein, 1994).

Despite the attention that self-disclosure has received in the therapy literature, the use of self-disclosure by supervisors in supervision has received very little attention. Therefore, we conducted a qualitative study in which we asked both supervisors and trainees to describe the risks and benefits of supervisor self-disclosure. We then used this feedback to develop guidelines for the appropriate use of self-disclosure on the part of supervisors. This appears to be the first published study on the subject.

METHODS: WHAT WE DID

We wanted to better understand the role that self-disclosure can play in supervision. To obtain the perspectives of both supervisors and trainees, two focus groups and one individual interview were conducted with nine supervisors, and three focus groups were conducted with 11 family therapy trainees. The supervisors included faculty supervisors as well as supervisors from community agencies that regularly supervised family therapy trainees. Seven were Approved Supervisors by the American Association for Marriage and Family Therapy; the other two were supervisors-in-training. The supervisors had a range from 2 to 19 years of supervision experience. The family therapy trainees were finishing or had just finished a master's program in family therapy. All focus group discussions (and the one individual interview) were audiotaped and transcribed for analysis.

RESULTS: WHAT WE FOUND

What Is Self-Disclosure?

In the study, supervisors and trainees were not given a specific definition of self- disclosure; instead they were asked how they would define self-disclosure. At one extreme, some individuals believed that any form of communication on the part of the supervisor technically contained some element of self-disclosure. Even choosing not to comment could reveal something about the supervisor. However, most individuals gave a response similar to a supervisor who said, "I think of self-disclosure as sharing any kind of information about one's own experience or background or life in the supervisory process." Two individuals also thought that self-disclosure could include a supervisor's reaction to the trainee or their interactions.

Many individuals pointed out that there are two types or levels of self-disclosure. One type has to do with sharing information related to professional experience or cases or situations that we've encountered in our own development, and the other area has more to do with personal, private information about one's own life.

Potential Benefits of Self-Disclosure

Supervisors and trainees alike indicated that there were numerous potential benefits to having the supervisor self-disclose during supervision.

Self-Disclosure Normalizes

One of the benefits most frequently mentioned by both trainees and supervisors was the power of self-disclosure by the supervisor to normalize the struggles of being a beginning therapist. Beginning therapists seemed to find the supervisor's self-disclosure of clinical struggles and mistakes to be most helpful. As one trainee put it, "When the supervisors talk about similar experiences with clients, and you hear about their mess ups, it gives you an idea that—'Okay, this is part of the growth process and I'll get over this hump.'"

Self-Disclosure Encourages Mutuality

One of the perceived benefits of supervisor self-disclosure was that it helped create a climate that made it safer and easier for the trainee to be self-revealing. It did this by reducing the power differential between the supervisor and trainee and suggesting that self-disclosure was going to be a two-way street. One trainee commented, "Just the fact that they are willing to share with you helps the student feel more comfortable." Another trainee said, "I got to see . . . a humanness to him rather than just the technical stuff he usually talks about. And I opened up more after he had opened up because . . . I felt more comfortable." Moreover, yet another trainee described a problem where self-disclosure was not mutual: "One of my supervisors expects some real self-disclosing from me. I am pretty open about things like that. But I don't feel that the same thing is going on with the supervisor. So it feels more like therapy, and that can be pretty uncomfortable to me."

Supervisory Self-Disclosure May Be a Modeling Process

Several supervisors believed that self-disclosure on their parts could serve as a model for how therapists in turn could appropriately self-disclose with their clients.

Appropriate Self-Disclosure Enhances the Credibility of the Supervisor

One trainee said he was able to see how his supervisor could be "down-to-earth and human with his clients" through his self-disclosure in supervision. The trainee added that the supervisor's credibility was also enhanced because he disclosed "just enough, but not too much." One supervisor felt that his own self-disclosure demonstrated that "you are not a hypocrite, that you are walking the talk." He added, "I think that gives you more solidity as a supervisor, more believability, more credibility, if you can treat them the way that you are asking them to treat clients."

In one focus group, trainees were asked specifically if supervisors lost credibility when they shared clinical examples in which they had made mistakes or had struggled with an issue. The trainees responded that this did not reduce the credibility of the supervisor in their eyes. However, it did make the supervisor seem more human, which increased the trainees' positive regard and comfort with the supervisor. "For me that hasn't changed their pedestal any more or any less. It makes them more likable I think, more real . . . and confident enough to show their own weaknesses."

Self-Disclosure Helps Supervisors Be Authentic

As one supervisor put it, sharing personal stories about herself enabled her to be "authentic wherever I am and not being a different person in my office from somewhere else." Moreover, it allowed supervisors to be more "up front" in their interactions. One supervisor said that he would self-disclose if something were gnawing at him so as not to be distanced from his trainees.

Self-Disclosure May Allow Insights into the Supervisor's Strengths or Limitations

A supervisor let it be known that her first husband had been an alcoholic, and that she had done her master's thesis on alcoholism. Her trainee thought that, in one particular case where the trainee was working with an alcoholic family, her supervisor "may have had a little bit more information or a little bit more insight to it."

Self-Disclosure Can Be Used for Emphasis

Some supervisors felt that self-disclosures could be an effective way of highlighting an important issue in supervision. It even might make trainees more receptive to what the supervisor is saying.

Self-Disclosure May Change Emotional Responses

One supervisor said she might use self-disclosure to elicit a different affective response from a trainee. "If I want to broaden their affective response to a client, I'll use my own life experience at times to hopefully encourage empathy." Likewise, she said she might use a personal story to help trainees connect to what they are feeling in regards to a case.

Self-disclosure validates and supports trainees. Self-disclosure was described as a powerful tool for giving a trainee confidence. Supervisors sometimes used it to convey that trainees' thoughts and feelings touched a responsive chord.

Potential Risks in Supervisor Self-Disclosure

Despite the numerous benefits that supervisors and trainees mentioned regarding supervisor self-disclosure, there was also a recognition that self-disclosure could be problematic, particularly if done for the wrong reasons.

Self-Disclosure May Promote Too Much Intimacy in the Training Relationship

Supervisors and trainees agreed that self-disclosure sometimes confused the nature of the relationship. Some supervisors created too much closeness in the relationship, seemed to redefine it as something more than or other than a training relationship, and diminished the hierarchy. In turn trainees felt confused and anxious and behaved accordingly. For example, one trainee described a supervisor who acted more like a friend than a teacher. The trainee said that when she is anxious about a case she does not go to this supervisor. Instead, she goes to another staff member "where there is this sort of hierarchy." Trainees described supervisory relationships that became too friendly or too sexual, which in turn interfered with their own ability to discern and respond to an authority figure.

Self-Disclosure May Be Self-Serving

Some trainees perceived that supervisors sometimes used self-disclosure to ask for help with a personal issue. In essence, this confused or inverted the hierarchy of the relationship. Because the supervisor was normally in the one-up position, the trainee now felt thrust into the one-up position relative to the supervisor: "I feel like it's a role reversal when they are talking about their lives. It's like I'm the therapist now, and I'm the person telling what to do here . . . and that's not comfortable." One trainee described how her supervisor shared personal stories about the supervisor's own struggles as a parent. The trainee didn't know ". . . if I should talk to her mother to mother, or . . . as if she were the boss, and not assume that I could share equally with her. I was uncomfortable. I didn't know how to handle that." Supervisors, too, spoke of the need to be careful about one's motives in self-disclosing. They felt that it must always be done with a specific training purpose.

It was interesting to note that a role reversal between supervisor and trainee was not always seen in a negative light, provided it was an isolated incident resulting from extraordinary circumstances. For example, one trainee described how her supervision group offered emotional support to a supervisor who had just been mugged. Another described a situation in which the trainees offered support to a supervisor who had just had a parent die. In the latter example, the experience was described as bringing the supervision group closer together. What was consistently described as detrimental, however, were situations in which supervisors looked to trainees for help on a repeated or consistent basis.

Self-Disclosure May Take Time Away from Supervision Issues

Another potential concern about self-disclosure is that it may take time away from more important issues that need attention. One trainee said, "I come in with a wheelbarrow full of things to talk about and if we start talking about dogs or kids or traveling or husbands or movies and stuff, it just makes more anxiety for me because I'm not getting my needs met that way." Of course, trainees sometimes may encourage supervisor self-disclosure to avoid getting supervision. One trainee admitted, "Sometimes I'd rather keep her talking about herself and her life."

Self-Disclosure Can Increase Dependence on Supervisors

Two supervisors feared that too much self-disclosure on their part could set them up as being experts, and reduce the trainee's willingness to explore their own ideas or creativity. One supervisor stated, "With less self-disclosure, that cuts down on them looking at me as having all the answers, and turns it back to the supervisee to find those answers."

Negative Disclosures Can Erode Trust in Supervisors

A supervisor who disclosed negative feelings about other trainees could reduce a trainee's sense of safety with that supervisor. One trainee said "If she was to talk about me behind my back when I wasn't there, I would be irate I think. . . Or if she talked to me about someone else, because then I would think that she would talk about me when I wasn't there."

Self-Disclosure Risks Privacy

Supervisors pointed out that self-disclosure was potentially risky for them. Not only did they have a right to and need for privacy but also a disclosure made in confidence to one trainee could be shared with others.

Self-Disclosure Risks Loss of Credibility

Supervisors can lose credibility if self-disclosures are inappropriate. For example, one trainee said he would lose respect if a supervisor made a rude comment about clients. Another said she would lose respect for a supervisor if he or she revealed some unethical behavior. Moreover, the trainees pointed out that supervisors also lose respect if they continually use self-disclosure to meet their own needs: "What was I getting out of it? Why would I want to go see her for supervision?"

Self-Disclosure May Limit Supervisor Maneuverability

Some supervisors feared that self-disclosure could limit their "maneuverability." One supervisor explained, "I think that the more the trainees know about me and my clinical work, the more likely they are to pigeon-hole me or to create biases about who I am as an individual. They will have preconceived notions about what type of questions they can come to me with, and what my responses will be."

DISCUSSION: GENERAL GUIDELINES FOR SELF-DISCLOSURE

Both supervisors and trainees articulated a number of possible benefits that could be derived from supervisors appropriately self-disclosing during supervision. Several trainees reported that self-disclosure on the part of the supervisor made them feel more connected with their supervisors and made it easier to self-disclose their own personal reactions to clients and to being a therapist. Indeed, it would be tempting to suggest that supervisors who expect self-disclosure on the part of trainees should be prepared to disclose themselves. Some supervisors felt that self-disclosure on their part could help them remain authentic or present in their interactions with their trainees. In addition to these relational benefits, self-disclosure also could be a powerful tool for normalizing the struggles of becoming a therapist, modeling appropriate self-disclosure with clients, highlighting important issues in supervision, eliciting a different affective response from therapists, and validating them as clinicians.

However, supervisor self-disclosure also was said to carry with it certain risks. Inappropriately done, self-disclosure could confuse the hierarchy by putting the trainee in a position of taking care of the supervisor. Self-disclosure also carried the risk of creating too much intimacy, which could make the relationship "too friendly or too sexual." Another potential concern about self-disclosure was that it could be an ineffective use of supervision time. Supervisors also expressed concern that self-disclosure could result in loss of privacy, increase trainees' dependence on them, and reduce supervisors' maneuverability. Finally, inappropriate supervisor self-disclosure could reduce trainees' trust and their own credibility.

Based on the results from the study, the following guidelines for supervisory self- disclosure are suggested:

1. Self-disclosure should have a clear clinical purpose. As one supervisor said, "I always ask what would be the point of me disclosing a given thing. If there isn't a good one . . . then I wouldn't self disclose." This helps ensure that supervisor self-disclosure will be relevant to trainees' needs, less motivated by supervisors' personal needs, and a constructive use of supervisory time.
2. Supervisors should not self-disclose material they have not worked through. One supervisor said, "I never share something that I am still

so much caught up in that I am not clear enough to see my way through it." Likewise, another supervisor shared, "The less emotionally charged it is, the more comfortable I may be in sharing it, because I'm less suspicious of my motives." Failure to follow this guideline increases the likelihood that disclosures may be self-serving.

3. Supervisors should be clear to the trainee that the supervisors are not asking for help. For example, after sharing some personal background information one supervisor told a trainee, "This is to let you know a little bit about who I am . . . but we're not going to spend your time on that. That's just so that you know a little bit of information about me to make you feel a little bit more comfortable when we are talking about your issues." One trainee offered, "I think that one way that a supervisor can get the message across—that it is self-disclosure and not asking for help—is to say that 'This is how I dealt with this issue myself,' instead of just saying 'I am struggling with this right now' and leaving it open-ended."

4. Supervisors should monitor the amount of time spent self-disclosing. Spending a lot of time sharing personal stories could be a warning signal that supervisors are trying to meet personal needs. Moreover, time spent in personal stories is time not spent on other supervisory tasks.

5. Supervisors should not disclose information they would be embarrassed for others to know. This may prevent supervisors from sharing information that is too intimate in nature, keep training relationships on a more professional level, and protect supervisors from trainees with an inclination toward gossip.

6. Supervisors should assess each trainee's ability to handle or benefit from self-disclosure. Trainees' personal maturity and stage of training may be important. For example, some supervisors indicated that they were most likely to use self-disclosure with advanced trainees who were looking at self-of-the-therapist issues.

REFERENCES

CORNETT, C. (1991). The "risky" intervention: Twinship self-object impasses and therapist self-disclosure in psychodynamic psychotherapy. *Clinical Social Work Journal, 19,* 49–61.

CURTIS, J. M. (1981a). Effect of therapist's self-disclosure on patients' impressions of empathy, competence, and trust in an analogue of a psychotherapeutic interaction. *Psychological Reports, 48,* 127–136.

CURTIS, J. M. (1981b). Indications and contraindications in the use of therapist's self-disclosure. *Psychological Reports, 49,* 499–507.

EDWARDS, C. E., & MURDOCK, N. L. (1994). Characteristics of therapist self-disclosure in the counseling process. *Journal of Counseling and Development, 72,* 384–389.

GOLDSTEIN, E. G. (1994). Self-disclosure in treatment: What therapists do and don't talk about. *Clinical Social Work Journal, 22,* 417–432.

HILL, C. E., MAHALIK, J. R., & THOMPSON, B. J. (1989). Therapist self-disclosure. *Psychotherapy, 26,* 290–295.

PALOMBO, J. (1987). Spontaneous self-disclosures in psychotherapy. *Clinical Social Work Journal, 15,* 107–120.

PART TWO

Integrative and Eclectic Supervision

CHAPTER 4

Getting Started

ROBERT E. LEE

Becoming a supervisor, like becoming a therapist, is a lifelong process. This chapter has very modest goals, yet very heroic ones. It has the task of describing how to do supervision when you are just getting started and perhaps so is your trainee (although beginner status is not necessary to the models presented here). That is, it suggests an approach to use before you've completed a formal class and had considerable experience doing supervision, and before you've attended the workshops and read all the books and articles. It suggests what to do before you fully know what you are doing. For an effective start (and a place where one may return when things get confusing), adhere to the transcendent rules of supervision, continuously observe and interview the therapist, and employ a two-stage integrative model of intervention (the "Minimalist Model").

THE BIGGEST PICTURE

How do you get started? You know that your job is to work with the therapist, while the therapist works with the client. That is, you are not to treat the client through the therapist. That's the therapist's job. Your responsibility is to make the therapist the best therapist he or she can be at this stage in development.

Theoretical schools of marital and family therapy differ in what they see as the goals, processes, and techniques of supervision (Liddle, Breunlin, & Schwartz, 1988). However, the ideas and instructions of the various theoretical schools may come second after generic considerations. Most reasonable people would probably agree that the following rules of supervision transcend the directives of the various theoretical schools:

- The goals of supervision, like the goals of therapy, depend not only on who the parties are and what they respectively know about human intercourse, but where they are in the process that is taking place between them. Whatever specific advice various theorists offer, two developments are seen as fundamental to the earliest stages of the interaction: the establishment of a working alliance and acceptance of the presenting problem in systemic terms.
- The supervisor does not treat the client. The proper level for the supervisor's intervention is the therapist-plus-client unit, whoever they are, at whatever developmental level. Supervisor and therapist in fact are a subsystem in a total "training system" that includes the therapist and client. In this context, the ideas and actions of each person influence those of everyone else. The supervisor is a transacting, shaping part of the system he or she is observing. The supervisor isn't observing a system but living the system.
- Supervision, like therapy, must be a safe place (see Emerson, Chapters 1 and 2). Individuals must feel safe if they are to take risks and disclose, learn, and change. If supervision is not a safe place, the therapist may not only be inhibited from taking risks in supervision, but also may create an environment that inhibits the client. A supervisor's requirement that a therapist "perform" ultimately may become a demand on the client to "measure up."
- A corollary to the above is that supervision, like therapy, should be competency based. Therapists who experience supervisors as "deficit detectives" tighten up. Supervisors who find resources in therapists allow them to feel realistically competent, and the therapist in turn may pass this attitude on to their clients. (Clients in turn make therapists feel competent, and this in turn makes supervisors feel competent!)
- Supervision, like therapy, and like most human relationships involving high interdependency, may develop through stages: dependency and idealism, rebellion, and emancipation. The individuals' expectations and needs should differ at each stage, just as the reader probably differs from what he or she wants and needs from a supervisor now as opposed to when he or she first started out as a therapist. What is appreciated in a supervisor now may not have been desirable then.
- As with any supervision consultation, effective therapy supervision depends on shared goals and a relationship sufficient to support work on those goals. If the relationship is not sufficient, or the parties are not "ready" for certain goals, the attempt is premature.

There are parallel processes in supervision and therapy. The interactional processes that take place between the supervisor and therapist will be played out between the therapist and client. These may involve structural variables. For example, an authoritarian relationship between supervisor and therapist is expected to lead to a problematic relationship between the therapist and the client. Blurred boundaries in the supervisory relationship may lead to dual relationships in the therapy. (A supervisor who goes beyond the supervisory relationship with a therapist may discover that the therapist, in turn, goes beyond the appropriate relationship with the employer and the client.) Replicating interactional patterns also may include perception and definition of problems. This may include contextual variables such as race, sexual orientation, and other subcultural variables. There also may be replication of affect and adaptive style, that is, what type and how much emotion (including anxiety) is experienced and how it is managed. This may include blind spots (see Lee, Chapter 8).

WHERE TO BEGIN?

An Initial Look at Affect

As the therapist meets with you and perhaps presents a case, you should look for anxiety in both the therapist and yourself. Is there too much or too little? Too little anxiety may be a mark of confidence, but at this stage of development such confidence likely could indicate denial or even sociopathy. You might benefit from thinking about having a lack of anxiety (which others typically experience) as an "unusual" situation, reflect on the implications of that, and see what develops. More likely, both you and the therapist feel anxious. The question is, have you both dealt with this anxiety constructively or destructively? That is, are both you and the therapist task oriented, or are either of you escapist or hostile? That needs to be addressed up front and handled through ground rules and a good interviewing technique. It is reasonable to inquire routinely about the supervisor's as well as the trainee's fears and anxiety, recognizing that these ideas and feelings are a normal part of the situation. It also may be comforting to you to remember that in supervision as in therapy the wisdom and skill of the "expert" may not be as important as the capacity of the client to let him or her be useful. The supervisor's resources, like the therapist's, may be negated by barriers within the other party.

Cultivating a Working Alliance

A working alliance is a complex thing. A working alliance involves agreement not only with the person of the therapist, but also with the goals of the process, the specific techniques being used, the theory that drives them, and the bond between the two parties (Bordin, 1979). A greater amount of one may compensate for a lesser amount of another, but each of these factors plays a role. Where there is a deficit, the working alliance is impaired. An initial step of supervision, then, is developing a constructive relationship, a working alliance, with the therapist, just as the first task of therapy is to develop a working alliance between therapist and client. Protecting that working alliance becomes a priority throughout the course of supervision. The first task of a supervisor, as well as that of a therapist, is to be alert to anything that might involve the working alliance and to address that before addressing anything else, no matter how persuasively the other party argues otherwise. In the absence of a working alliance, work cannot proceed. Fortunately, development and maintenance of a working alliance is a product of good fundamentals: observational skills, interviewing technique, and social grace.

Working on Effective Communication

Supervisors and therapists, and therapists and clients should speak clearly and listen actively, hear objectively and with equanimity, and validate communications. This, then, should lead to appropriate behavior. If it doesn't, and skill training does not resolve impediments—on the part of supervisor or therapist—this needs to be addressed appreciatively and may even require therapy for one or both parties.

BEGINNING AND DOING

An "integrative" therapist needs to be able to explain whatever he or she is doing. Therapists should have a rationale underlying each of the various interventions or approaches to therapy that are formulated for his or her clientele (Nichols & Everett, 1986). Therapy may be endangered by intuitive approaches, which may reflect the unconscious needs and fears of the therapist. Therefore, it is important for the integrative therapist to be guided by a systematic, logical plan of intervention.

No matter how sophisticated the supervisor, trainees, or both, there are two important things to do in the initial sessions. The first is to conduct an appreciative interview of yourself as well as of the therapist. The second is to use "the minimalist model"—described later in this chapter—to guide your work with the therapist and the therapist's work with the client.

Interviewing the Supervisory Subsystem

Experienced supervisors often begin a new training relationship by interviewing themselves and the new trainee. This is done from a strengths, resources, and success posture. Your interview of yourself is covert and involves reflection about what you are doing when things are going well with a trainee and client. Moreover, you yourself have been in supervision and have some sense of what things were helpful, and what were not, at various stages of your career. The interview of the therapist is similar. If he or she had previous supervision, what was he or she doing and what was the supervisor doing when things were going well? And, if trainees had been in therapy themselves, what were they doing and what was the therapist doing when things were going well? The implication is that if things are to go well in supervision and therapy, there is much that they already know how to do. According to Quinn (1996), these probably will include a good, mutually affirming personal bond, sensitivity to the client's needs, and a climate promoting discovery. At the heart of these are social grace and acumen and a good interviewing technique: "active listening" in the service of an exploratory orientation (seeking to learn rather than to teach); asking about the cognitive and affective aspects of an experience; paying attention to tone, body language, and the context of what is being said; seeking validation that the other means what one is receiving; combating the obscurity of abstractions by seeking further definition and examples; and questioning generalizations and assumptions (after Satir, 1983). In summary, to be effective a supervisor should work on observational skills, active listening skills and interview skills, and actively work at interviewing the therapist. This is true not only in the initial stages of supervision but throughout, debriefing therapists by asking them what the supervisor is doing that they find helpful. Through role modeling and parallel processes continuous self-assessment will benefit the entire training system.

THE MINIMALIST MODEL

The minimalist model is a way of beginning and structuring one's interventions. It is an approach to use while you are learning about and deciding what models are best for you and your clientele. It also is a framework for intervention using an eclectic or integrative approach.

Change occurs through a number of channels: educating, altering perceptions, responding to the change in others, developing insight, releasing constricted emotions, confiding in others, coming to terms with painful experiences, clarifying communications, exercising one's will, lowering anxiety, and resolving grief, to name a few (Nichols, 1988).

In the most basic way, a therapist helps clients identify and remove those things that keep them from being able to solve problems. Therapists and clients need to become aware of blockages, identify them as problems, and take appropriate action to remove the obstacles (Pinsof, 1994). This is the same goal of supervisors with therapists. They too have to be aware of obstacles—to therapy and to supervision—and have the motivation and capacity to remove them. Moreover, it is likely that the barriers most available to mutual view and change are behavioral and involve a lack of sensitivity and knowledge or skill, (e.g., anxious people who talk too much and ask too little). However, the prudent supervisor should recognize that such obstacles are not the sole possession of trainees. Just as the therapist may not carefully observe or listen to a client or a supervisor, a supervisor may not carefully observe or listen to a therapist.

Sometimes, despite awareness and careful skill training, constructive communication does not occur. Individuals still don't listen and speak effectively. At other times, although successful communication is taking place—clear messages are sent and received—the behavior labeled problematic doesn't change. A vignette given by Lee, Emerson, and Kochka (see Chapter 10) illustrates how this can typify both therapist and client. When ineffective communication occurs, because senders don't speak effectively, receivers don't hear accurately or, having heard, don't change behavior, it is reasonable to assume that "something else" is operating. That "something else" may be contradictory goals or, quite likely, "baggage": unvoiced, conscious or unconscious expectations, of selves or others, based on present or past experience, which unduly influence what people perceive, think, decide and, therefore, do.

The Minimalist Model: Stage 1

The "minimalist model" suggests that supervisors with therapists, and therapists with clients, begin by focusing on the here and now behavior that is taking place between them. This is behavior that is being created in the dyad and can be experienced, observed, and labeled. At first meeting, a sample of behavior and a vehicle for interaction are required. Both supervisors and therapists can acquire these by asking each other to state and clarify their goals for the session. While establishing rapport one can observe the dyad solving problems. Ideally, communication would involve "I statements," clear and consistent focus, appropriate qualifiers (e.g., "Never say 'never' "), and validation of accurate reception. It also should demonstrate systemic thinking and a sense of circular causality.

Whenever these desirable skills and ways of looking at things do not appear, one party draws the attention of the other to that occurrence. Initially this is most likely to be a supervisor with a therapist, just as it would be a therapist with a client. The problematic nature of the behavior is described and appreciated, and training specific to that skill may be indicated. If the problematic behavior then is replaced by something more desirable, the dyad moves on. If other encumbrances arise, they are treated in similar fashion.

The Minimalist Model: Stage 2

If constructive talking and listening aren't possible, or don't change behavior, the assumption is that nonverbalized contradictory goals are operating. These may involve "baggage," that is, conscious or unconscious expectations from an individual's present or past life. Based on their past academic and clinical experiences, supervisors may have unrealistic ideas about what they and therapists can and should be able to do. Likewise, therapists may have unrealistic expectations or distorted perceptions of either supervisors or clients. (Lee gives an elaborate example of both supervisor and therapist reinforcing each other's misperceptions and expectations in Chapter 8.) Often the misperceptions and expectations may come from outside the academic and clinical sector. They may stem from contemporary and past relationships, including those with families of origin. The author has painful memories of supervisory behavior that felt abusive at the hands of a faculty member who was having problems with a late-adolescent son. This included an atmosphere of hostility and authoritarianism, alongside accusations of disobedience and lack of respect. Presumably, at the extreme, if "baggage" lost a therapist or supervisor sufficient degrees of freedom, a referral to therapy would be in order. Here the assumption is that supervision is something other than, and apart from, therapy, Aponte (1994), notwithstanding.

Just as with clients who misperceive or act on faulty expectations, the stuff of supervision—like the substance of therapy—may be co-editing that particular version of reality. How that is seen and done involves the particular theoretical model the supervisor feels fits the case, just as it would a therapist with a client. The supervisor's and the trainee's theories of problems and change dictate where they go next. These theories determine what each thinks the problem is, and hence what their goals are.

What theory to use to drive one's interventions is a complex question. Based on the various theoretical models, there are many possible ways of conceptualizing matters and of intervening. However, an integrative approach (Nichols & Everett, 1986) emphasizes "fit." The theory represents an accommodation to who the client is and what problems the client presents. One cannot consult effectively if one lacks the ability to engage the client. (Again, successful consultation requires shared goals and a relationship sufficient to support work on those goals.) The author remembers a glaring lack of influence when providing consultations to an allergist on the psychological and contextual aspects of asthma—until he discovered that the allergist himself was asthmatic and viewed his malady in a narrow biological fashion! However, the theories through which a case is viewed and the attendant interventions also must incorporate the therapist's strengths, including depth of knowledge and enthusiasm.

Problems of differentiation may require work with the trainee's family of origin, but Schnarch (1991) has demonstrated that effective work can occur in an affected dyad. The author can envision the following interchange between supervisor and therapist. First, the supervisor would draw the trainee's attention to an inappropriately intense emotional response to a critical comment. "You used 100 pounds of dynamite where 10 pounds might have been more appropriate. What else is going on here?" The therapist might respond that she recently had a bad experience with a very critical professor. The supervisor then could ask questions designed to promote reality testing in order to get the supervisor's identity untangled from the professor's. "In what ways am I like your old professor? In what ways am I unlike that person? What did I just do? Under similar circumstances, what would your old professor have done?"

In other situations, there may be actions and inhibitions best understood in terms of relational ethics, that is, justice, fairness, loyalty, and merit. The supervisor may need to proceed in a way that allows the trainee to express loyalty to and admiration toward other faculty or supervisors, perhaps those who played formative roles in the trainee's inchoate career. There also may be an unwillingness to try new ways if the trainee does not feel that he or she was treated fairly in the past. This may include appreciation of the trainee's ideas, acknowledgment of the trainee's contributions inside and outside of the therapy and supervision rooms, issues about performance evaluations, and matters of equity.

Others may be impressed by an apparent ambivalence of the trainee toward forming a training bond, or by persistent projection of positive or negative traits. The techniques suggested by object relations theory may be indicated. The supervisor would work to create a safe "holding" supervisory environment while questioning apparent projections and encouraging the trainee to take appropriate emotional risks.

At times a trainee might be handicapped by a lack of information or alternate perspectives. The supervisor's response would be to use questions, reframing, and the observations and hypotheses of others to generate more information. One way to raise consciousness about too narrow a construing of reality is to use a case presentation and exploit the "story" metaphor. What is the client's "table of contents"? What events were put in and which left out? Who are the "cast of characters" and what are their "roles"? What are the "dominant themes"? Are these the same for the therapist, is there an editing process occurring, and what is necessary to arrive at a common reality? Are other constructions possible, and what would be the implications of exploring them?

Case Examples

Where Skill Training Worked Well

"I don't know if I'll be able to talk to you!" was the opening statement, given with an air of alarm, by Mrs. B., aged 65. "You're so young!" Mr. B., also 65, did not seem inclined to disagree. The therapist shared their doubts. They said that they wanted sex therapy and, as he looked at their aging faces and overweight, aging bodies, he could not picture them finding each other sexually attractive. Indeed, he felt squeamish about the very idea of robust sexuality in any couple that age. He directed their attention toward constructing a genogram while he obtained a family history.

The therapist seemed unsettled at the subsequent supervision session, and the supervisor commented on that. "You're having trouble looking me in the eye, you came late to this session, and you're finding it hard to talk. I suspect that you are uncomfortable about something." The therapist readily agreed. It was the case with the older couple. He felt extremely youthful and inexperienced relative to their status in life. Moreover, they were the same age as his parents. In fact, he did not feel that he could empathize with Mrs. B. because he had little experience with older women: His mother and father divorced when he was a child and he stayed with his father, his mother moving to another state. He and his mother had never been close; their visitations were stilted. As he spoke, his anxiety seemed to decrease and he was verbally fluid. However, his speech became somewhat disjointed again as he tried to describe his discomfort about doing sex therapy with this couple. He was embarrassed to admit it, but he could not imagine a couple having sex at age 65 with the lights on. (This was an important feature for Mr. and Mrs. B. Mr. B. needed to see her body in order to maintain his arousal.) It all seemed faintly repelling, perverse, and even funny to the therapist. With this attitude, and at this stage of his training, what could he know and offer?

Throughout this session the supervisor practiced active, reflective listening. As this was done, the therapist appeared to be instructing both of them quite well in what was problematic, venting anxiety, and getting centered. The supervisor brought the session to a close with a final reflection: "You are wondering how you can be useful to them?" The therapist agreed. However, this session had been helpful. Just talking about things made the therapist feel much better.

The therapist began the next session by saying "I'm glad you came back. I felt that you were wondering if I have enough experience to be helpful to you. Talk about that." The couple agreed and Mrs. B. spoke at length about her discomfort with a therapy situation. She was not comfortable talking about sex and, in her family of origin, one was careful never to talk about personal matters with outsiders. As she spoke, and the therapist and her husband listened attentively, Mrs. B. seemed to forget that she was uncomfortable. "Well!" she said in surprise. "I don't seem to be having any trouble talking to you!" Her husband interjected that this wouldn't last long, once the focus was on their sex life. His wife, he volunteered, was not one to talk to him about that, better yet to strangers. On cue, Mrs. B. nodded her agreement. The therapist picked up on that. "What do you imagine happening if you were to share your concerns with me?"

Mr. and Mrs. B. both looked thoughtful, and then puzzled. They then began to talk about the specifics of the sexual problem—Mr. B.'s impotency. In pursuing the context of this, the therapist learned about Mr. B.'s massive coronary 2 years ago and two coronary bypass operations, the last one preceded by a near-death experience in an emergency room. Over the next few sessions, traditional sexual therapy was interspersed with talk about Mr. B.'s changing attitudes about life and his impending retirement in a few months. Mrs. B. was worried at the prospect of such a busy man being at home full time. She also was worried about a proposed move to a retirement community in another state at a time when their youngest daughter, very close to her mother, was getting a divorce. Several grandchildren would be involved in this situation.

As the supervision paralleled the therapy, the supervisor had to do very little—just as the therapist had to do very little. The couple were talking productively with each other. Each was listening and validating, and responding nondefensively, and this corresponded to accommodation of one to the other outside the session. So there was no need for the therapist to get involved except when the process was not ideal. At such a time, the therapist might caution that each party should speak only for himself or herself, not assume that the other knew what she or he was thinking and feeling, make sure that a communication was being received accurately, and allow the other person without argument to own individual thoughts and feelings. This was precisely the process that also was taking place in supervision. Therapist and clients developed a very close and open relationship such that the therapist and clients expressed sincere regret at termination, and met again just to say good-by when the couple moved out of state. The supervisor and therapist also felt a special bond in their relationship.

Where Skill Training Was Not Enough

A woman called for marital treatment and the case was assigned to a post-practicum male therapist. Mrs. C. was an extraordinarily attractive young woman and to the therapist's amazement voiced her frustration at the lack of physical affection in her marriage. She complained that her husband was not physically intimate in any way and that she was very frustrated. The therapist immediately took sides. He felt personally attracted to Mrs. C., was excited about her unfulfilled yearning, and he thought that the husband's behavior was outrageous. He was amazed that Mr. C. would leave his wife unfulfilled, resentful, and feeling entitled. Surely another man would leap at the chance to make her happy.

The supervisor, also a male, was not surprised that the therapist would find the woman's presentation sexually arousing. However, he was concerned that the therapist did not maintain his neutrality and did not think of her presentation of self as a therapeutic ploy, that is, as a way of inducting the therapist into the dysfunctional family system, seducing him into a triangle, or distracting him from observing or thinking about other things.

Accordingly, the supervisor began by interviewing the therapist about the couple, asking questions that would require more information than the therapist had to date or that would require thinking in terms of complementarity. For example, he observed how unusual it seemed for such a physically expressive woman to woo and marry an emotionally barren and undemonstrative mate. The supervisor noted that Mrs. C. dominated the session and that Mr. C. contributed little. Would not things be better served if the therapist interviewed both parties, getting each to speak for self, and making certain that each not only felt that she or he was getting a fair shake in the session, but also presented his or her full set of concerns about the marriage?

The situation did not improve, neither outside of the therapy session nor in it. Nobody, including the therapist, changed their behavior in the sessions. Mrs. C. complained bitterly to the therapist about her husband, he sat quietly and did not defend himself, and the therapist was critical of him in supervision. Soon it appeared that Mr. C. would not be coming in with his wife. They both agreed that she needed the sessions to work on her own concerns.

Because the therapist seemed incapable of constructive, balanced, reflective communication with both members of the marriage, and the case was worsening, the supervisor became more directive. He insisted that instead of seeing Mrs. C. by herself, the therapist meet with Mr. C. The therapist was angry at this and felt that the supervisor clearly did not understand him or the situation. The supervisor was impressed by the therapist's apparently irrational emotion and his continuing inflexibility. Calling attention to the therapist's anger, and its amount, the supervisor began a line of questioning designed to untangle the present situation from what he suspected were influential events of the past. This intervention elicited disbelief on the part of the therapist, attacks on the credibility and objectivity of the supervisor, and a sense that the rapport between therapist and supervisor was irrevocably harmed. However, in the following supervisory session, the therapist volunteered that he had been in a similar situation before: when his parents divorced and his father's family tried to defend his father's treatment of his mother. (His father was invested in his occupation and his mother complained that he was not there for her. She subsequently had an affair.)

The supervisor asked how he was similar to, and different from these relatives, and how Mr. and Mrs. C.'s marital situation compared to his parents'. The therapist decided that the supervisor was not defending Mr. C., but was simply asking context-establishing questions. However, he asserted that their marital situation was quite similar to his parents'. The session ended with the supervisor's question, "Do you have enough information to say that?"

Clearly there was no great "Aha!" of insight, or even an admission that the supervisor might have some credibility after all. However, the therapist subsequently conducted three individual sessions with Mr. C. and discovered that Mr. C. experienced Mrs. C. as a very critical and managing individual who quickly took over any area of her life that she thought was important. To reinforce that position, she allegedly found fault with any of Mr. C.'s attempts to handle their affairs; and, not particularly secure or anxious to do more work than he needed to do, Mr. C. let her take responsibility for many things. She, however, complained of being overworked and unappreciated, and he disliked her pervasive hostility and controlling ways. This picture of marital complementarity served as the basis for future conjoint sessions and the couple made substantial progress.

A COMFORTING THOUGHT

It may be important to remember that a supervision session, like a therapy session, by its very nature is bound to be helpful. Two or more individuals have set aside a block of time to look appreciatively at how they are working together and to make plans. That act reflects their mutual commitment, and the subsequent time of reflection is better than no reflection at all, or attempts to think about things in a less systematic way in a more cluttered time. The supervisor should draw comfort from this, let the situation itself "do its thing," and think of how to augment it.

REFERENCES

APONTE, H. J. (1994). How personal can training get? *Journal of Marital and Family Therapy, 20*, 3–15.

BORDIN, E. S. (1979). The generalizability of the psychoanalytic concept of the working alliance. *Psychotherapy: Theory, Research and Practice, 16*, 252–260.

LIDDLE, H. A., BREUNLIN, D. C., & SCHWARTZ, R. C. (Eds.). (1988). *Handbook of family therapy training and supervision*. New York: Guilford Press.

NICHOLS, W. C. (1988). *Marital therapy: An integrative approach*. New York: Guilford Press.

NICHOLS, W. C., & EVERETT, C. A. (1986). *Systemic family therapy: An integrative approach*. New York: Guilford Press.

PINSOF, W. M. (1994). An overview of Integrative Problem Centered Therapy: A synthesis of family and individual psychotherapies. *Journal of Family Therapy, 16*, 103–120.

QUINN, W. H. (1996). The client speaks out: Three domains of meaning. *Journal of Family Psychotherapy, 7*, 71–93.

SATIR, V. (1983). *Conjoint family therapy* (3rd ed.). Palo Alto, CA: Science and Behavior Books.

SCHNARCH, D. A. (1991). *Constructing the sexual crucible*. New York: Norton.

CHAPTER 5

Mirrors, Cameras, and Blackboards

Modalities of Supervision

WILLIAM C. NICHOLS
ROBERT E. LEE

Mirrors, cameras, and blackboards are terms used here to symbolize, albeit roughly, three major modalities of supervision in family therapy. "Mirrors" refer to what has been called "live supervision." Live supervision originally referred to supervision in which a supervisor or supervisory team observed from behind a one-way mirror as the therapist worked with a client system. Subsequently, this process changed and the observers actively intervened in the therapy process to make observations or to give directives (Liddle & Schwartz, 1983; Montalvo, 1973; Schwartz, Liddle, & Breunlin, 1988).

Today, live supervision typically refers to supervision in which the supervisor or supervisory team intervenes periodically through telephone call-ins, "bug in the ear" communications, midsession breaks, and sitting in on the session. Variants include co-therapy involving the therapist and supervisor and bringing a supervisory team into the therapy room to conduct supervision of the therapist in front of the clients (Ron, 1996). The clients sometimes enter into the discussion (see Dwyer, Chapter 12).

"Cameras" symbolize the use of supervision based on videotapes or audiotapes of the therapist's work with clients. The supervisor and therapist view or listen to the electronic recordings of sessions or portions of sessions and engage in discussion of pertinent matters.

"Blackboards" refer to the case presentation approach. This involves the presentation of verbal and written reports by the trainee and case discussion between the supervisor and trainee.

Although all three approaches appear to be used extensively, sometimes in combination with one another (Everett, 1980; Nichols, Nichols, & Hardy, 1990; Wetchler & Vaughn, 1992), institutional marital and family therapy regards live supervision the most highly and videotape or audiotape methods next. In the absence of live supervision, for example, the training standards of the Commission on Accreditation for Marriage and Family Therapy Education (1997) recommend that supervision based on audiotapes or videotapes be used. Moreover, at least half of all supervision in accredited programs must involve these modalities. The perceived advantages of "mirror" and "camera" supervision also are well described in the literature. In contrast, little is said about the case presentation method, and the implication on the part of some seems to be that it is an inferior training modality, perhaps not to be used. A notable exception with regard to case consultation is found in the voices of McCollum and Wetchler (see Chapter 6).

In this chapter we will take a brief but appreciative look at all three modalities. Each has its uses and limitations. We will compare and contrast live, videotape or audiotape, and case presentation approaches to supervision. In so doing, we will recognize the value of what appears to be a neglected approach by institutionalized marital and family therapy, the case presentation approach.

LIVE SUPERVISION

What does live supervision offer that is unique? Very simply, it allows the supervisor to affect both the trainee and the family client system by altering the course of therapy as therapy occurs. Consequently, there is one major reason to use a live approach as opposed to any other—immediacy. Other reasons to use a live approach are as follows:

- To view and experience the immediacy of the therapeutic situation.
- To obtain cognitive or affective data from the therapist, the client, or both.
- To provide immediate instruction.
- To implement a theoretical persuasion that holds that the training team (supervisor-therapist-client) functions best "on line" (that is, while the therapy actually is occurring, with the supervisor able to affect the process immediately).

There certainly are other benefits from using a live approach. It is a good teaching tool, especially for students observing from behind the mirror who are not affected by anxiety in the same ways that the student therapist may be affected. It also may be entertaining, intriguing, or reassuring to clients and therapists.

The use of reflecting teams is purported to bring several advantages to training in family therapy. This form of live supervision is thought to incorporate the perspectives of clients, therapist, and supervisor in an "equitable, recursive, and empowering way," and to provide guidelines to speed up the therapy process and increase therapists' and clients' options for change (Young, Perlesz, Paterson, O'Hanlon, Newbold, Chaplin, & Bridge, 1989). A reflecting team may also afford neutrality and support hypothesizing while providing a good division of labor (Andersen, 1993; Tomm, 1984a, 1984b). For example, the interviewer does not have to make sense of everything in the session. Somebody else can do that, leaving the interviewer free to work on interviewing technique.

However, there are some negative characteristics of live supervision as it generally is used. These include the following:

- Dilution of the relationship between the client and the therapist. This approach typically makes the team into the therapist. That is, rather than being the sole therapist, the therapist essentially becomes subject to the instruction and influence of a larger therapy team that makes significant input during the course of the session.
- Implications for the therapist that he or she is not able to function on his or her own in a session, but requires the presence and intervention of a supervisor or supervisory team.
- Absence of time or opportunity for substantial reflection. The therapist must respond to the questions or directives immediately, deciding quickly how to proceed in response to the intervention from the supervisor or team.
- Distraction of the therapist, the client, or both.
- Focusing on a single session. The telescopic view makes it difficult—if not impossible—to give adequate consideration to wider system issues such as culture, gender, and other contextual matters (Hoffman, 1981; McCollum & Wetchler, 1995).

The Intervention/Interruption Issue

Surprisingly, there has not been a large amount of question in the literature regarding the effects of interruptions on the therapeutic process, the client system, and the trainee. Instead, there seems to have been an assumption that interruptions are good; they contribute to better therapy and learning. However, empirical studies suggest that we need to be cautious. Although in one study trainees viewed telephone call-ins and during-session consultations as "valuable and complementary supervisory tools" (Liddle, Davidson, & Barrett, 1988, p. 391), they nevertheless were ambivalent. They complained of performance anxiety and lack of autonomy. In another study, participants were affected to differing degrees by interruptions of sessions by supervisors or therapists (Smith, Smith, & Salts, 1991). However, the latter researchers concluded that interruption was not disruptive enough to warrant not using this approach.

One point that does not seem to have been considered is that if there is supervisory intervention during the course of therapy, the opportunity for the therapist to make his or her own decisions in that situation is lost. Thus it is impossible to know what the therapist would have done if he or she had been permitted to proceed without any interference from the outside.

The fact that a facility possesses one-way mirrors and can place observers behind the mirror does not mean that the observers inevitably must interrupt the therapy session. Beginning more than three decades ago, when involved in extensive use of observation of therapy sessions by postdoctoral interns, we made the decision to refrain from making interventions into the therapeutic process unless there were indications that the parties in the therapy room were at risk of being harmed (Nichols, 1988). Goldenberg and Goldenberg (1996) indicated that, although strategic therapist Jay Haley teaches and trains by observing from behind a one-way mirror, in recent years he has provided feedback after the therapy session. He leaves the therapist in charge of the actual session.

Despite the high regard in which live supervision has been generally held, there is reason to question whether providing supervision in this fashion actually is a better approach than using self-report methods. Fennell, Hovestadt, and Harvey (1986), in a comparison of delayed feedback and live supervision models, found that live supervision was not superior to delayed trainee self-report. Similarly, Wetchler and Vaughn (1992) indicated that the results of their study of supervisory critical incidents did not support the belief that raw data supervision is superior to self-report methods. Certainly, the advent of electronic taping of sessions, particularly the use of videotaping, makes it possible for the supervisor to learn what has occurred in therapy without being physically present behind a one-way mirror or inside the treatment room.

VIDEOTAPE OR AUDIOTAPE SUPERVISION

What does this approach offer that is important, if not unique? Videotapes capture the actions, and audiotapes the verbal productions of all participants in the therapy session. The videotape or audiotape approach offers the following:

- Provides the potential for review of the actual events in the session. This can be done at leisure and contrasts with "live" supervision in which the moment occurs and passes and with case presentation in which the supervisor and therapist are restricted to the therapist's recall. The supervisor can audit the tapes or parts of the tapes prior to the supervisory session. (Although this is costly in terms of time, our experience indicates that it may be well worth the expenditure of time and effort, particularly in instances in which supervisor or supervisor and trainee have isolated learning problems or there are case dynamics that need to be elucidated and further explored.)

- Captures the actions of all parties (therapist and clients), although not necessarily the cognitive and emotional processes that drove them.

- Offers the opportunity for comparison and reflection about what one says one did or felt as contrasted with what can be seen or heard in the recording. Therapists often remember only selective parts of sessions (e.g., where they think things went well or where they were problematic). Video- and audiotapes aid recall and correct bias by permitting things missed by the therapist to be picked up subsequent to the session by the therapist and the supervisor.

- Offers the opportunity for trainees to gain additional self-awareness by observing their patterns of behavior in the emotional intensity of therapeutic sessions (Keller & Protinsky, 1984).

- Provides material exemplary of good therapy or on which further teaching can be based. Tomm and Wright (1979) have described how trainees can be helped to improve their perceptual and conceptual skills with the aid of videotapes. After monitoring a tape, they can be asked to describe what they have witnessed in the client system, to reflect on interventions that might be effective in similar situations with client systems in the future, or to share what they have learned regarding marital and family therapy from the session.

- Permits distance learning in that the supervisor does not have to be present for the session.

- Is economical. The entire session does not have to be reviewed in order to isolate patterns, touch on various topics of interest, and focus on specific parts of the session. The supervisor also can sample many cases by the same individual or, in group supervision, sample cases from several different individuals in one supervisory session.

- Allows for repeated use. Things that were missed initially can be picked up subsequently by the therapist, the supervisor, or supervisory team. Also, tapes can be stored, allowing comparisons between sessions—over time with the same client, or at different times in the training process.

- Selected incidents may be important stimuli to which a therapist can "free associate" and thereby discover his or her internal processes during the supervisory session.

The use of taped materials is not all positive, of course. Several drawbacks or limitations of using videotapes in supervision are noted as follows:

- Focusing on a single session rather than on larger contextual issues. If the session is to be contextualized, the therapist and supervisor must do so by reconstructing through discussion what transpired previously (Breunlin, Karrer, McGuire, & Cimmarusti (1988).

- Focusing on discussion of the specific events seen on the tape, rather than engaging in more extensive issues of therapeutic issues and case planning (McCollum & Wetchler, 1995).
- Making the therapist very anxious and defensive, which may hinder learning (Breunlin et al., 1988).

The preceding limitation can in some instances be converted to an asset. For example, the supervisor can determine whether the therapist has "learning problems" (things he or she needs to learn) or "problems with learning" (e.g., emotional blocks to recognizing and dealing with issues presented by the client system) and proceed to work appropriately on the problems thus elucidated.

The use of videotapes can be enhanced by adding additional features to this mode of supervision. Chapter 11 by Quinn and Nagirreddy contains many excellent examples.

CASE PRESENTATION SUPERVISION

Supervision based on case presentations has been around for a long time. Until the 1950s and even later in some instances, supervisors were largely dependent on written and spoken reports of trainees for their information on what had transpired in clinical sessions. Raw data were not available. In an effort to fill this void, supervisors frequently required trainees to reconstruct from memory "verbatim" reports of each session. Those of us who were subjected to such requirements can attest to the distasteful nature of the task of "writing verbatims." But they were an excellent teaching tool. They provided experience in thinking about and reporting on events and dynamics. Subsequently, trainees would be asked to conceptualize what had transpired and plan for future sessions. Often this was an opportunity to integrate case history with theory.

When technology changed and audiotapes and videotapes became available, there was no longer any excuse for foisting on trainees the task of providing verbatim reports. However, it is possible that, in some settings, as the amount of writing diminished so did the attendant reflection. Being observed through a one-way mirror or captured on film was novel and glamorous. And, since the raw data was "right there," trainees were freed from the hard mental work of determining and writing down the essential features of a session and considering their implications.

Consequently, our practice of supervision in formal training settings has generally included the requirement that trainees prepare a written report for each clinical session, regardless of whether audio- or videotapes are available. Typically, the reports have three sections and are a page or less in length. First, trainees are asked to write a brief descriptive paragraph of what occurred in the session. This can be a brief summary of what transpired or a critical incident report. Second, they are asked to compose a paragraph describing the dynamics of the session—among family members, and between the client system and the therapist. Third, trainees are given the option of including a brief paragraph of personal reactions, fantasies, predictions about future sessions, and so on. This section is regarded as "the growing edge," in that trainees are encouraged to think about what happened, its meanings, and what could be done in future sessions. In addition, at the beginning of supervision trainees are provided with outlines for preparing treatment plans that form frameworks for conceptualizing events and process, and contain flexible guidelines for planning treatment and evaluating progress toward goals. Implementation of the plan, progress toward achievement of the stated goals, and planning for the next session with clients are then discussed in supervision, and the flexible treatment plan is amended as appropriate.

We believe that this commitment to reporting, evaluating, and planning is quite valuable to a trainee's development. Where the focus otherwise might be limited to the acquisition of interview skills, this approach aids in the comprehension of human behavior and the understanding and application of theory.

Special Features of the Case Presentation Method

The case presentation approach:

- Provides a broader perspective than do modalities that highlight a single session. McCollum and Wetchler (1995) use the metaphor of a zoom lens to refer to the view provided by the case presentation approach.
- Provides the opportunity to examine the wider contextual issues of the therapy, the clients, and the therapist. This ability is enhanced by the use of genograms and ecomaps in which family processes, including the trainee's (Deveaux & Lubell, 1994), can be depicted and explored more extensively than is possible in tightly focused "do it now," live supervision, or is likely to occur in videotape-focused supervision.
- Provides the opportunity to talk, ventilate, and conceptualize based on trainee observations and experiences with multiple sessions of therapy. This includes comparing and contrasting what has occurred and been learned in previous sessions with what has occurred in and been learned from the most recent session. Similarly, the trainee and supervisor can compare and contrast different client systems for

learning purposes, and explore the vicissitudes of the trainee with multiple settings and cases.

- Provides the opportunity for a considerable amount of didactic work regarding the nature of therapy, the needs of clients, and skill development.
- Is economical. The supervisor does not have to be present when therapy is provided. A large number of cases can be reviewed at times convenient to the supervisor.
- Permits the creation of a mutual questioning process between the supervisor and trainee that assists the trainee in organizing information about client families into useful frameworks for consideration (West, Bubenzer, Pinsoneault, & Holeman, 1993).
- Permits involvement of the client system in the supervisory-therapy process. The client system can be asked to discuss how therapy has been and could be going. The clients also can furnish responses, evaluations, and so on immediately subsequent to the therapy session or periodically during the treatment process. Lee, Emerson, and Kochka describe a variant of this in Chapter 10.
- Provides the opportunity for supervisors and trainees to explore the influence of important contemporary issues, gender, culture, social class, and larger social systems (McCollum & Wetchler, 1995). It also provides an opportunity to consider radical constructivism, social constructionism, and power and hierarchy (Hardy, 1993).

Uses of the Case Consultation Method

There are indications that case consultation is used as often as, or more often than, the other two approaches. Saba and Liddle (1986), for example, found that most supervisors in their sample used trainee self-report. Moreover, individual case consultation was the technique most often identified by both supervisors and trainees as the most helpful supervision technique in a study of American Association for Marriage and Family Therapy (AAMFT) approved supervisors by Wetchler and Vaughn (1992). Nichols, Nichols, and Hardy (1990) surveyed supervisors in all types of practice and teaching settings and discovered that case presentation methods ranked second in frequency of usage, behind the use of video or audio recordings, and ahead of live supervision. In another study, in which individual case consultation was not given as an alternative, McKenzie and associates (McKenzie, Atkinson, Quinn, & Heath, 1986) found that most of the supervisors in their sample used audiotapes as the basis for supervision.

In a study of AAMFT approved supervisors, Nichols, Nichols, and Hardy (1990) discovered that the use of videotape and live supervision both increased dramatically in the decade ending in 1986. The increase was thought to be related to the growth of accredited graduate programs in universities. Within university based family therapy training programs live supervision and videotape methods are more likely to be used than case consultation or audiotape methods (Henry, Sprenkle, & Sheehan, 1986; Kaplan, 1987; Sprenkle, 1988).

There are a large number of references and positive attributions to live supervision in the family therapy literature. This probably is because of its popularity among university faculty, who make disproportionately large contributions to the literature when compared to practitioners and supervisors who use other methods of supervision. At any rate, the case for claims that live supervision is superior to other supervisory methods appears to rest on shaky foundations. Moreover, when evaluating the efficacy of a supervisory technique, there is a need to be concerned with which technique "for which trainee under which situation" (Wetchler & Vaughn, 1992, p. 135). The level of development of the trainee may be an important variable (see Dwyer & Lee, Chapter 9; Liddle, 1991) .

SOME OBSERVATIONS, THOUGHTS, AND COMMENTS

Each of the three approaches to supervision sketched in this chapter has values and purposes. In our judgment, it is not necessary to debate which is best or to become an advocate, spokesperson, or apologist for any one of the three. The statements that follow are not intended to spark debate. We feel that it is exceedingly easy to generate too much heat and not enough light by taking dogmatic and authoritarian stances and daring others to prove us wrong if they can. Rather, our intent is to propose a more careful examination of the values of case presentation as a supervisory approach to facilitate a more thoughtful approach in general to marital and family therapy supervision. We would caution against purism and purity in approach, and favor integration; caution against apprenticeship training in narrowly defined methods or schools, and encourage more integrative education and training in family therapy, which focuses on the learning of the trainee and increased opportunity for the student to be more self-directive than is possible in an apprenticeship context (Nichols, 1997).

Supervision from Three Perspectives: Service, Teaching, and Learning

Supervision has sometimes been cast in terms of a debate over personal growth versus skill development. Haley (1988) has been adamant about the importance of skill development and opposed to dealing with the personal development of the therapist. Others (Aponte, 1994) have emphasized the need to attend to the person of the therapist. There are indications that the field is moving toward integrating self-awareness and skill in the delivery of therapy and, hence, in programs preparing family therapists. McDaniel and Landau-Stanton (1992) have described integrative efforts in a postgraduate training program for family therapists at the University of Rochester. Watson (1993) has pointed out that as the field moves toward such integration, critical issues arise. These include the preparation of culturally and gender sensitive therapists, and the possibilities of dual relationships in the training and supervisory process.

When we consider what we are trying to accomplish with supervision, a central issue may be who—trainee, therapist, supervisor, or reflecting team—determines what is considered important. In this regard, probably the method of supervision is less important than the attitudes and behaviors of the supervisor. It certainly is possible for a supervisor to observe a trainee working with a client system without interrupting the session and making interventions into the process. On the other end of the line, it is possible for a trainee to present the material—description, content, and dynamics—that he or she considers significant and, in a worst case scenario, to have the supervisor discount the report and enter into a mode of interrogation and issuance of directives that strips the trainee of the learning responsibility and privilege. In either instance, it should be possible for supervisor and trainee to engage in respectful dialogue in which meaningful learning occurs.

The issue isn't whether or not a hierarchy exists. The issues appear to pertain to attitudes and behaviors rather than structure. Liddle and associates found that many trainees in their study of supervision believed that "it was possible to have a collaborative supervisory relationship within a hierarchically organized relationship" (Liddle, Davidson, & Barrett, 1988, p. 389). Similarly, Edwards and Keller (1995) have proposed that a "heterarchical" alternative be instituted so that there can be "partnership discourse" in family therapy supervision. In this regard, a study of trainees trained through live supervision in essentially a structural-strategic therapy model (Liddle, 1985) found that trainees emphasized the need for supervisors to "be flexible and change over the course of training" as well as to show respect to trainees and to provide increasing opportunity for trainee independence (Liddle, Davidson, & Barrett, 1988, p. 395). These also are the findings reported by Dwyer and Lee in Chapter 9.

A therapist can bring in written reports and tapes and select places where he or she wishes to focus. Alternately, a supervisor can suggest what is done with the tapes, that is, determine which tapes shall be audited and how that will take place. This might involve straightforward auditing of a session without selection, selection of excerpts from the beginning, the middle, or the ending, or skimming the tape and searching for critical incidents.

When addressing the focus of supervision issues, instead of thinking about hierarchy, it may be more productive to think in terms of teaching, learning, and service perspectives. Although there is some inevitable overlap among these perspectives, we are pulling them apart here for clarity.

The Service Perspective—Focusing on the Client System

Jay Haley (1975) once wrote a provocative article titled "Why A Mental Health Clinic Should Avoid Family Therapy." Analogously, one could make an equally provocative statement that clinics primarily interested in the delivery of services should avoid training therapists. When one decides to use trainees in the delivery of services, it is necessary to permit the trainee to progress at his or her own pace if the training is to provide the trainee with the best opportunity to learn.

At some point, one needs to examine a critical question: "Who is the therapist?" Is the trainee the therapist, or is she or he part of a therapy team, which may include the supervisor in a co-therapy arrangement, a reflecting team, or a supervisor who interrupts the treatment through one or more methods? The question of who is responsible for working with the client system is not necessarily the same as who is ultimately responsible for the outcome of the treatment and for the welfare of the clients. The supervisor can have legal and ethical responsibilities without being required to deliver the services personally. Despite discussions in the literature about erasing the hierarchy between supervisors and trainees, co-constructions of reality, and related matters, supervisors remain legally liable for how their trainees handle cases and remain responsible for the evaluation of their trainees' therapeutic work and development as therapists.

Clients deserve to be informed that the therapist is a trainee and that his or her work is being supervised by a knowledgeable professional in order to help the trainee learn and thus better serve the clients. It is not necessary to introduce the supervisor to the clients (as recommended in an ethics and legal issues book by Vesper and Brock, 1991) to provide the clients with adequate basis for deciding whether to enter into therapy with a trainee. It is persuasive to us that good service generally can be rendered to the client system by therapists working under supervision, and that such therapy in many instances possibly is superior to the treatment provided by some more experienced practitioners who work independently. Certainly, the examination of cases in supervision probably is more extensive than the examinations conducted by solo practitioners in busy outpatient practice.

Of course, the supervisor probably can "do it better" than the trainee. At least, we would assume so, or else he or she should not be in the supervisory role. This holds true in all approaches to dealing with clients— in traditional "therapist expert" situations and in contemporary, constructivist, narrative approaches in which the therapist co-constructs a narrative in conjunction with the client system. But is the primary issue one of service or is it one of education?

A distinction can be made between supervising for administrative purposes and supervising for educational purposes. It is understandable that agencies committed to public service be concerned with providing the best service possible to clients. The argument was made early that live supervision provides better services, as well as more complete and accurate information than presumably is obtained from trainee self-reports (Rickert & Turner, 1978). The salient question, however, is not where and how the supervisor secures data but what the supervisor does with regard to the therapy. If you argue that a supervisor can secure better data through live supervision, you also might reason that a supervisor's direct interventions in a session are for "the good of the clients" and for the benefit of the trainee. However, the trainees at times may feel that the case is not "theirs" and that they are an extension of the supervisor (Liddle, Davidson, & Barrett, 1988).

The Teaching Perspective—Focusing on the Supervisor

Historically, many family therapists were rebels, discoverers of new approaches to working with human beings who were eager to teach what they had discovered or invented to trainees. The traditional "see one, do one, teach one" pattern characteristic of medicine was essentially the approach taken by many of the family therapy pioneers. As the pioneers have begun to pass from the scene, marital and family therapy has ceased to be an obstreperous newcomer to the therapy field, and as formal educational programs have developed, there is less reason to involve the second and subsequent generation supervisors directly in the treatment process. There is less need to assume that family therapy knowledge is restricted to a small number of persons and no good reason to rely exclusively on supervision for learning family therapy, as was often the case in early years. There is immensely more content and substantive family therapy material available for students and trainees to master in their educational experience prior to and during their clinical training work.

Also, as the "schools" phase of the family therapy movement grows older, it becomes more evident to some theorists and practitioners that there are many ways to perform therapy, and to focus naively and uncritically on the approaches and techniques of one school, supervisor, or team perhaps is not the most desirable path to follow. The systems concept of equifinality implies that one may start from any one of several different points and use any one of a variety of techniques to reach a desired goal or secure a given result (Nichols, 1996). Consequently, we see a slowly emerging tendency in the therapy field to be more reflective (Schon, 1983, 1987).

It seems evident that either the service or the teaching perspective will be favored in supervision. Some kind of compromise is desirable and probably necessary. For example, one can take the stance that providing the best possible service to clients is the goal which, at the extreme, provides the supervisor and observing/reflecting teams with a license to intervene and give orders and directives to the trainee/therapist about how to proceed. This can be done immediately in live supervision and also with audio or video and case consultation approaches. The effects that heavy directiveness can have on trainees deserves more attention than it typically receives. Our observations over the years support the idea that zealous supervisory focus on "what ought to be done" may have unintended consequences for the trainee.

The Learning Perspective—Focusing on the Trainee

One of us (Nichols, 1988) has described an educational focus for supervision based on the principles of *educere,* a progressive leading out of knowledge and skill on the part of the trainee, as opposed to "pouring in" or imposition of knowledge and skill from the outside. At the extremes, the differences between these two approaches can be described as education versus indoctrination. Both are respectable approaches to learning, but they have different purposes and outcomes.

As already noted, one can take the stance that adequate supervision will result in adequate services to clients—assuming that at least a moderate degree of care is taken in the assigning and matching of clients and therapists and that the supervisor adequately monitors the therapy. Can one assume that adequate learning and trainee development will occur if the supervisor takes part in the therapy process?

We think a career development perspective should take precedence over a limited view of single session focus, skill training, and apprenticeship goals. A training program should prepare a student therapist for future, "real-world" practice. How well does this occur when therapists are trained primarily in a therapy team setting? If what occurs is heavily determined by supervisory teams, or if trainees largely function in treatment teams or with a cotherapist, how do those trainees learn to function independently once "graduated" from the training setting and program? How many of them are going to practice with a team behind a mirror or in the room with a family? Where is this done outside of subsidized settings, particularly training settings? How many outpatient treatment facilities provide multiple therapists for each client system?

Even more important, how much unnecessary "baggage" goes with the trainee into the real world of practice and clinical service? Inevitably, a graduate of any educational program needs to "unpack his or her (cognitive and emotional) bag," taking out parts that have been taken over uncritically from others—either as a result of unexamined identification with others or through coercive pressure—and "repack the bag" with materials (theory, ideas, techniques) that have become his or her own.

We have worked with and observed trainees, both during and after their clinical training experiences, for more than three decades. We have discovered that the early reactions of trainees to their training experiences often differ from their later reactions and evaluations. Trainees initially may be accepting and even enthusiastic with respect to highly directive and frequent supervisory interventions into their therapeutic work. Later, however, trainees can be fairly negative about such an experience. A few years after training they may retrospectively describe "coercive" supervisory experiences, which "interfered with my growth, especially with developing my own identity as a therapist."

Multiple Choices in Theoretical Approaches to Supervision

A logical case can be made for using purist approaches in the training of beginners in the field. If the focus is on learning a particular approach and mastering the skills consistent with that orientation, there is a tendency to use an apprenticeship orientation, with live supervision. The latter permits the teacher or supervisor to intervene in the therapy process and to immediately direct and correct the therapeutic work of the learner. Similarly, some trainers have used co-therapist arrangements in which the apprentice worked with clients alongside the teacher, observing the work of the master and having his or her performance observed and corrected. At times the co-therapy model has been one in which the two—teacher and student—have learned from each other. However, it seems evident that the emphasis tends to remain on the mastery of skills that are consistent with the theoretical orientation of the teacher or supervisor.

Nevertheless, we believe that clinical and educational experience support the notion that different levels of trainee knowledge and experience require different supervisory models. These are beginning to accumulate. For example, some clinical educators have developed solutions focused models which, of course, begin with what trainees and supervisors consider to be current strengths. What subsequently occurs is based on incremental changes in trainees' confidence, resources, and knowledge (Marek, Sandifer, Beach, Coward, & Protinksy, 1994). However, Wetchler (1990) points out the need for supervision to incorporate a developmental approach to both education and skill training, because less experienced trainees require more focus on technique and "answers." Similarly, others have observed (e.g., Dwyer & Lee, Chapter 9; Keith, Connell, & Whitaker, 1992), a more "consultative" approach works best with senior level trainees or therapists in practice.

REFERENCES

ANDERSEN, T. (1993). See and hear, and be seen and heard. In S. Friedman (Ed.), *The new language of change: Constructive collaboration in psychotherapy* (pp. 303–322). New York: Guilford Press.

APONTE, H. J. (1994). How personal can training get? *Journal of Marital and Family Therapy, 20,* 3–15.

BREUNLIN, D. C., KARRER, B. M., McGUIRE, D. E, & CIMMARUSTI, R. A. (1988). Cybernetics of videotape supervision. In H. A. Liddle, D. C. Breunlin, & R. C. Schwartz (Eds.), *Handbook of family therapy training and supervision* (pp. 194–206). New York: Guilford Press.

COMMISSION ON ACCREDITATION FOR MARRIAGE AND FAMILY THERAPY EDUCATION. (1997). *Manual on accreditation* (Version 9.0). Washington, DC: Author.

DEVEAUX, F., & LUBELL, I. (1994). Training the supervisor: Integrating a family of origin approach. *Contemporary Family Therapy, 16,* 291–299.

EDWARDS, T. M., & KELLER, J. F. (1995). Partnership discourse in marriage and family therapy supervision: A heterarchical alternative. *Clinical Supervision, 13,* 141–153.

EVERETT, C. A. (1980). An analysis of AAMFT supervisors: Their identities, roles, and resources. *Journal of Marital and Family Therapy, 6,* 215–226.

FENNELL, D. L., HOVESTADT, A. J., & HARVEY, S. J. (1986). A comparison of delayed feedback and live supervision models of marriage and family therapist clinical training. *Journal of Marital and Family Therapy, 12,* 181–186.

GOLDENBERG, I., & GOLDENBERG, H. (1996). *Family therapy: An overview* (4th ed.). Pacific Grove, CA: Brooks/Cole Publishing Company.

HALEY, J. (1975). Why a mental health clinic should avoid family therapy. *Journal of Marriage and Family Counseling, 1,* 3–13.

HALEY, J. (1988). Reflections on supervision. In H. A. Liddle, D. C. Breunlin, & R. C. Schwartz (Eds.), *Handbook of family therapy training and supervision* (pp. 358–367). New York: Guilford Press.

HARDY, K. V. (1993). Live supervision in the postmodern era of family therapy: Issues, reflections, and questions. *Contemporary Family Therapy, 15,* 9–20.

HENRY, P. W., SPRENKLE, D. H,. & SHEEHAN, R. (1986). Family therapy training: Student and faculty perceptions. *Journal of Marital and Family Therapy, 12,* 249–258.

HOFFMAN, L. (1981). *Foundations of family therapy.* New York: Basic Books.

KAPLAN, R. (1987). The current use of live supervision within marriage and family therapy training programs. *The Clinical Supervisor, 5,* 43–52.

KEITH, D., CONNELL, G., & WHITAKER, C. A. (1992). Group supervision in symbolic-experiential family therapy. *Journal of Family Psychotherapy, 3,* 93–109.

KELLER, J. F., & PROTINSKY, H. (1984). A self-management model for supervision. *Journal of Marital and Family Therapy, 10,* 281–288.

LIDDLE, H. A. (1985). Five factors of failure in structural-strategic family therapy: A contextual construction. In S. B. Coleman (Ed.), *Failures in family therapy* (pp. 152–189). New York: Guilford Press.

LIDDLE, H. A. (1991). Training and supervision in family therapy: A comprehensive and critical analysis. In A. S. Gurman & D. P. Kniskern (Eds.), *Handbook of family therapy* (Vol. 2) (pp. 638–697). New York: Brunner/Mazel.

LIDDLE, H. A., DAVIDSON, G. S., & BARRETT, M. J. (1988). Outcomes of live supervision: Trainee perspectives. In H. A. Liddle, D. C. Breunlin, & R. C. Schwartz (Eds.), *Handbook of family therapy training and supervision* (pp. 386–398). New York: Guilford Press.

LIDDLE, H. A., & SCHWARTZ, R. C. (1983). Live supervision/consultation: Conceptual and pragmatic guidelines for family therapy trainers. *Family Process, 22,* 477–490.

MAREK, L. I., SANDIFER, D. M., BEACH, A., COWARD, R. L., & PROTINSKY, H. O. (1994). Supervision without the problem: A model of solution-focused supervision. *Journal of Family Psychotherapy, 5*(2), 57–64.

McCOLLUM, E. E., & WETCHLER, J. L. (1995). In defense of case consultation: Maybe "dead" supervision isn't dead at all. *Journal of Marital and Family Therapy, 21,* 155–166.

McDANIEL, S. H., & LANDAU-STANTON, J. (1992). The University of Rochester family therapy training program. *American Journal of Family Therapy, 20,* 361–365.

McKENZIE, P. N., ATKINSON, B. I., QUINN, W. H., & HEATH, A. W. (1986). Training and supervision in marriage and family therapy: A national survey. *American Journal of Family Therapy, 14,* 293–303.

MONTALVO, B. (1973). Aspects of live supervision. *Family Process, 12,* 343–359.

NICHOLS, W. C. (1988). An integrative psychodynamic and systems approach. In H. A. Liddle, D. C. Breunlin, & R. C. Schwartz (Eds.), *Handbook of family therapy training and supervision* (pp. 110–127). New York: Guilford Press.

NICHOLS, W. C. (1996). *Treating people in families: An integrative framework.* New York: Guilford Press.

NICHOLS, W. C. (1997, September). *Advanced seminar: The maturing of family therapy.* Presentation at the meeting of the American Association for Marriage and Family Therapy, Atlanta, GA.

NICHOLS, W. C., NICHOLS, D. P., & HARDY, K. V. (1990). Supervision in family therapy: A decade restudy. *Journal of Marital and Family Therapy, 16,* 275–285.

RICKERT, V. C., & TURNER, J. E. (1978). Through the looking glass: Supervision in family therapy. *Social Casework, 59*(3), 131–137.

RON, K. (1996). Open live supervision in family therapy. *Contemporary Family Therapy, 18,* 69–83.

SABA, G. W., & LIDDLE, H. A. (1986). Perceptions of professional needs and practice patterns and critical issues facing family therapy trainers and supervisors. *American Journal of Family Therapy, 14,* 109–122.

SCHON, D. A. (1983). *The reflective practitioner: How professionals think in action.* New York: Basic Books.

SCHON, D. A. (1987). *Educating the reflective practitioner.* San Francisco: Jossey-Bass.

SCHWARTZ, R. C., LIDDLE, H. A., & BREUNLIN, D. C. (1988). Muddles in live supervision. In H. A. Liddle, D. C. Breunlin, & R. C. Schwartz (Eds.), *Handbook of family therapy training and supervision* (pp. 183–193). New York: Guilford Press.

SMITH, C. W., SMITH, T. A., & SALTS, C. J. (1991). The effects of supervisory interruptions on therapists and clients. *American Journal of Family Therapy, 19,* 250–256.

SPRENKLE, D. H. (1988). Training and supervision in degree granting programs in family therapy. In H. A. Liddle, D. C. Breunlin, & R. C. Schwartz (Eds.), *Handbook of family therapy training and supervision* (pp. 233–248). New York: Guilford Press.

TOMM, K. (1984a). One perspective on the Milan systemic approach: Part 1. Overview of development, theory and practice. *Journal of Marital and Family Therapy, 10,* 113–125.

TOMM, K. (1984b). One perspective on the Milan systemic approach: Part 2. Description of session format, interviewing style and interventions. *Journal of Marital and Family Therapy, 10,* 253–271.

TOMM, K., & WRIGHT, L. (1979). Training in family therapy: Perceptual, conceptual, and executive skills. *Family Process, 18,* 201–210.

VESPER, J. H., & BROCK, G. W. (1991). *Ethics, legalities, and professional practice issues in marriage and family therapy.* Boston: Allyn & Bacon.

WATSON, M. F. (1993). Supervising the person of the therapist: Issues, challenges and dilemmas. Special Issue: Critical issues in marital and family therapy education. *Contemporary Family Therapy, 15,* 21–31.

WEST, J. D., BUBENZER, D. L., PINSONEAULT, T., & HOLEMAN, V. (1993). Three supervision modalities for training marital and family counselors. *Counselor Education and Supervision, 33,* 127–138.

WETCHLER, J. L. (1990). Solution-focused supervision. *Family Therapy, 17,* 129–138.

WETCHLER, J. L., & VAUGHN, K. A. (1992). Perceptions of primary family therapy supervisory techniques: A critical incident analysis. *Contemporary Family Therapy, 14,* 127–136.

YOUNG, J., PERLESZ, A., PATERSON, R., O'HANLON, B., NEWBOLD, A., CHAPLIN, R., & BRIDGE, C. (1989). The reflecting team process in training. *Australian & New Zealand Journal of Family Therapy, 10*(2), 69–74.

CHAPTER 6

Case Consultation

The Cornerstone of Supervision

Joseph L. Wetchler
Eric E. McCollum

Early family therapists made an important contribution to family therapy training through the use of live supervision (Liddle, 1991; Nichols & Schwartz, 1998). This was a revolutionary step in that it challenged the veil of secrecy that shrouded the therapeutic encounter. Supervisors were now free to observe their trainees' in-session behavior and directly intervene in the clinical process. This provided important learning opportunities for novice therapists as well as aiding trainers in correcting therapist mistakes before they caused damage. Montalvo (1972) first described this process in a now classic paper, and it has become a hallmark of family therapy training. Unfortunately, the favored status of live supervision, and other forms of "raw data" training, has pushed the discussion of case consultation to the periphery. In fact, with two notable exceptions (McCollum & Wetchler, 1995; Stewart, 1997), the only mention of case consultation within the family therapy supervisory literature is to focus on its weakness in relation to live supervision (Berger & Damon, 1982; Montalvo & Storm, 1997). This is an important omission, as we contend that live supervision does not supersede case consultation in the supervisory process, but that it is only helpful if it works in harmony with case consultation. In fact, case consultation serves as the cornerstone of supervision from which all "raw data"' supervisory modalities follow.

"Case consultation consists of an individual supervisor and supervisee discussing a particular case without the use of raw data. Such a discussion addresses the specific practice of an individual therapist and his/her interaction with specific clients" (McCollum & Wetchler, 1995, p. 156). Through case consultation the trainer and trainee attempt to expand the context of therapy. While raw data supervision focuses on the content of a single session, case consultation takes a wider perspective toward the therapeutic process. As the contextual issues related to clients' lives and trainees' development are often complex, supervision typically requires an integration of case consultation, live supervision, and videotape review. In fact, the boundaries between raw data supervision and case consultation are not so rigid. For example, supervisors may wish to stop the viewing of a videotape segment to engage in extended case consultation about a therapeutic issue, or they may choose to incorporate live supervision to correct a clinical problem that was discovered in case consultation.

While the process of supervision is never as clear as black and white, we focus on the technique of case consultation to highlight its use within the training context. This is especially important because case consultation is the most used training technique by American Association for Marriage and Family Therapy (AAMFT) Approved Supervisors (Wetchler, Piercy, & Sprenkle, 1989), and is most associated with supervisory incidents that had a positive effect on trainee development (Wetchler & Vaughn, 1992). The process of training supervisees is far more complex than the content of an individual session. Much as the early family therapists believed that clinicians could not deal with individual problems without focusing on the larger context of the family, we too believe that the narrow focus of the raw data approaches cannot succeed unless they are grounded within the larger context of case consultation.

A BRIEF OVERVIEW OF RAW DATA APPROACHES

In keeping with our view of supervision as a contextual process, we will first provide a brief overview of live supervision and videotape review. While our discussion will focus on the advantages and disadvantages of these approaches, it is not meant to imply that they are ineffective techniques. In fact, they are crucial to the supervision process. There also are advantages and disadvantages to the use of case consultation. It is recognizing when to appropriately integrate these techniques into the training process that supervisors can tailor training to fit their supervisees' specific needs.

Live Supervision

Live supervision offers the trainer the opportunity to observe the family, the therapist, and the therapist and family interaction directly as opposed to relying on a trainee's reconstruction of the events. It also enables supervisors to correct supervisee mistakes as they happen (Berger & Damman, 1982; Liddle & Schwartz, 1983; Montalvo, 1972). This provides trainees with an in vivo learning experience and protects clients from potential harm. For example, live supervision can be extremely useful for helping a trainee keep a couple's conversation on track, or teaching a supervisee how to appropriately time an intervention with a specific family.

The strength of the telescopic view of live supervision is also its weakness. Its very structure creates a necessary focus on behavioral sequences that exist within a 1-hour session while pushing broader issues to the periphery. While it is easy to identify brief interactional patterns among family members and between therapists and clients, it is harder to focus on larger systems issues such as gender, culture, family of origin, and the environmental context for both clients and their therapists.

Further, the speed at which live supervision allows a trainer to correct a supervisee's mistake is a double-edged sword. Information is usually given quickly over the telephone, during midsession breaks, or through the supervisor entering the room to demonstrate a technique. While this can dramatically alter the course of a session, little time is available for supervisees to reflect on the purpose of the supervisory directive or where it fits within the overall therapy plan. Following a live supervision session, it is not uncommon for trainees to be confused about why their case improved or how they will proceed in subsequent sessions.

Videotape Review

In contrast to live supervision, videotape review allows therapists and supervisors to observe the raw data of a specific session at a more relaxed pace. They are able to view the session as an interactional event, placing therapist behaviors, family patterns, and the results of specific interventions in context (Breunlin, Karrer, McGuire, & Cimmarusti, 1988; Protinsky, 1997; Whiffen, 1982). Further, supervisee's observations of themselves on videotape can lead to increased self-awareness about interface issues that often go unnoticed during the emotionality of a therapy session (Keller & Protinsky, 1984; Kramer & Reitz, 1980). Finally, as with live supervision, trainers are able to identify actual clinical events without the filter of therapist reconstructions.

Videotape review also has several limitations. As with live supervision, it limits the supervisory focus to the events within a single session, which may inhibit discussion of larger contextual issues. Further, it is questionable whether supervisors actually see relevant, or complete, interactional sequences as trainees often choose what segments they present in supervision. This is especially true if the trainee is stuck due to a limited view of the interactional process. Finally, viewing oneself on videotape in an evaluative setting can promote defensiveness that inhibits learning for some trainees (Breunlin et al., 1988).

CASE CONSULTATION

We believe that the primary strength of case consultation is its ability to focus on broad contextual issues that impact the therapy system. This requires that it be a thoughtful and organized process with tasks dependent on the unique properties of this medium. We propose four broad supervisory areas that can be addressed by this method: (a) understanding the "architecture" of the therapy process, (b) helping trainees develop theoretical models of change, (c) understanding the clients' broader context, and (d) understanding the therapist's broader context (McCollum & Wetchler, 1995). While we are aware that different training environments, supervisor preferences, and specific trainee needs might lead to a different emphasis in the use of these tasks, we believe that each of them can be profitably addressed in the supervisory process. Finally, we wish to emphasize again that it is the interplay of the broad view of case consultation with the narrow focus of the raw data approaches that leads to a contextually sound training package. However, raw data approaches tend to lose much of their effectiveness without the necessary groundwork that is established in case consultation.

The Architecture of Therapy

Much as an architect creates the master plan for the construction of a building, so must a therapist have a clear understanding of the therapeutic process. In therapy, "architecture" represents how the therapist works across several sessions with the same client and how he or she incorporates the many facets of therapy into a coherent whole. Therapy begins with specific goals and hypotheses that serve as the initial blueprint for treatment. It then unfolds as subsequent sessions and interventions are both guided by these goals and serve in the evolution of new hypotheses. Supervisee growth requires an ability to see connections between what is happening in the present session, what has happened in the past, and what is expected to happen in subsequent sessions. Further, it is the ability to recognize deviations from the master plan that enables therapists to get back on track. Without this sense of architecture, therapy can unravel into a meaningless series of unrelated interventions or lose its appropriate pace. It is within the case consultation setting that supervisees can develop hypotheses and treatment goals, unify the therapy process, try out different theoretical frames with stuck cases, and maintain an appropriate pace for treatment (McCollum & Wetchler, 1995).

Developing Goals and Hypotheses

While conducting family therapy can be difficult for the advanced practitioner, it often is overwhelming for the beginner. The continuous bombardment of information can seem never ending to a new trainee. It is crucial that supervisors help beginners organize discrepant clinical data into a coherent whole if they are to be of service to their families. Particularly important is to teach them to relate what is happening in their sessions to what they are learning in their readings.

It especially is important for supervisors to help trainees develop hypotheses and treatment goals for raw data supervision to be effective. Live supervision and videotape review often become unraveled if the supervisor and supervisee lack a mutual understanding about what is going on with a specific family. Communication in live supervision is extremely difficult if the supervisor lacks a clear picture of the family and the supervisee lacks a reference point to organize a supervisor's input (McCollum & Wetchler, 1995). Further, videotape review can degenerate into a random viewing of meaningless segments if the supervisee cannot relate them to specific hypotheses (Breunlin et al., 1988).

It is the slower pace of case consultation that allows trainers and trainees to develop an organized assessment out of the huge amount of data that often spans several sessions. For example, one beginning trainee complained of being completely overwhelmed by a family with a conduct disordered adolescent. As the supervisor inquired about the various relationships within the family and about how they had tried to resolve the problem, it became clear that the parents worked at cross-purposes with the child. The mother attempted harsh punishment while the father tried to be a friend. The supervisor then tied this information to the theory of triangles and helped the trainee set a goal of having the parents work together on parenting their child. Supervision then flowed smoothly around this case as the supervisor and supervisee had a theoretical reference point on which to base their discussion. Further, videotape review was productive as the trainee could present segments on how she was working toward uniting the parents.

Unifying the Therapy Process

It is the slow pace and ability to focus on multiple sessions that makes case consultation an excellent method for helping supervisees unify the therapy process. Case consultation permits trainees the time to reflect on whether their current plans fit with their hypotheses and treatment goals. Much as trainees face a huge amount of seemingly discrepant data in their therapy sessions, so they also run the risk of being overwhelmed by the number of techniques and theories that exist within the field. Many supervisors face the "intervention of the week" phenomenon as their trainees read about new theories in their coursework or return with new techniques from workshops and conferences. To maintain coherent therapy, trainers must actively help their trainees focus on the larger picture, and decide whether new learnings are consistent with the goals of therapy. Questions that tie the current plan to past and future sessions are helpful in this regard. We have found the following questions to be especially useful:

- How does this plan fit the general goal toward which you and your clients are working?

- What steps are involved in getting from where the clients are today to where they/you want to go?
- How does what you are doing today relate to what you did last session? Five sessions ago?
- If your plan works well today, what will you want to do next session?
- How will you explain, both to yourself and to the client, why you are introducing a new direction in therapy now? (McCollum & Wetchler, 1995, p. 159)

Supervisors also can teach trainees to develop coherence in their therapy by helping them define the therapy model they are using with a particular case. Questions can then focus on how new ideas fit within the theoretical context of the treatment. Does a specific technique fit with this theory or these hypotheses? For example, a trainee who was using a narrative approach to treat a case of obsessive compulsive disorder had read a book on strategic therapy and wanted to incorporate paradoxical interventions into the case. He and his supervisor used case consultation to engage in a discussion on the theoretical assumptions of narrative and strategic therapies. As the trainee's original decision to use a narrative approach stemmed from the hypothesis that giving his client personal control over his symptoms would alleviate his anxiety, he decided that the directive nature of paradoxical techniques ran counter to his stronger desire to be collaborative with this case.

Trying Different Theoretical Frames

While beginning family therapists are more likely to focus on an individual model of therapy, advanced practitioners are more likely to see doing therapy as a "frame experiment" (Schon, 1983). Advanced practice is not a rigid set of rules applied to a narrowly defined problem. Rather, it is a reflective encounter in which a professional applies a variety of theoretical stances to see which one will best guide him or her in a specific situation (Stewart, 1997). For advanced therapists, supervision often examines a variety of hypotheses to see which would fit best for a specific client.

Advanced supervision becomes a process in which the supervisee presents his or her knowledge about the case while the supervisor presents alternative hypotheses. Together the supervisor and supervisee evaluate the different theoretical "frames" to see which appear most useful. Schon (1983, p. 133) suggests answering the following questions to gauge the usefulness of a hypothesis:

- Can I solve the problem [as it is now framed]?
- Do I like what I get when I solve this problem?
- Have I made the situation coherent?
- Have I made it congruent with my fundamental values and theories?
- Have I kept inquiry moving?

As one hypothesis begins to emerge as the most potentially useful, the advanced supervisee is then free to develop a plan for the upcoming sessions. The model is then evaluated over subsequent sessions and appropriately modified.

Developing an Appropriate Pace for the Therapy Process

"Pacing involves knowing what one can expect in a certain amount of time in therapy and assessing whether a particular case is 'on schedule' or not" (McCollum & Wetchler, 1995, p. 160). Beginning clinicians are often unsure about how much time is needed for clients to resolve certain issues. One of our beginning students angrily commented that his client should get on with her life after talking for three sessions about her husband abandoning her. While this student needed to learn to slow down his timetable, other trainees discover that their therapies are drifting aimlessly. This typically happens when the original goals are forgotten or resolved and therapy slips into a pattern of insight for insight's sake.

Through case consultation, the supervisor and supervisee are able to gauge the appropriate pace for a specific case. Therapists can be referred back to the original treatment contract to evaluate their progress. As client goals are resolved, trainers and trainees can discuss whether to work towards new goals or move towards terminating the case. Those trainees who find themselves drifting can again strategize about how to make their interventions more consistent with their client's goals. Some trainees need to learn what an appropriate pace entails for specific problems.

Finally, a sense of the pace of therapy allows supervisors to counter the belief held by some students that therapy must always be dramatic and exciting. This idea is often strengthened through viewing training tapes by master clinicians or reading about brilliant case studies. Case consultation allows supervisors and supervisees to place the immediate session in the larger scheme of the therapy context. For example, one trainee needed to be reminded that the three "boring" sessions she recently experienced were a sign of stability in a chaotic family she had been treating. Understanding the architecture of therapy enables trainees to recognize whether a low-key session is a sign of stagnation or progress.

Building Theoretical Models

While the previous section focused on helping trainees see the broader picture within a specific case, theoretical model building proposes that it is important to generalize across cases. Meaningful growth necessitates that therapists be able to take what was learned with one family and apply it to their subsequent cases. Otherwise, they must "reinvent the wheel" with every case. Developing a personal theoretical model (Liddle, 1982) is the best means for trainees to generalize what they have learned in supervision to their posttraining practice.

The case consultation process should help trainees develop their personal theory of therapy and apply it in their sessions. Supervisors need to ask therapists how their in-session behavior fits within their evolving model and how new experiences serve to alter their theory. One trainee had developed a clearly articulated solution-focused model that she had developed working with individuals and couples. However, she found herself in a clinical crisis when she began a practicum at an adolescent treatment center and several of her teens had no desire to change their behaviors. This led to an interest in structural therapy as she and her supervisor discussed the concept of parent and child hierarchy and cross-generational coalitions (Minuchin, 1974) in adolescent treatment. Through case consultation, she developed an integrative model that incorporated both solution-focused and structural components.

Regular discussion of a supervisee's model also offers the supervisor the opportunity to focus on any neglected aspects of the theory-building process. Students often apply new techniques without understanding how they fit into the overall picture. One trainee, new to the structural approach, was shocked at an "overinvolved" mother's anger after she assigned her to watch while her husband took care of the children for a week. This led to a supervisory discussion of the mother's possible feelings of being demeaned for doing an inadequate job and for being moved out of a position that she saw as her role in the family. The supervisee was then advised to integrate her client's feelings and gender issues into her family assessments. This enabled her to view her new theoretical model as less of an abstract map and more of an interpersonal guideline.

The Client's Broader Context

Larger Systems Issues

Because the therapy relationship takes place within a structured time frame, it is easy to forget the numerous outside experiences that can impact a client's behavior within the therapy hour. Learning to recognize the larger systems that impinge on clients' lives can make all the difference between success and failure in a given case (Imber-Black, 1988; Schwartzman, 1985). A family who is referred for mandatory therapy by the courts or a woman who must attend to regain custody of her child present different situations than a voluntary client. Trainees must learn to think about the relationship of these systems to their clients' lives as they develop their treatment goals.

Case consultation is the technique of choice for helping trainees deal with larger systems issues. Supervisors and supervisees can discuss the impact of these larger systems on the presenting problem and how the trainee can intervene in the broader context. This includes learning how to work with probation officers, case managers, child protective workers, judges, and attorneys. These discussions often must include specific ethical problems such as therapist responsibility to report abuse, therapist duty to warn, and when to report suicidal behavior. Further, supervisors must focus on the pragmatic issues regarding how trainees can reestablish a relationship with their clients after filing a report of sexual abuse or informing a probation officer of nonattendance.

One trainee was extremely frustrated with a client who had failed to come to several scheduled initial therapy sessions. This mother had lost custody of her child until she could successfully gain steady employment and learn to parent effectively through court-ordered therapy. The therapist stated that the woman's child protective services caseworker agreed that the woman was noncompliant. After first discussing the therapist's anger at how this woman refused to fight for her child, the supervision focused on possible larger systems issues that might be impeding therapy. While many ideas were discussed, three larger systems hypotheses became relevant for this trainee. First, the mother might assume her therapist had already prejudged her as a bad parent and not be supportive of her. Second, there might be real issues within the woman's life that were preventing her from attending sessions. Third, much of the therapist's information about the woman had come from her case manager, who might have a biased view of this woman. Several weeks later, the student reported that she had successfully engaged the mother in therapy by scheduling therapy sessions at the group home where her child was placed, when she made supervised visits. This helped to improve the woman's attendance because she could save on bus fares, which was especially important since she was on welfare. The woman also became more trusting after seeing the therapist make special arrangements for her therapy. Furthermore, several months later the therapist discovered that much of her initial perception of the woman was filtered through the caseworker's biases. New strategies had to be developed to work with the caseworker when he refused to allow more supervised visits even though the woman had become successfully employed and was making steady improvement with her parenting skills.

A few of the many questions we use in helping trainees assess their clients' larger context include the following (McCollum & Wetchler, 1995):

- Who referred the clients to therapy and why?
- What other institutions are involved in working with the clients on this problem—school, church, court, social services, and so forth?
- How do the clients' economic and work situations affect the problem they are coming for help with?

- What other family members might be involved in trying to help with this problem?
- Besides therapy, who do the clients feel they can rely on for support when they need it?

Gender and Culture Issues

In addition to social institutions, which have a powerful effect on clients' lives, other contextual issues relate to race, gender, and culture. These issues pertain to how problems are developed, defined, and solved. Their relationship to therapy can challenge even the most advanced therapist because their impact often is subtle as well as profound. While our field stresses the inclusion of these issues when conducting an assessment (Goodrich, Rampage, Ellman, & Halstead, 1988; McGoldrick, Giordano, & Pearce, 1996), it is the responsibility of trainers to make this an active part of supervision.

For example, one trainee was extremely upset about the religious views of a fundamentalist Christian family with a disobedient daughter. The trainee felt that the parents' refusal to allow their daughter to date or wear makeup was stifling her emotional development and causing her behavior problems. When her supervisor asked if all children of fundamentalist parents were emotionally disturbed, she immediately answered, "Yes!" and began to laugh at her obvious cultural bias. This led to a discussion of the various child rearing practices of diverse cultures. Through this conversation, the supervisee concluded that the problem was not one of religious orientation, but rather one of the parents' ability to enforce their beliefs with their daughter. Further discussion also revealed that the parents disagreed about how strictly to enforce their values. Based on this, the therapist chose to stay out of the discussion on what constitutes appropriate parenting practices, and instead helped the family negotiate this issue (McCollum & Wetchler, 1995).

The Trainee's Broader Context

Like clients, trainees' experiences impact the work they do as therapists. Pursuing the present-based and transgenerational issues that affect supervisees' work is an important part of case consultation.

Present-Based Contextual Issues

One of the most important present-based influences is the environment in which a trainee conducts therapy. How a therapist proceeds with a case can differ greatly depending on whether he or she practices in an inpatient hospital, an outpatient mental health center, a probation department, an in-home therapy project, or a school setting. It can be frustrating for trainees to discover that some of the concepts they are learning must either be modified, or are not appropriate, for their work environment. Supervision must include a focus on how students can apply their new ideas to their clinical setting (Boscolo, Cecchin, Hoffman, & Penn, 1987). This is especially true when they experience value conflicts between themselves and their agencies, try to introduce a system model in a symptom-focused setting (e.g., drug and alcohol treatment), encounter various economic realities such as limited insurance and managed care, and find they must work with other professionals who do not believe in family therapy.

One trainee became completely lost when she transferred from an outpatient facility to a short-term, inpatient program. She was uncomfortable with the switch from having weekly sessions over an extended span of time to having multiple sessions within less than a 2-week period. Further, she was extremely frustrated with several members of the unit staff who had different theoretical orientations than hers. Case consultation first focused on helping this supervisee apply her knowledge of triangles and hierarchy to her work environment. From this discussion she was able to develop strategies for negotiating joint treatment plans with coworkers and for how to discuss clinical concerns with the supervising psychiatrists and her unit director. As she became more comfortable with these interactions, she realized that it was more important that the treatment team function as an integrated whole than winning the battle over who had the best ideas.

The second supervisory concern dealt with how to apply her theoretical orientation in a shorter time period. Case discussion focused on how to distinguish between brief, achievable goals that could be accomplished in the hospital, from long-term ones that were best dealt with in outpatient aftercare. Further, she and her supervisor discussed how to work as a team member with the aftercare therapists and how to prepare her clients for outpatient therapy.

Trainee's Interface Issues

Some clinical problems do not pertain as much to the client as they do to a therapist's response to that client. Supervisors can help trainees address interface issues either through helping them establish emotional empathy for their clients (Wetchler, 1998) or through exploring their own family systems (Bowen, 1978; Keller & Protinsky, 1984; Kramer, 1985; McCollum, 1990). Obviously, these issues cannot be dealt with during a midsession break. Case consultation is the method of choice for addressing these problems as it provides trainees with the space and time to focus on their personal concerns.

Some interface problems result from trainees and clients becoming involved in interactional patterns that inhibit their ability to bond with each other. As a result, both exhibit defensive behaviors that further hinder their therapeutic attachment (Wetchler, in press). One way to help therapists reconnect with their clients is to help them identify personal emotions they may be avoiding by keeping their client at a distance. For example, one therapist could not join with an abused client until she became aware of her own feelings of sadness and anger towards her client's situation.

A second way to promote a therapist and client bond is to help trainees identify the emotions that underlie their clients' defensive behavior. One of our female trainees wanted to discontinue treatment with a couple because the husband made disparaging comments about women. A discussion about the times these comments were most likely to happen revealed that he tended to insult his wife when he was about to ask her for a favor. The trainee softened her opinion of her client when her supervisor proposed that he might be using sexist insults as a way to defend himself because he feared rejection. She then developed strategies to help the husband express his underlying fears when he caught himself beginning to insult his wife.

Clinical problems also arise when trainees' family-of-origin issues become entangled in the therapy process. Helping students identify which issues belong to their clients and which belong to their own families can be a powerful way to move a stuck case forward. This especially was obvious with one young trainee who had great difficulty interrupting argumentative parents, but was easily able to silence their children. It was clear from her ability to quiet the most belligerent teenager that she had the necessary skills to maintain control. When asked about her family's rules regarding parent and child relationships, she responded that "children should never interrupt their parents." In fact, she and her brother were likely to be sent to their rooms if they "talked back!" Armed with this information, she developed a strategy to catch herself when she responded to adult clients as her own parents. This led to her being more assertive and subsequently more empathic as she could see her adult clients as individuals and not representations of her parents.

CONCLUSION

Case consultation is a valuable component to the complete training package. In fact, the ability of case consultation to focus on the broader issues of therapy makes it the ideal cornerstone for the supervision process. Our hope is that this chapter will compel other supervisors to both examine and write about their experiences with this method. It is through continued dialogue that this overlooked technique can regain its place alongside the raw data approaches.

REFERENCES

BERGER, M., & DAMMAN, C. (1982). Live supervision as context, treatment, and training. *Family Process, 21,* 337–344.

BOSCOLO, L., CECCHIN, G., HOFFMAN, L., & PENN, P. (1987). *Milan systemic family therapy.* New York: Basic Books.

BOWEN, M. (1978). *Family therapy in clinical practice.* New York: Jason Aronson.

BREUNLIN, D. C., KARRER, B. M., MCGUIRE, D. E., & CIMMARUSTI, R. A. (1988). Cybernetics of videotape supervision. In H. A. Liddle, D. C. Breunlin, & R. C. Schwartz (Eds.), *Handbook of family therapy training and supervision* (pp. 194–206). New York: Guilford Press.

FRAMO, J. L. (1982). *Explorations in marital and family therapy.* New York: Springer.

GOODRICH, T. J., RAMPAGE, C., ELLMAN, B., & HALSTEAD, K. (1988). *Feminist family therapy.* New York: Norton.

IMBER-BLACK, E. (1988). *Families and larger systems.* New York: Guilford Press.

KELLER, J. F., & PROTINSKY, H. (1984). A self-management model for supervision. *Journal of Marital and Family Therapy, 10,* 281–288.

KRAMER, J. R. (1985). *Family interfaces: Transgenerational patterns.* New York: Brunner/Mazel.

KRAMER, J. R., & Reitz, M. (1980). Using video playback to train family therapists. *Family Process, 19,* 145–150.

LIDDLE, H. A. (1982). On the problem of eclecticism: A call for epistemological clarification and human-scale theories. *Family Process, 21,* 243–247.

LIDDLE, H. A. (1991). Training and supervision in family therapy: A comprehensive and critical analysis. In A. S. Gurman & D. P. Kniskern (Eds.), *Handbook of family therapy* (Vol. 2) (pp. 638–697). New York: Brunner/Mazel.

LIDDLE, H. A., & SCHWARTZ, R. C. (1983). Live supervision/consultation: Conceptual and pragmatic guidelines for family therapy trainers. *Family Process, 22,* 491–500.

McCOLLUM, E. E. (1990). Integrating structural-strategic and Bowen approaches in training beginning family therapists. *Contemporary Family Therapy, 12,* 23–34.

McCOLLUM, E. E., & WETCHLER, J. L. (1995). In defense of case consultation: Maybe "dead" supervision isn't dead after all. *Journal of Marital and Family Therapy, 21,* 155–166.

McGOLDRICK, M., GIORDANO, J., & PEARCE, J. K. (Eds.). (1996). *Ethnicity & family therapy* (2nd ed). New York: Guilford Press.

MINUCHIN, S. (1974). *Families and family therapy.* Cambridge, MA: Harvard University Press.

MONTALVO, B. (1972). Aspects of live supervision. *Family Process, 12,* 343–359.

MONTALVO, B., & STORM, C. L. (1997). Live supervision revolutionizes the supervision process. In T. C. Todd & C. L. Storm (Eds.), *The complete systemic supervisor: Context, philosophy, and pragmatics* (pp. 283–297). Boston: Allyn & Bacon.

NICHOLS, M. P., & SCHWARTZ, R. C. (1998). *Family therapy: Concepts and methods* (4th ed.). Boston: Allyn & Bacon.

PROTINSKY, H. (1997). Dismounting the tiger: Using tape in supervision. In T. L. Todd & C. L. Storm (Eds.), *The complete systemic supervisor: Context, philosophy, and pragmatics* (pp. 298–307). Boston: Allyn & Bacon.

SCHON, D. A. (1983). *The reflective practitioner: How professionals think in action*. New York: Basic Books.

SCHWARTZMAN, J. (Ed.). (1985). *Families and other systems*. New York: Guilford Press.

STEWART, K. (1997). Case consultation: Stories told about stories. In T. C. Todd & C. L. Storm (Eds.), *The complete systemic supervisor: Context, philosophy, and pragmatics* (pp. 308–319). Boston: Allyn & Bacon.

WETCHLER, J. L. (1998). The role of primary emotion in family therapy supervision. *Journal of Systemic Therapies, 17*, 2.

WETCHLER, J. L., PIERCY, F. P., & SPRENKLE, D. H. (1989). Supervisors' and supervisees' perceptions of the effectiveness of family therapy supervisory techniques. *American Journal of Family Therapy, 17*, 35–47.

WETCHLER, J. L., & VAUGHN, K. A. (1992). Perceptions of primary family therapy supervisory techniques: A critical incident analysis. *Contemporary Family Therapy, 14*, 127–136.

WHIFFEN, R. (1982). The use of videotape in supervision. In R. Whiffen & J. Byng-Hall (Eds.), *Family therapy supervision: Recent developments in practice* (pp. 39–46). Orlando, FL: Grune & Stratton.

CHAPTER 7

Getting Down and Dirty
Using a Sandtray in Supervision

PATRICIA A. MARKOS

Sandplay therapy is a play therapy technique that has been used successfully with children, adolescents, and adults (Oaklander, 1989). I have found that sandplay can be very useful in supervision as well.

Lowenfeld (1939, 1979) first developed what has come to be known as sandplay therapy. It consists of a sandtray and an assortment of symbols and objects, including vehicles, animals, human figures, and scenic pieces. The ways a participant places these figures in the sandtray and plays with them are believed to express conscious and unconscious thoughts and feelings. However, how well this activity goes doesn't just involve the apparatus and the client. It also requires a safe setting, a creative therapist who can consider complex things symbolically, and a therapeutic alliance (Kalff, 1980).

Why add a sandtray to your supervisory resources? For therapy, the advantages of and indications for nonverbal, action-oriented techniques—be they sculpting (Papp, Silverstein, & Carter, 1973), kinetic drawing (Burns, 1982), or sandplay—are well recognized. Such techniques can cut through excessive verbalization and other forms of defensiveness, involve tongue-tied participants, and unlock deeper levels of experiencing (Kalff, 1980). Because each party arranges himself or herself and the others in a tableau that physically symbolizes their emotional relationship with each other, one's experience in and with the group is condensed and projected into a visual picture. There is a spatial and pictorial display that can be explored for actions, motives, and feelings. Each of these methods allows participants to stand back and to get a new look at themselves in relation to the others. Such an exercise has the potential to reveal things that have remained hidden and to give form to vague and confused feelings and impressions on the periphery of awareness (Papp, et al., 1973). They may provide new information and therefore the opportunity to see new connections (Tomm, 1984).

Sandplay is particularly appealing as a training tool. Like other methods it gives the unconscious an opportunity to express itself more clearly, and delivers metaphors to explore. Like the other methods, too, it negates an attempt to focus on individuals and instead presents interrelationships. However, sandplay may be unique in its playful quality. Properly employed, sandplay involves a "free and sheltered space" (Kalff, 1980, p. 29), in which a playful participant has an opportunity for self-expression and learning. Moreover, it encourages a playful, comfortable, and unguarded approach to self-expression and exploration of human relationships. This comfort is important to therapy trainees who will need to be in touch with their own selves, appreciate the nuances of the training system (supervisor, therapist, and client), and comfortable in talking about these things. Certainly, sandplay will help self-conscious trainees manifest less guarded forms of expression and highly verbal trainees think of and move to other forms of expression. In so doing, it has the potential for substantial learning.

CASE ILLUSTRATION

During the second week of supervision in a beginning practicum class, I asked a trainee to describe her first therapy session in which she met with and took a history from an 18-year-old female. The student seemed very reluctant about sharing her experience and stated that the session had been uncomfortable for her. I brought out a sandtray and assorted human figures, animals, and inanimate objects. I asked her to "put" this first therapy session in the sandtray. While the student was setting up the sandtray, I and the other members of the class sat quietly and observed.

When the trainee indicated that she was through, I asked her to tell us about what she had constructed. In the tray the trainee had portrayed herself with a very small figure. In contrast, the 18-year-old female client was represented by a cartoon character that was much bigger than the trainee. I asked her why she chose a small figure for herself and a big figure for her client. The trainee was startled. Her immediate reaction was that she had not even been aware of that until I pointed it out. Reflecting on it, she then said that this after all was her first therapy session and she felt very small and nervous about dealing with what seemed a very difficult client problem. The trainee then described her feelings of inadequacy. Her self-disclosure stimulated a lively discussion in the practicum group. All of her colleagues were feeling much the same way at the prospect of meeting with clients for the first time. I pointed out how the sandplay brought unconscious thoughts and feelings into awareness, and then returned to the therapy session represented in the sandtray.

The 18-year-old girl's presenting problems centered around her relationship with her mother and her stepfather. The girl and her stepfather were ordered by the court to obtain family counseling following an incident in which she physically attacked him. She reported a consistently bad relationship beginning when her mother married the man when the girl was 10 years old. She felt that her mother should have asked her permission to marry him. The girl recently had moved out of her parents' home, but still was financially tied to them. She needed their monetary support to "live on her own."

As the trainee described this background information, she stated that the reason she was feeling so uncomfortable was because this situation was so similar to her own life story and she was having strong personal feelings. I asked her to place in the sandtray the girl's family situation as reported in the therapy session. The trainee worked for several minutes, trying to represent the family as accurately as possible. When she was through, I asked her to describe her re-creation. In the sandtray were the girl, her mother, her stepfather, and a grandmother. The grandmother, with whom the girl had a close relationship, was in the far left-hand corner of the sandtray. The stepfather and mother were positioned on the right side of the tray, near the lower edge. The stepfather was represented by a powerful-looking cartoon character, and the mother was represented by a diminutive female figure. The girl, represented by another petite female figure, was placed in the middle of the sandtray, all by herself.

The trainee explained. The family had moved to the Southwest to be closer to the grandmother. Initially, the grandmother had been living with the family, but then moved out because of conflict with the stepfather. The girl described him as generally "irritating" but not abusive. The grandmother, in turn, was said to often take the side of the girl, defending and supporting her. The mother, however, preferred either to ignore the conflict of her husband with the grandmother and the daughter, or to take his side and defend him.

The 18-year-old had stated that she did not want any relationship with her stepfather, but also did not want to give up the financial support he gave her. She was angry with her mother for staying with him, and felt that she was not being supported by her mother. However, her mother reportedly replied that she loved her husband and wanted her daughter to try to get along with him.

After the trainee described the family situation, I asked her to look at the sandtray and talk about her own family. The trainee immediately said that she understood "exactly" what the girl was feeling because the trainee had experienced the same kind of feelings growing up in her own family. The trainee had a stepfather with whom she did not feel close, and a mother who appeared to support the stepfather rather than her. Growing up, she felt very isolated and apart from her family.

I asked the student, given her own experiences, how she might best be helpful to this particular client family. I expressed my concern that the trainee might not be objective, would project her own family situation onto this case, and lose her neutrality and ability to hypothesize freely. I wanted to be sure that the student would be dealing with the clients' concerns and not her own. Because of the strong argument presented by the sandtray experience, the trainee could clearly understand my concerns. However, she thought that her own life experiences actually might be helpful in building a therapeutic relationship with the family.

The entire practicum group then discussed what was taking place and the implications. They talked about transference and countertransference issues, projective identification, hypothesizing, circularity, and neutrality. Finally, they thought about what appropriate self-disclosure might be, and how it could be used in this case.

MAXIMIZING THE VALUE OF SANDPLAY

Sandplay goes best in supervision, just as in therapy, when it takes place in a setting conducive to self-expression and exploration. That means that the setting must be experienced as safe (see Emerson, Chapter 1). In addition, trainees and supervisors both need to have the capacity for playful self-expression and relatively uninhibited appreciation for what may be revealed. There should be a sense of "unconditional positive regard," valuing of creativity, openness to new information, the capacity to think on a symbolic level and give that clear expression, and the ability to see new connections. Participants should resist premature closure and rejection of possibilities, and feel free to pursue and fully explore the various symbolic possibilities and their ramifications.

Tomm (1984), Andersen (1991), and others have appreciated the importance of a supervisory group to hypothesizing, circularity, and neutrality. I have found my supervisory group invaluable to sandplay supervision. They have provided support to their peers and to me in the form of courage, ideas, self-disclosure, laughter, and consolation. They have continued to be enthusiastic about sandplay as a tool. They feel that it has enabled them to be more self-revealing, more relationship conscious, and more playful with each other and with their clients. They also feel that sandplay has played a buoyant role when the gravity of training has seemed overwhelming. Finally, they feel that my use of sandplay in supervision has modeled for them not only how to get down on the floor and play with a child, but also how to be open to their own inner selves.

REFERENCES

ANDERSEN, T. (1991). *The reflecting team: Dialogues and dialogues about the dialogues.* New York: Norton.

BURNS, R. C. (1982). *Self-growth in families: Kinetic family drawings (K-F-D) research and application.* New York: Brunner/Mazel.

KALFF, D. M. (1980). *Sandplay.* Santa Monica, CA: Open Court Publishing.

LOWENFELD, M. (1939). The world pictures of children. *British Journal of Psychology, 18,* 65–73.

LOWENFELD, M. (1979). *The world technique.* London: George Allen & Unwin.

OAKLANDER, V. (1989). *Windows to our children: A Gestalt therapy approach to children and adolescents.* Highland, NY: Gestalt Journal Press.

PAPP, P., SILVERSTEIN, O., & CARTER, E. (1973). Family sculpting in preventive work with "well families." *Family Process, 12,* 197–212.

TOMM, K. (1984). One perspective on the Milan systemic approach: Part II. Description of session format, interviewing style and interventions. *Journal of Marital and Family Therapy, 10,* 253–271.

CHAPTER 8

Seeing and Hearing in Therapy and Supervision

A Clinical Example of Isomorphism

ROBERT E. LEE

Therapists have always believed in the importance of "separating one's own issues from those of the client." For example, psychodynamic theorists emphasize that the introjects and projections of both client and therapist need to be identified and kept from obscuring current relationships and events (Scharff & Scharff, 1987). Bowen theory in turn recognizes that a therapist can be helpful to a family only to the extent that he or she remains neutral and untriangled while relating to the emotional issues of the family (Papero, 1988). Accordingly, much supervisory attention is given to the personality of the therapist (Aponte, 1994; Storm, 1991). Likewise, Milan-strategic therapists speak of neutrality (Tomm, 1984), and structural supervisors understand the importance of clear boundaries at all levels of the training system (Minuchin & Fishman, 1981). Finally, postmodern theories emphasize the importance of getting "unstuck" by appreciative listening and the coediting of alternative constructions of reality (Andersen, 1993).

There are clear and uncomfortable signs that both therapist and client are locked into joint, unhelpful, and too narrow constructions of reality. For example, both therapist and client may experience themselves as "stuck." They may not see something that is "obvious" to a third party. There may be a narrowness or distortion of perception, a loss of choice about or control over behavior, and over- or underreaction to things. There also may be over- or underinvolvement in relatedness, or goals of relatedness that are inappropriate to the parties involved. When a client behaves in this fashion, it is a cue to the therapist to ask questions that will alert the client to the "baggage" involved. However, if the therapist is not able to do this because the therapist also is not able to see things in other ways, or perhaps feels the same way as does the client, then no change is possible. A therapist not only

Source: This chapter originally appeared in *Journal of Family Psychotherapy*, 1997, *8*, 51–57. Reprinted by permission of the Haworth Press, Inc.

needs to join a client, but also needs to challenge the client's conscious reality in order to bring change. If one is inducted into the family system, one is rendered useless as a change agent (Minuchin & Fishman, 1981).

One role of the supervisor, then, is to help the therapist become a more flexible observer of self and the family. The supervisor perhaps best accomplishes this by becoming a very alert self observer. In this regard we can appreciate the wisdom of those who feel that a primary focus of training must be the emotional maturity of the supervisor and therapist (Aponte, 1994; Storm, 1991).

Isomorphism is the hypothesis that the supervisor-therapist relationship mirrors the therapist-family relationship, and vice versa (Liddle, 1988; Nichols & Everett, 1986). This has both diagnostic and intervention value. On the one hand, if there is replication across the subsystem boundaries, then what a supervisor observes between self and therapist may reflect what obtains in the therapist-client subsystem. On the other hand, a change made in the supervisor/therapist subsystem should result in change in the therapist/client subsystem. Therefore, if one allows the boundaries to become muddied between self and supervisee, the latter in turn may become confused and ineffective in his or her relationship with clients. And, if one clears them up with the supervisee, the latter may be empowered.

Therefore, a worst-case scenario might be one in which the entire training system— supervisor and his or her peer consultants, supervisee, and client—all rigidly accept the same construction of reality. This may preclude the possibility of change. The following case study exemplifies this worst-case scenario. However, the eventual enlightenment of the supervisory peer subsystem allowed the liberation of the supervisory subsystem and, in turn, the treatment subsystem. The whole training system became empowered.

SETTING

In the present situation my role was that of "consultant" to pastoral counselors who were viewed by their employer as fully trained family therapists. The employer was a family counseling center funded, sponsored, and staffed by white fundamentalist Christians. It serviced an isolated small rural town with which it was compatible. It seemed to me that relationships were restricted by narrow and rigid ideas about the roles of men and women, and common ideas about what is sinful or morally dangerous. The setting also struck me as characterized by blurred boundaries and a lack of privacy. Therapists, clientele, administrators, and referral sources lived on the same streets and attended the same churches, and the latter comprised a fundamental social network. In contrast, I and my colleagues saw ourselves as urban, nonfundamentalist Christians and sophisticated professionals, and we viewed the treatment setting as narrow, closed, and rigid.

CASE HISTORY

The therapist was a new employee, who had had one year's prior experience in an urban adolescent inpatient unit. Her employment was noteworthy because she was a graduate of a Commission on Accreditation for Marriage and Family Therapy Education (COAMFTE)-accredited MFT program, and the first female professional ever hired by this agency. Also unusual to this environment, she was a newly divorced, single mother of a 7-year-old son. Her former husband had been alcoholic and physically abusive, as had been her father.

Although a fundamentalist Christian (and aware of and accepting of many attitudes unique to this setting with regard to gender roles, hierarchy, and the role of scripture), she said she was aware of and concerned by some gender-related characteristics of the current setting. She was annoyed by her perception that she was related to in limited ways. However, although assertive, which she expected would not be an acceptable feminine trait in this setting, she also could be diplomatic and patient.

She welcomed me as a fellow, sophisticated professional—vaguely contrasted with her colleagues—and I quickly allied with her. I at first did not recognize the triangle: Her assumptions about pastoral counseling education matched my own and her affirmation of my identity and worth in this setting felt very good. Moreover, in contrast to the case consultation requested by the other therapists, she specifically asked for "supervision." Feeling that she was just a beginner in her chosen profession, she wanted increased knowledge and skill training. We thought that I brought a unique opportunity. Neither of us thought that her colleagues were very knowledgeable and she pointed out that, instead of getting help from them, her colleagues sought her advice.

She had solid strengths: She had the ability to join many client families very well. She was alert to details, quick to understand the implications systemically, and quick to find interventions. However, she also had blind spots. For example, she was prone to forego systemic thinking. Instead, she would conceptualize a problem in a psychological way and would shift to working individually and sympathetically with those who triangulated her. She also lacked differentiation in two specific circumstances. She would too readily assume gender bias, lack of sophistication, or some other form of closedness within the system (setting, and family-within-setting), and take sides unthinkingly. She also uncritically allied with women in circumstances apparently like her own: divorced or divorcing women, single parents, and women with abusive husbands.

I had been discussing this therapist and the setting with a colleague who was a former Episcopal priest. We had smugly traded knowing stories about the "religious right wing," talked sympathetically of this therapist's plight, and observed how she might prove to be a change agent in what we saw as a relatively closed system. However, as we spoke of this therapist's lack of differentiation, my colleague began to question our own. Maybe, isomorphically, we ourselves were taking sides and assuming too much about the setting.

As this self-discovery took place, I found that I began to occupy a more differentiated position relative to the therapist. Accordingly, I could ask her questions which challenged her position when she was entangled with a certain client family, ineffective, and sometimes in pain. For example, the therapist began one supervision session by not wanting to talk. I pursued that and she said that she "dreaded" seeing a single mother and child. The mother, she said, didn't do what the therapist had asked her to do. I asked her about that: Her telling a client what to do and her irritation when the client wouldn't obey. Although both women had been molested as children, and both were divorced mothers of young sons, the therapist said that she was confident that she had separated her "issues" from her client's. Instead, she said, the problem was that the mother was willing to "drop everything" and take the ex-husband back, a man who in this case also had abused the child. The therapist emphasized that this was destructive. After all, she herself had been reared in a household where the parents "ripped each other up," and she could not believe that her client would leave her child with a man who had abused him. I drew her out further and she noted two additional problems, which were a function of the setting. The family lived across the street from her, so that her boy played with the client family's child. So she feared for the safety of her own child but didn't feel free to break off that relationship. In addition, she had been invited to the couple's upcoming remarriage.

The therapist said that she could talk to no one at the agency about this because, unconcerned about multiple relationships, none would understand her predicament. I appreciated her sense of isolation. She agreed: "It's hard when I stand alone." She stated that she could not change the system, and all she could do was tolerate what was occurring or leave. She observed further that either to stay or to leave was problematic. On the one hand, she couldn't rely on the agency because it made bad judgments. It wasn't just the problem of blurred boundaries and dual relationships. She cited examples of alleged incompetence, characterized by insensitivity to the children under the agency's purview, for example, a homosexual resident of a group home was said to have molested several boys for 10 months before he was discovered. On the other hand, she observed that recently, when a staff member was discovered looking for other work, his employment was abruptly terminated. These events said to her "It's not safe to stay, and it's an act of treason to leave."

I listened sympathetically, but consistently asked questions focused on alternative ways she could perceive things or steps she could take. I wanted to be with her, but to work against the triangulation. It took many such sessions before the therapist began to see herself as having choices. I confronted her with her reactions and expectations and questioned both. Should a therapist give orders? Should a client be a "good little girl" and obey? Is the agency as inept, insensitive, and unprofessional as she perceives, and will the authorities not support her if she brings concerns to their attention? On close inspection, does the evidence support the agency as inept, insensitive and enmeshing? Must she do therapy with a neighbor? In addition, although she seems to be experiencing herself almost as a child within the agency, could it be that she has had, or potentially could have had, more of a voice and a choice?

I wondered about her perception of standing alone. Even if the head of the agency were dysfunctional, was everyone else as well? Was the therapist alone because she hadn't voiced her concerns with anyone else? Was her isolation a matter of emotional cut-off? Might she not have been able to find some other, better-differentiated people to join her in working on the system? If not, if she had fewer blind spots could she not have stood alone better—with more conviction, less fear, and less baggage? In fact, she was so preoccupied with such cases, and so immobilized, I recommended that she explore her own family of origin with a therapist, which she subsequently did.

In dealing with her own struggles for autonomy and intimacy, the therapist became more aware of her own circumstances, as well as those of the other members of the larger system. In the process, changes in her personal life were mirrored by growth in her client families. She felt renewed energy and degrees of freedom as she again met with total families, and viewed things systemically. At about the same time she began to challenge the closedness of the agency and found that it was not so closed. She also went on vacation with her mother and sister, whom she normally avoided, and brought back snapshots.

More recently the therapist has begun to have more comfort in more therapy sessions of varying types. She has begun to ask differentiating questions of her clients in areas where formerly she did not. She has been less likely to take refuge in individual psychotherapy to avoid facing families. A preponderance of clients continue in treatment with her and develop skills, and she herself has become more adept with specific skills, for example, defocusing and reframing. Her clients have referred many cases to her. She also has found more freedom in her personal life.

DISCUSSION

This therapist had triangulated me initially in order to pull back from the agency. It explicitly saw itself as a "family" and investment in it made her anxious. Presumably, based on her previous experiences, she feared enmeshment in a dysfunctional family run by incompetent adults, having custody of trusting or impotent children. Unhappily, in my own undifferentiated and arrogant stance, I myself was blind to alternate constructions. Besides, the agency did have some dysfunctional features, abetting her fears. However, to the extent that my colleague became self-conscious, and began to question his own assumptions, and then mine, I was able to do this with the therapist. She in turn was better able to observe the therapy system (self-family-setting) and ask questions of them. Isomorphically, as I the supervisor made progress appropriate to my own level of development, the therapist began to increase her own level of differentiation and mobility, and the client-family was then able to do the same.

The most influential supervisory tool was my own position of differentiation, wherein I could pose questions, challenge her perceptions, and allow the therapist to differentiate herself. Accordingly, I needed to look to my own level of comfort and seek feedback as to whether I was as alert and technically helpful as I should have been. I needed to observe my relationship with the therapist for the presence and absence of telltale cues, keeping an eye out for what the therapist brought to me, or didn't bring to me: affective displays, material on a certain theme, only stories of success. I needed to become aware of my own interests, lack of interest, and blind spots. My supervisee's development as a therapist seemed to parallel mine as a supervisor. To the extent that I was a better observer of myself as a member of a large, treatment system, so was she.

Clearly the simple presence of a supervisor is not enough. That supervisor needs mechanisms to enable her or him to increase personal levels of awareness and cognitive and emotional fluidity. That may come from explicit work on the person of the supervisor (Aponte,1994; Storm,1991), use of a reflecting team (Andersen,1991), or peer consultation or supervision of supervision (Nichols & Everett, 1986).

REFERENCES

ANDERSEN, T. (1991). *The reflecting team: Dialogues and dialogues about the dialogues.* New York: Norton.

ANDERSEN, T. (1993). See and hear, and be seen and heard. In S. Friedman (Ed.), *The new language of change: Constructive collaboration in psychotherapy* (pp. 303–322). New York: Guilford Press.

APONTE, H. J. (1994). How personal can training get? *Journal of Marital and Family Therapy, 20,* 3–15.

LIDDLE, H. A. (1988). Systemic supervision: Conceptual overlays and pragmatic guidelines. In H. A. Liddle, D. C. Breunlin, & R. C. Schwartz (Eds.), *Handbook of family therapy training and supervision* (pp. 153–171). New York: Guilford Press.

MINUCHIN, S., & FISHMAN, H. C. (1981). *Family therapy techniques.* Cambridge, MA: Harvard University Press.

NICHOLS, W. C., & EVERETT, C. A. (1986). *Systemic family therapy: An integrative approach.* New York: Guilford Press.

PAPERO, D. V. (1988). Training in Bowen theory. In H. A. Liddle, D.C. Breunlin, & R. C. Schwartz (Eds.), *Handbook of family therapy training and supervision* (pp. 62–77). New York: Guilford Press.

SCHARFF, D., & SCHARFF, J. S. (1987). *Object relations family therapy.* New York: Jason Aronson.

STORM, C. (1991). Changing the line: An interview with Edwin Friedman. *The Commission on Supervision Bulletin, IV* (3), 1–2.

TOMM, K. (1984). One perspective on the Milan systemic approach: Part II. Description of session format, interviewing style and interventions. *Journal of Marital and Family Therapy, 10,* 253–271.

CHAPTER 9

A Picture Is Worth a Thousand Words

Exploring Metaphors in Training

TIMOTHY F. DWYER
ROBERT E. LEE

Metaphors of supervision are social constructions that can be both liberating and constraining and can hold significant influence over the course of the supervisory relationship. When metaphors used to describe supervision are pursued and appreciated as an explicit part of training, the training system is more likely to be an open and reflexive one. Specific metaphors can have different implications for the way in which a supervisory relationship is experienced. In this chapter we briefly describe the role of metaphors in language and interactionist theory. A clinical vignette offers a window into the reflexive process and discovery of multiple metaphors in therapy with a consulting supervisor. Finally, we summarize a series of reflexive discussion group meetings exploring the metaphors used by students and faculty in a doctoral level marriage and family therapy program. The narrative themes connected with these operative metaphors have implications for other training systems.

Family therapy training can be described, understood, planned, and conducted by means of images and language. Therefore, it is important that family therapy trainers give substantial thought to the images, icons, and words that authors, trainers, and students use to make sense of the experience. Some authors (Andersen, 1993; Anderson, 1993) have encouraged clinicians to consider the metaphors that frame their relationship with those who consult them, and also have encouraged reflexive dialogue ("conversation"). We encourage a similar sensitivity to and conversation about the metaphors and words used to make sense of training and supervision.

LEANING ON LANGUAGE AND MEANING

The act of labeling something may sensitize one to and capture certain aspects of that entity while excluding and blinding one to other aspects.

Wittgenstein (1922) observed that the act of using language "captures" a person's reality and "holds it hostage" because language is a form of "picturing" reality. This notion is at the core of narrative approaches to therapy (Anderson, 1993; Anderson & Goolishian, 1988). A metaphor in turn is a specific use of language: ". . . a way of speaking in which one thing is expressed in terms of another, whereby this bringing together throws new light on the character of that being described" (Kopp, 1971, p. 17). As such, metaphors become a primary vehicle through which attributes of an object or person are included and excluded in one's thinking and perceiving about that object or person (Cassirer, 1946). For example, calling the family a "system" may heighten our attention to its relational nature while causing us to lose sight of the individual who is a constituent part of that system (Nichols, 1988). In fact the metaphors we use to give thinghood to relationships are especially powerful (Thomas, 1923). We make relationships "real" by naming, categorizing, and orienting ourselves to constellations of objects, including the self as an object. Moreover, how we "define these situations"—using a symbolic or metaphorical construct—shapes their consequences (Thomas, 1972). So, if we make a relationship real (for example, we talk about a "supervisory relationship"), and we picture it in a certain way, there are very real consequences to both of these actions.

Social psychologists (Kelley, 1950; Warr & Knapper, 1968) demonstrated empirically how words used in anticipation of an individual's appearance subsequently shaped how that person is perceived and received. Similarly, Schnitzer (1993) found that, in therapy, the beliefs and expectations attendant on a specific metaphor influenced how individuals felt about themselves and their world and how they related to one another. In marriage and family therapy training, the expectations of trainee and trainer are defined in part by the metaphors each uses uniquely to describe the experience. These expectations can include ideas about what training should look like in terms of both the style and direction of training, the roles of the participant parties, and what needs to be accomplished.

Piaget's (1954) concept of constructing schemas is another way of understanding the assimilative and adaptive systems of metaphors in the training relationship. Each individual uses his or her own language and history to make sense of things (Schnitzer, 1993). The metaphoric nature of language governs a large part of what will take place and how the individuals feel about the training situation and training relationship (Rosenblatt, 1994). Thus, it seems only prudent to identify the various metaphors being used, explore them, and to ascertain whether or not they are similar, congruent, and constructive. Presumably one goal of the training system is for all parties to be "on the same page" and in pursuit of compatible goals! Similarly, whether a compelling metaphor is held individually or collectively shared, it may be the only reality that will be seized if individuals do not take a more reflexive stance, observe themselves, and consider alternative metaphors, which in turn may offer other information about "reality."

If trainers and trainees are to appreciate the ambiguity and complexity of constructed meanings, relationships and realities, it is essential that they be (a) aware that relationships and tasks are governed by the language used to present them and that language consists of metaphors (Cassirer, 1946), (b) alert to the metaphors being used, and (c) open to alternative metaphors (and can create them). For example, if a trainer felt that a student who did not follow directives had "problems with authority," what might be seen and not seen, expected and not expected? How would all of that change if that trainer thought of training as "consultation" and the student as exhibiting "precocious autonomy"? The shift in metaphoric description may invite a different perception, and that may change the experience of "difficulty" between the parties to something much more benign. The reflexive process of conjointly exploring the metaphoric schema from which each was operating can foster that sense of being "on the same page."

Awareness of language and how it constructs meaning requires a collaborative and conversational approach (Andersen, 1993; Anderson & Goolishian, 1988). Using a narrative approach therapists actively listen to another's story of his or her situation and ask appreciative questions. Whether in therapy (Nichols & Schwartz, 1998) or training (Zimmerman & Dickerson, 1994), as one listens, validates, questions, and reframes, one eventually becomes a coauthor (White & Epston, 1990) or coeditor (Hoffman, 1993) of a mutual story. Through this mutual "storying" in training we at times are forced to appreciate the limits of some constructions of reality. For example, the supervisor and trainee must accept the difference of their experiences and training, and cannot fully deny the asymmetry of the relationship, although they may aim for non-hierarchical collaboration. In this way, awareness of metaphors in training grows out of the realization that we initially may have at least "two separate pages" to be read and perhaps coedited. A mutual task is then to collaborate in the creation of other interpretations or, in Thomas's (1923) view, alternative "definitions of the situation" that offer a different sense of self, relationship, and the shared problems that may exist (or arise).

Metaphors, as we are describing them, are viewed as "small stories" contained in larger narratives: They may give instructions or suggestions for action, present various frames for viewing situations, and offer possible solutions to problematic situations. In what follows, metaphors are further explored in light of their influence and use in therapy training. Examples will highlight the rich variety of different narrative constructions and the implications of metaphor in other training systems.

METAPHORS IN THERAPY AND TRAINING

Without denying that there are a host of contextual factors that can influence the structure and process of training (e.g., gender and experience), the role of language and metaphors remains a critical variable in shaping relationships and experience. How supervisors, trainees, and clients view each other, and therefore their initial and ongoing expectations and feelings, can depend largely on the metaphors each uses to make sense of the therapeutic relationship. Similarly, how trainers and trainees view each other, and the ramifications of those narratives, also are bound by the metaphors each uses to make sense of the supervisory relationship. In each situation, the metaphors capturing those relationships may be conscious and verbalized, conscious and nonverbalized, or unconscious (generalized from Sager, 1976). Moreover, an explicitly defined metaphor may be decided on by fiat or be more mutually constructed, negotiated, and contracted. In addition, because it is not likely that any relationship will be static, the metaphors used to capture it at one point in time may need to be reexamined at another.

As a trainee and supervisor establish a workable training contract they begin to coevolve in their training relationship. Their individual metaphors of that relationship often unfold developmentally (e.g., moving from a hierarchical structure to a more collaborative and collegial model). However, the developmental path is not always linear and sequential, but oscillates over time regulated by patterns of both continuous and discontinuous change. Given the shaping power of metaphors to mark meaning and context, it is important to actively traverse the narrative course in the training relationship. By reflexively identifying and appreciating the ramifications of particular role definitions, their attendant images, and mutual goals, the trainee and supervisor can more effectively maintain a common frame throughout the training process.

When one participant's metaphors of therapy or training are incongruent and even contradictory with another's picture and definition of the situation, then therapy, training, and morale can suffer. However, when the members of a therapy and training system appreciate their use of multiple and diverse metaphors, they may each come to realize they have divergent expectations of self and the others. If they subsequently explore those metaphors conjointly, awareness of those definitions and images will lend understanding to each other's feelings and behavior.

ON THE ROAD TO FINDING OUT:
EXPLORING METAPHORS IN A
SUPERVISORY CONSULTATION

In the clinical vignette that follows, Joe requested his supervisor, Lisa, to come into the session for a consultation because "I'd just like to open things up more between us, and clarify what we're all experiencing in there." Earlier Joe expressed in the presession, with not just a little exasperation, "Each time this couple comes in they seem completely different from one session to the next. I don't know how to plan ahead for them because I never know what they're going to be like." Lisa asked Joe if he thought he was different each session. "Well, I guess I am, because I don't really know what they want from me."

Joe introduced the idea to Tom and Deborah in this way: "I've asked my supervisor, Lisa, to come into the therapy room to talk with us about how therapy is going." He described her role to them as being "like an obstetrician, or a midwife, to the therapy process because she remains present and watchful for us all, yet is ready to step in when needed to help things along."

Lisa began by asking Tom, "How do you feel about coming to this room, about coming to therapy." Tom paused for a moment and then said "I feel like I'm coming to work." Lisa pursued this a little further. "Is this 'work' some place you like and want to go, or do you feel like you must go because you have to?" After thinking for a moment, Tom said, "I don't like the fact that we need to come here, but it's not a bad place to come. I know it's a place that we'll get something done, and I feel good about that. So, this work is worthwhile. It's meaningful. Similar to what my job affords. I know this work will allow me and Deb to get more of what we want out of life, to get more of what we need from each other."

Lisa continued to explore the metaphor of therapy-as-work. "So, how do you think Joe figures into this for you then? Is he a colleague? Your boss? Or perhaps a subordinate? Or is there another role that seems to fit for him in this job, in this work you come to?" Tom thought long and deeply about this. "Well, he's not my boss. But I'm not his either . . . I don't know. I think he's like a 'salesman.' But he didn't just call, or knock on the door. He came because I asked him to, because I knew he had something we needed. His task is to try and match our needs with his best product, his best strategies, his best ideas for us to meet our own needs."

Lisa then turned to Deborah. "And how do you feel about coming here, Deborah?" She immediately replied, "I'm always excited about coming here. I like this because, well, I can't say it's fun, but it's so interesting to me! It's not like work to me, but more like 'school.' Because I always learn something here that I can take home and think about. I'm learning new skills too, so it's kind of like a trade school. Yeah, that's it! We're trading in some old ideas and some really bad habits for some new skills. Some new life skills that will make it possible for us to build a different future than the one we were heading for, to build something better together."

Lisa clarified. "So the therapist is the 'teacher' at this school then?" "Exactly."

Lisa then invited Joe to identify his operative metaphor. "Can you tell us, Joe, how do you feel about coming here and meeting Tom and Deborah in therapy?" Joe was somewhat surprised by Tom and Deborah's responses. In contrast, he doubted their commitment to therapy and had been feeling frustrated! However, he needed to reframe his doubt and frustration. "I feel like a bus driver for Tom and Deborah. I sense them pulling the stop cord sometimes when it feels to me like we're out in the middle of nowhere. I wonder whether this is really where they want to get off, or if they are ambivalent about the direction in which we're heading I stop the bus so they can get their bearings, until they give me the signal to go a bit farther down the road. At the end of each session, I let them out. They are usually at some completely different spot then next session, but still they flag me down and climb aboard. They tell me they want to head west, but they're standing at the east-bound station, so we clarify the direction and head north. I might invite one of them to drive, and offer to narrate the road and navigate."

Lisa gently mines Joe's metaphor a bit deeper. "Is the 'bus' in pretty good running condition?" Joe replies, "Yes, it really is." Lisa continues, "Then tell us about the road conditions, Joe. Do they seem hazardous to you?" Joe takes a long pause to reflect on this. He notices himself experiencing a shift from his earlier frustration to see the "road" more clearly. Then, with clarity and compassion he notes, "Actually, there are a few hairpin turns and switchbacks on this road. I urge us to proceed cautiously and go slow. Otherwise, the road is well maintained. I think they trust my driving." Tom and Deborah's heads are nodding, "but sometimes the road is foggy, and I'm not so sure where we're going. When I ask them they say, 'we don't know, Joe, but please drive faster, faster, faster . . .' like the destination might become clearer to them quicker. Yet I keep wondering if they don't know where they are, how do they know where they should be? It seems they might appreciate where they've come from, and recall some of the beautiful places they've been in their 15 years of marriage."

This brief vignette highlights not only the role of metaphors, which can be explored in therapy and training, but also illustrates the importance of the training context of the supervisory relationship (Sprenkle & Piercy, 1986). Here, the isomorphism between therapy and live supervision is framed by the "consultant" role of the supervisor. The opportunities to model and explore relational metaphors embedded within a client-therapist system, in situ, through live supervision offer an experiential context in which the metaphors can be identified and come to life. Important facets of that context are sometimes derived from the metaphors constructed to inform and interpret it. In the preceding situation, Joe's operative metaphor of his supervisor as "midwife" allowed him to request her presence in session, thus sharing that relationship in an experiential way with his clients.

The mutually reflexive stance in the supervisory relationship affirmed the value of asking for, recognizing, and pursuing the various metaphors of the treatment system, and provided useful and validating information to both the treatment and the supervisory systems. First, Joe's metaphor for Lisa both affirmed her role and invited Tom and Deborah to share in his trust of her. The "therapy as work" metaphor clarified the therapeutic relationship and recast the alliance in collaborative terms. It is interesting to note both the similarities and the differences in Tom and Deborah's metaphors. Although there may be important differences between Deborah's "teacher" and Tom's "salesman," the images are similar in that teachers and sales consultants both impart information. In each metaphor role, Joe is conferred with "expert knowledge" and special tools and skills. For the clients, their metaphors put the focus on what the therapist was saying or doing, rather than their taking explicit ownership for their own expert experience. They may have been blind to their own influence, and the cross-purposes they may have exhibited in the expression of their needs. With the therapist's metaphor uncovered, however, the contract between client and therapist became open for clarification and perhaps renegotiation. Without understanding their current operative metaphors, there existed the potential for the therapist not to utilize his position effectively (i.e., teaching, selling, driving) toward the unexpressed goals of the couple. In making this more explicit through the shared metaphors, the different ways in which the couple had been requesting their goals—however unspoken or unconscious—became more clear.

Depending on supervisory philosophy and therapy situation, the implication of the therapist's metaphors could be further explored at that time or in a private supervisory session. In either case, this vignette illustrates how not only the supervisory system but also the therapy system can benefit from identifying and exploring clients' and trainees' metaphors in a live supervision session. Moreover, further extending this reflexive process may have proved both beneficial and informative to the therapy-and-supervisory system, vis-à-vis exploring the supervisor's metaphors from her vantage point of the in-session consultation as well as from behind the one-way mirror.

EXPLORING METAPHORS WITH TRAINEES IN REFLEXIVE DISCUSSION GROUPS

It is important for families and therapists in therapy to coevolve acceptable visions of how they will work together. Similarly, trainers and trainees also need to develop a frame for their working together

(Schwartz, 1988). This "frame for training" needs to reflect the degree of fit between the individual, idiosyncratic expectations held by the trainer and trainee for the aims and purposes of the training experience. Trainees tend to enter supervision holding a variety of motives and expectations, and a moderately opaque sense of their own needs. These motives, expectations, and sense of needs may be quite different from those held by supervisors.

Of course, all trainees do not share the same needs or expectations for supervision. Researchers have found that trainees are likely to vary according to experience (Liddle, Davidson, & Barrett, 1988; Pike-Urlacher, 1995), gender (Caust, Libow, & Raskin, 1981; Wheeler, Avis, Miller, & Chaney, 1986), and learning style (Hoffman, 1990; Perlesz, Stolk, & Firestone, 1990). Other important factors also can influence the trainer-trainee relationship. Among these are culture (Falicov, 1995), preferred theoretical style and epistemological stance (Liddle, 1982), emotional maturity and differentiation (Papero, 1988), developmental level (Pike-Urlacher, 1995), and theoretical model (Liddle, Breunlin, & Schwartz, 1988). Each of those variables can invite the construction of a different kind of metaphor, with different relational implications. For example, gender and culture may press toward metaphors of the supervisory relationship expressing ideas about hierarchy and collaboration. Similarly, metaphors created by trainees at different developmental levels will incorporate disparate ideas about hierarchy, directiveness, and emotional support. In addition, one may expect trainees' metaphoric constructions of the training relationship to change consistent with their shifting perceptions of their needs.

Supervisors

Supervisors' metaphors also are shaped by cultural variables, including ideas about gender, pedagogical style, theoretical orientation, personality, personal life stage, and their perceptions of trainees' developmental level. For example, supervisors focused on stage of training issues might emphasize their role as "teacher," "coach," or "colleague" depending on the educational level of the trainee. Each metaphor has specific implications for how the relationships are structured and enacted, and what the supervisor's expectations are for a particular relationship. Each metaphor also may contain within it a reciprocal role. If there is a "teacher," there is a "student." A "coach" has a "trainee," and a "colleague" has a "peer." Similarly, the supervisor's definition of the training relationship may incorporate personal metaphors which are not always obvious to trainees. For example, metaphors regarding a supervisor's birth order and family roles may become enacted along with expectations for reciprocal trainee roles, as parent-child or sibling-sibling.

Agreement of Metaphors

Supervisors and trainees may not share the same metaphors for the process/event in which they are mutually engaged. Accordingly, there is opportunity for confusion and disappointment for both parties. A supervisor may subscribe to an authoritarian, trainer-as-expert metaphor, and the trainee's perception of training may be training-as-collegial-conversation. Conversely, a supervisor may conceptualize training as helping a trainee to appreciate the supervisor's solutions while the trainee may be looking for specific advice. Moreover, even if both supervisor and trainee do share a similar metaphor for training, they nevertheless may still feel at odds because of how that metaphor is enacted. For example, a trainee's expectations of the supervising "coach" may not match the coaching role enacted by a supervisor who shares that same metaphor. Does a boxer's coach share the same idea of his or her role as does a cheerleader's coach or an acting coach? It is the nature of language that each individual has his or her own personal sense of what a metaphor means, and that sense is based on his or her personal experiences.

Using Sager's (1976) ideas about marriage contracts (i.e., that each partner brings to the relationship expectations about the institution itself), metaphors may contain implicit contracts of goals and purposes that guide the training relationship. Each person's metaphor includes the framer's perception of "who I am" and "who you are." In turn, each person has a unique expectation that, "if I do this, you should do that." The difficulty is that, if supervisor and trainee have incongruent metaphors of the training relationship, each may be working very hard only to be disappointed. Each may feel betrayed because, having done his or her part, he or she did not experience the expected payoff.

The opportunity for confusion and disappointment appears to be substantial. The metaphors of training predictably are as diverse as the supervisors and trainees who create them. However, those individual metaphors rarely are explicitly stated and explored, and congruent metaphors rarely are negotiated and contracted.

Reflexive Discussion Groups

One way the authors found to accomplish the task of metaphor identification and exploration was through reflexive discussion groups. That is, supervisors and trainees were asked to share their metaphors for training, and then to reflect on what they had said. They were to give their metaphors and then the connotations of their metaphor. (To say that training is "teaching" is not enough. There is a need to know what each party involved thinks that "teaching" is.) Specifically, the authors facilitated discussion groups with 20 master's and doctoral level trainees and three clinical faculty members in a university-based marital and family therapy program.

We hosted three sessions, with each discussion group lasting about an hour. In the first discussion group session both faculty and trainees were asked to generate metaphoric ideas that for them captured some of the relational dynamics of supervisory relationships and of faculty-student positions in the program. In the two subsequent follow-up sessions, the ideas and metaphors generated in the first session were explored more fully, along with some reflective consideration of the variation between a particular student's program level and individual supervisory relationships. In the first follow-up discussion group the generated metaphors were explored in terms of their fit with the variety of needs and experiences of these trainees and supervisors. In the third and final session, a set of open-ended questions was posed to identify what trainees thought was expected of them in training, and what they expected to get in return. Similarly, the supervisors were asked what they expected of trainees, and what they in turn should bring to the enterprise.

Metaphors of Training

The intensity and concentrated focus of the academic program provided a wealth of instructive metaphoric constructions. When asked to consider and share their metaphors for supervisors and supervision, trainees' responses reflected their level of training. Beginning- and intermediate-level trainees offered metaphors that highlighted the hierarchical nature of supervision, and invested the supervisor with a superior level of knowledge: "teacher," "expert," "coach," "boss," and—a precursor of a popular program metaphor ("family," below)—"parent." Doctoral trainees, on the other hand, offered metaphors of supervision that did not readily incorporate hierarchical relationships. For example, they described the clinical supervisor as a "teammate," "partner," and "colleague."

Supervisors held metaphors as disparate as "master craftsmen," "watchdog," and "mentor." Supervisors agreed that the metaphors they held were bound by the unique relationship they had with specific trainees. Yet, they also maintained that trainees' developmental level, "openness for supervision," and ability to articulate needs were the factors from which their metaphors arose. For example, one faculty member identified enacting the role of "case manager" for one trainee, "compatriot" for another, and "protective, big sister" for yet another.

Other creative metaphors identified were the trainee as artist in training with a master; supervisor as a gardener planting mystery seeds and nurturing the potential of growth (being careful to discern weeds from desirable shoots), and supervision as a "police state." The trainee who perceived supervision as a "police state" experienced supervision as a constraint to individual, personal creativity. This revelation highlights the importance of this exercise.

Regarding the training program itself, the metaphor of "family" was discussed at length in the first discussion group. Many common systemic features were highlighted (e.g., rules, roles, norms, and loyalty issues), as well as different family configurations (e.g. adoptive or stepfamily) and relational connections (e.g., parent-child, mother-father, brother-sister). The participants observed that projections of one's own family of origin, rooted in experience and perceptions of family roles and emotional process, unwittingly were superimposed on the supervisory process. Some trainees also said that they expected certain classmates to perform stereotypic family roles, such as big brother, mother hen, the hero, clown, scapegoat, rebellious adolescent, and compliant child. Finally, just as in a family, each participant was thought to have a different structural position with regard to his or her level of experience, and a different emotional position according to their preferred distance.

For some the metaphor of training-program-as-family included the idea of its being an "island of sanity" or a "haven." To them the training program was a place where people support you, care about your troubles, and make time to help in moments of need. However, program-as-family also suggested some dysfunctional attributes with the potential to inhibit individual development. For example, children could be parentified, enmeshment could lead to the loss of individuality and to loyalty conflicts, or a collective push for autonomy might cost the inhabitants the cohesion necessary for individual growth.

Some trainees objected to the idea of considering themselves a "family." To them, this would add even more obligation to the already substantial demands of their training. Furthermore, they rejected the implied notion of emotional process as fundamental to the program or to training, and considered it an imposition on their conceptual view of therapy. They preferred to construct their metaphors around individual supervisory relationships, rather than a polymorphous system like a university training program. Their reaction clearly demonstrated the power of a metaphor, and the emotional charge attendant upon "family."

Some discussants thought that the training program wasn't so much a family as it was a "team." Exploration of this metaphor was illuminating. On a team there are various kinds of interdependence with both individual and group goals. Individuals serve in different positions, yet are able to form a more or less cohesive unit. The success of the team depends on the directives and intuition of the "coach." Moreover, the coach not only teaches fundamentals, but also plays a part in keeping the players' spirits up. Finally, it is essential that both the players and the coach trust each other.

Implicit Contracts in Training: Expectations of Self

Another way to discover and explore the metaphors for training held by the discussion group participants was to inquire about the implicit contract each brought to the enterprise. The participants were asked what they thought was expected of them as trainees, and what they expected to get in return.

Trainees' feelings about what should be expected of them varied with their level in the program. Congruent with hierarchical metaphors—specifically, someone operating under the authority of and through the guidance of an expert—beginning trainees identified "coming prepared to present concerns" and "alerting supervisors of duty to warn issues and crisis cases." However, they also had a perception of supervision as an educational process involving self-actualization. Some trainees indicated they should be "committed to (my) own growth" by "listening with an open mind" and "being willing to take risks." The latter included "sharing mistakes openly" and "speaking up when needs aren't being met."

All the trainees, beginning through advanced, felt that training is "active and collaborative learning" (Johnson, Johnson, & Smith, 1991). They specified the high value of every student, at every level, sharing case material and participating in case discussion. However, intermediate and advanced trainees more emphatically stressed the contribution of the student as a collaborator in that process. They emphasized self-organization and self-determination ("identifying own goals," "identifying needs of self and issues that get activated"). They spoke of their obligation to be firmly grounded in theory and to be able to articulate an evolving personal theory of therapy and change.

More advanced trainees, while visioning training as collaborative learning, had a more complex picture of what that is. For example, they stressed the importance of coming to supervision equipped with a "working hypothesis to be continually testing and assessing" and having a "prepared treatment plan, with interventions designed to meet the goals and objectives." They also expected that each trainee would bring a "developing vision" of the kind of therapist he or she hoped to become. Moreover, it was thought important that all participants recognize that supervision is a multifaceted enterprise which includes clients, therapists, supervisors, and the training context.

Supervisors expected trainees to remain current with theoretical knowledge and to "continue to grow in the process of training." Some noted the ever pressing dialectic of "giving ideas and interventions" and "eliciting" them from the trainee's own repertoire and developing knowledge base. Similarly, balancing personal, self-of-the-therapist issues with executive and technical skill was described as a perennial expectation of supervisors. One supervisor noted, "sometimes it's a tough call between supervising the case and supervising the trainee. You can't always do both simultaneously. At those times, I try to go with the trainee."

Implicit Contracts: Expectations of Training

When trainees were asked what they expected to get in return for their efforts, their images of training involved three metaphorical domains: training as a source of information, a place, and the art of pedagogy.

Training as a Source of Information

First, trainees identified a number of content expectations. For example, beginners expected explicit ties to theory ("make the theory come to life"), concrete clinical examples ("tell me exactly what to say and do"), guidance in administrative procedures ("tell me when to administer what assessments"), and professional practice issues ("show me how to make a child protection report" or "how and when to refer a client for further evaluation").

Intermediate trainees identified more advanced content issues. They expected to be taught "how to apply different theoretical models" and "multiple ways of conceptualizing cases," and "how to use, and stick with, interventions that are consistent with one particular model." However, they also expected to "expand our repertoire of intervention ideas," and "to incorporate different assessment tools." Several trainees also expected opportunity both to see others—including supervisors—do therapy, and to work in teams with other trainees.

Advanced trainees expected "flexibility and respect for different ideas" and "freedom to disagree and discuss theoretical differences." They felt that supervisors should provide feedback based on a good understanding of the trainee at this stage in his or her development, and they expected work on the person of the therapist (e.g., "my self reflected back to me"). Finally, they expected to be socialized into the profession. This included being shown how to interact with "and even confront" other professional colleagues.

Again, supervisors voiced needing to know what trainees themselves saw as their particular needs. The following comments reflect similar themes: "I need evidence that trainees are actively monitoring and reflecting on their own growth." "I always try to ask, 'what did you like about the session and what didn't you like? ' " One supervisor recalled in his own training that "my supervisor always wanted us to bring in an example of where we 'screwed up.' He'd say, 'remember, a bad tape is a good tape in supervision.' " Thus, it appeared that supervisors wanted to know how to be helpful—from the eyes of their trainees.

Training as a Place

All of the discussion members thought of training as a specific kind of place conducive to growth. The ambiance imagined varied by level of training. Beginning trainees imagined training to be a "safe place" that included empathy and support. However, their place also had an "uplifting" quality. Training was a place in which strengths were identified and "growing edges were watered." It was ". . . a place to come and vent,. . . a place to laugh,. . . a place to go when I'm all confused,. . . a place of inspiration, with clear evidence of the supervisor's own joy and value of doing therapy." Intermediate trainees, perhaps because they were ready to venture out on their own, emphasized supervision as a safe haven, including an honest mirror that offered protection and guidance in the process of that. "I want constructive feedback, but I still need a safe place."

Intermediate trainees, like beginners, also saw supervision as a place that promotes growth. However, this image included "empowerment." For the intermediate trainees, supervision was a place". . . where we can feel competent. . . and find solutions to being stuck."

The environment of supervision for the advanced trainees was viewed as a co-constructed place. These trainees expected empowerment through the expression of their own efficacy and self-knowledge: "Space to exercise my creativity,. . . articulate my growing vision of my own personal theory of therapy,. . . to have creative license in developing treatment plans." They wanted to "respectfully disagree" in an open and nondefensive way, and wanted the supervisor to set the norm for doing that, "by modeling acceptance of difference."

Supervisors agreed with the trainees' descriptions of "place." However, they noted there are "necessary constraints" on that space when trainees did not perform the duties as expected (i.e., following procedures, protocols, etc.). Thus, they described the place as "democracy to a point" but with ample room for "genuine dialogue, and even debate."

Training as an Art of Pedagogy

Not only did the discussion group members conceptualize supervision as active, collaborative learning, requiring different kinds and amounts of contribution by trainee, they also had reciprocal images of supervisors. That is, supervision was universally conceived as an "act of teaching." However the individual visions of teaching could be placed on a continuum ranging from hierarchical structure, strict direction, and specific instruction to collegial consultation. Beginning trainees expected more concrete guidance and direction, in contrast to the advanced trainee who envisioned mutual interaction and diversity of theoretical input. Intermediate trainees, in turn, expected training-as-teaching to be sensitive and responsive to their oscillating needs. Advanced trainees held the view that supervision was a mentoring process, with the supervisor as "more seasoned collaborator."

The supervisors in turn felt that what was taught and how it was taught depended on each trainee's developmental path. However, each supervisor drew from different stylistic traditions. The traditions seemed to be largely informed by the manner in which they themselves were trained or by the theoretical models they were inclined to embrace. For example, one faculty member not only drew heavily from his narrative and constructivist therapy models but employed an experiential frame. He would invite the use of reflecting teams and in-session language consultations. Another faculty member drew from a background in play therapy and psychoeducational models. Thus, each pedagogic style shaped and influenced the coevolving metaphors of the training relationship.

A MODEST PROPOSAL

The variety of images and meanings the discussion groups generated around the supervisory context highlights the importance of identifying and exploring the metaphors of training. The narrative character of language suggests that metaphors are categories, unique to each individual, into which experiences are sorted and defined. Through them trainees draw lessons from the past, interpret the present, and predict the future. These metaphors define what trainees will and will not see, and how they will react to the experiences to which they are sensitized. Moreover, metaphors of training are neither universal nor static. Rather, they are fluid, dynamic, idiosyncratic, and shaped by the perceivers who define their situation as it is coevolving in relationships. At the very least the metaphors themselves, or the images subsumed under the label, differ according to ecosystemic factors and students' progress through the training process. Individuals involved in the oftentimes intense interpersonal process of therapy training may hold multiple metaphors for their experiences, and these may or may not be congruent across situations.

All members of the training system, in whatever training context they find themselves, need to have conversations about therapy and training (Andersen, 1993) and to negotiate common, or at least congruent metaphors for that in which they are engaged. The participants also need to consider the implications of the metaphors that influence their interactions in training relationships—thus inviting a change that deepens those relationships, clarifies the vision of training, and enhances the commitment to professional development.

REFERENCES

ANDERSEN, T. (1993). See and hear, and be seen and heard. In S. Friedman (Ed.), *The new language of change: Constructive collaboration in psychotherapy* (pp. 303–322). New York: Guilford Press.

ANDERSON, H. (1993). On a roller coaster: A collaborative systems approach to therapy. In S. Friedman (Ed.), *The new language of change: Constructive collaboration in psychotherapy* (pp. 323–344). New York: Guilford Press.

ANDERSON, H., & GOOLISHIAN, H. A. (1988). Human systems as linguistic systems: Preliminary and evolving ideas about the implications for clinical theory. *Family Process, 27,* 371–393.

CASSIRER, E. (1946). *Language and myth.* (S. K. Langer, trans.). New York: Dover.

CAUST, B. L., LIBOW, J. A., & RASKIN, P. A. (1981). Challenges and promises of training women as family systems supervisees. *Family Process, 20,* 439–447.

FALICOV, C. J. (1995). Training to think culturally: A multidimensional comparative framework. *Family Process, 34,* 373–388.

HOFFMAN, L. (1993). *Exchanging voices.* London: Karnac.

HOFFMAN, L. W. (1990). *Old scapes, new maps.* Cambridge, MA: Milusik Press.

JOHNSON, D. W., JOHNSON, R. T., & SMITH, K. A. (1991). *Active learning: Cooperation in the college classroom.* Edina, MN: Interaction Book.

KELLEY, H. H. (1950). The warm-cold variable in first impressions of persons. *Journal of Personality, 18,* 431–439.

KOPP, S. (1971). *Guru: Metaphors of a psychotherapist.* Palo Alto: Science and Behavior Books.

LIDDLE, H. A. (1982). Family therapy training: Current issues, future trends. *International Journal of Family Therapy, 4,* 81–97.

LIDDLE, H. A., BREUNLIN, D. C., & SCHWARTZ, R. C. (Eds.). (1988). *Handbook of family therapy training and supervision.* New York: Guilford Press.

LIDDLE, H. A., DAVIDSON, G. S., & BARRETT, M. J. (1988). Outcomes of live supervision: Trainee perspectives. In H. A. Liddle, D. C. Breunlin, & R. C. Schwartz (Eds.),. *Handbook of family therapy training and supervision* (pp. 386–398). New York: Guilford Press.

NICHOLS, W. C. (1988). An integrative psychodynamic and systems approach. In H. A. Liddle, D. C. Breunlin, & R. C. Schwartz (Eds.), *Handbook of family therapy training and supervision* (pp. 110–127). New York: Guilford.

NICHOLS, M. P., & SCHWARTZ, R. C. (1998). *Family therapy: Concepts and methods* (4th ed.). Boston: Allyn & Bacon.

PAPERO, D. V. (1988). Training in Bowen theory. In H. A. Liddle, D. C. Breunlin, & R. C. Schwartz (Eds.), *Handbook of family therapy training and supervision* (pp. 62–77). New York: Guilford Press.

PERLESZ, A. J., STOLK, Y., & FIRESTONE, A. F. (1990). Patterns of learning in family therapy training. *Family Process, 29,* 29–44.

PIAGET, J. (1954). *The construction of the child.* New York: Basic Books.

PIKE-URLACHER, R. A. (1995). *Towards the development of the supervisee developmental needs scale (SDNS): An instrument for assessing the developmental needs of family therapy supervisees.* Unpublished doctoral dissertation, Purdue University, West Lafayette, IN.

ROSENBLATT, P. C. (1994). *Metaphors of family systems theory: Toward new constructions.* New York: Guilford Press.

SAGER, C. J. (1976). *Marriage contracts and couple therapy: Hidden forces in intimate relationships.* New York: Brunner/Mazel.

SCHWARTZ, R. C. (1988). The trainer-trainee relationship in family therapy training. In H. A. Liddle, D. C. Breunlin, & R. C. Schwartz (Eds.), *Handbook of family therapy training and supervision* (pp. 172–182). New York: Guilford Press.

SCHNITZER, P. K. (1993). Tales of the absent father: Applying the "story" metaphor in family therapy. *Family Process, 32,* 441–458.

SPRENKLE, D. H., & PIERCY, F. P. (1986). Supervision and training. In F. P. Piercy and D. H. Sprenkle and Associates (Eds.), *Family therapy sourcebook* (pp. 293–297), New York: Guilford Press.

THOMAS, W. I. (1923). *The unadjusted girl.* Boston: Little, Brown.

THOMAS, W. I. (1972). Definition of the situation. In J. G. Manis & B. N. Meltzer (Eds.), *Symbolic interaction* (2nd ed.) (pp. 331–336). Boston: Allyn & Bacon.

WARR, P. B., & KNAPPER, C. (1968). *The perception of people and events.* London: Wiley.

WHEELER, D., AVIS, J. M., MILLER, L. A., & CHANEY, S. (1986). Rethinking family therapy education and supervision: A feminist model. In F. P. Piercy (Ed.), *Family therapy education and supervision* (pp. 53–71). New York: Haworth.

WHITE, M. & Epston, D. (1990). *Narrative means to therapeutic ends.* New York: Norton.

WITTGENSTEIN, L. (1922). *Tractus logico-philosophicus.* London: Harcourt Brace.

ZIMMERMAN, J. L., & DICKERSON, V. C. (1994). Using a narrative metaphor: Implications for theory and clinical practice. *Family Process, 33,* 233–245.

PART THREE

Enlisting the Voice of the Client

CHAPTER 10

Using the Michigan State University Family Therapy Questionnaire for Training

ROBERT E. LEE
SHIRLEY EMERSON
PATRICIA B. KOCHKA

The Michigan State University Family Therapy Questionnaire (MSU/FTQ) is a way for clients to give marital and family therapists feedback about the effectiveness of their therapy. It is highly structured and comprised of the major systemic theorists' ideas about how therapy works. Clients indicate whether or not they remember specific interventions having taken place and, if so, they rate the "importance" of that experience.

Ascertaining the perceptions of clients of their unique therapy experiences is important. It "offers an alternative to the expert stance taken in traditional psychotherapy" (Bailey, 1996, p. 287), it may generate testable hypotheses about the nature of therapy, and it is very helpful in training. That is, debriefing a client can tell therapists something about what they are doing and not doing (Quinn, Nagirreddy, Lawless, & Bagley, 1996). Recently there have been both qualitative and quantitative attempts to obtain feedback from clients about their therapy.

The qualitative studies (Bischoff, McKeel, Moon, & Sprenkle, 1996; Quinn, 1996; Quinn, et al., 1996; Sells, Smith, & Moon, 1996) employed more or less open-ended questions in a variety of formats (e.g., debriefing interviews of clients and therapists by therapists or third parties). The transcripts then were systematically explored for themes. Such openness to the variety and richness of human experience typifies qualitative work (Sells, Smith, & Sprenkle, 1995) and in the present case empowers clients relative to therapists and theorists. Clients give their personal construc-

Source: This chapter originally appeared in *Contemporary Family Therapy,* 1997, *19,* 289–303. Reprinted by permission of Plenum Publishing Corporation.

tions of their therapeutic reality, and say what they think is important in the resolution of their own problems.

There also have been highly structured, quantitative approaches. Dumka, Martin, and Sprenkle (1995) assessed therapeutically induced change as a function of clients' outcome optimism, perceived progress, and self-agency. Pasley, Rhoden, Visher, and Visher (1996) asked stepfamily clients how much expertise their therapists had in stepfamily issues and related that to the clients' ratings of the helpfulness of therapy. Although these studies had a narrow focus, one value of a more structured, quantitative approach is that it is driven by theory and "accepted practices," and therefore gathers data about therapy as a professional construct. The clients are asked to evaluate things theorists say are important to successful therapy based on formulations about symptom formation, behavioral maintenance, and systemic changes. Although some theorists (Anderson, 1993; Hoffman-Hennessy & Davis, 1993) would encourage therapists to do so, it does not seem prudent to overlook decades of reflection and practice, deconstruct therapy, and begin anew with what the client says. Instead, it is more reasonable to formally put clients in the context of the profession and its theory-driven assumptions and ask them their experience of these. The MSU/FTQ does precisely that.

THE MICHIGAN STATE UNIVERSITY FAMILY THERAPY QUESTIONNAIRE

The MSU/FTQ is a mechanism for recursivity. Based on the entire body of family systems therapy, it is a relatively exhaustive list of 74 family therapy interventions. It asks clients what interventions they remember having occurred in their current or recently completed therapy and to estimate each intervention's importance to them. When the MSU/FTQ is used for training the assumption is that, if the client tells the therapist that something is "important," the therapist should pay attention to that and continue to do it. The MSU/FTQ also can alert the therapist to things considered important by theorists but not being done.

Like qualitative approaches, the MSU/FTQ is expected eventually to lead to testable hypotheses about "what works." However, unlike the qualitative researchers, the present investigators chose to go in the direction of measuring established clinical theories and getting clients' reactions to interventions based on them, as opposed to discovering the unique realities of the clients. The MSU/FTQ takes theory and turns it into concepts the clients can use to evaluate the effects of theory. Similar to others, the present investigators think of the client as having expert status. However, they disagree with those who ask the clients to generate the criteria of effective therapy. Instead the client is given a list of the interventions held by theorists to be important to family therapy, and asked which were important to the resolution of their problems, and to what extent. Finally, in contrast to other surveys of client experience, which have looked at the more global ("macro") process (therapist relationship skills, meeting client needs, cultivation of a context for discovery, therapist knowledge, client expectations of change, client agency), the MSU/FTQ deals with marital and family therapy "micro" process interventions.

DEVELOPMENT OF THE MSU/FTQ

The MSU/FTQ was compiled through a modified Delphi process (Jenkins & Smith, 1994). The initial inventory was built on the efforts of others, using listings they had obtained from experts in specific theoretical orientations, and from respected scientist practitioners. For example, the Basic Family Therapy Skills project (Figley & Nelson, 1989, 1990; Nelson & Figley, 1990; Nelson, Heilbrun, & Figley, 1993) used a national sample of marital and family therapy supervisors to generate lists of "the most important skills for beginning family therapists." These included generic marital and family therapy interventions as well as interventions specific to structural, brief, strategic, and transgenerational family therapy. These interventions were compiled into a master list and to it were added contextual interventions culled from the Contextual Family Therapy-Therapist Action Index (Bernal, Flores-Ortiz, Rodriguez, Sorensen, & Diamond, 1990). Finally, the pool of generic interventions was expanded by adding the items of the national marital and family therapy role delineation study (reported in Lee, 1993), resulting in a compiled list of 399 interventions. Redundant items were then removed, resulting in a reduced master list of 114 interventions.

Two problems then needed to be solved. First, such a lengthy list of interventions did not seem "consumer friendly." However, because these interventions were generated by theorists and might involve subtle distinctions that clients would not appreciate, it was decided that some could be combined. Second, many interventions needed to be reworded so that they would match the vocabulary and perception of the client. A panel of four experts were recruited to do these tasks on an empirical basis (Shirley Emerson, University of Nevada, Las Vegas; David Imig, Michigan State University; William C. Nichols, adjunct, University of Georgia; Candyce Russell, Kansas State University).

First, the developers (Lee and Kochka) tried to subsume similar interventions under one common statement. In addition, an intervention had to be something that a client could recognize. This process reduced the master list of 114 items to 74 interventions, which were worded to match the hypothesized perception and vocabulary of a client. Next, the proposed items were given to the panel of experts. Under each proposed statement of an intervention were listed those of the original 114 items that it was thought to subsume. The task of each panelist was to rate the goodness of fit between the translation and the items each was meant to translate and subsume. This was done on a 6-point Likert scale ranging from "extremely dissimilar" to "extremely similar." The panel was encouraged to edit items as needed, with an eye toward presenting things from the frame of reference of a client. The developers decided that one way to keep the number of items small was to strive for "good enough," and not "perfect." Therefore, an acceptably worded intervention should be rated "very similar" and "extremely similar." A lower rating would require rewriting. Subsequently, differences between the panelists in their ratings were identified to ascertain which items needed revision or deletion.

Four rounds of consultation, editing, and rewriting resulted in the final version of the MSU/FTQ: 74 interventions, described in consumer-friendly language, all of which were rated by the panel either as "very similar" or "extremely similar" to the interventions originally culled from the literature and which they were meant to subsume. These items, and the instructions to be given to clients for responding to them, are shown on pages 111–114.

THE USE OF THE MSU/FTQ
AS AN ADJUNCT TO TRAINING

The MSU/FTQ is considered a helpful training aid. For one thing, the very perusal of the 74 items performs a "consciousness raising" function. The trainee and supervisor are reminded how therapeutically rich the marital and family therapy situation is and can be. The MSU/FTQ can be used as a checklist of interventions to guide one's own work and to teach others. In addition, when used in the midst of a course of therapy or on its conclusion, the MSU/FTQ can provide a feedback loop between client and therapist. The tone is positive: The implication is, "These are the things you are doing that are helpful." In short, the MSU/FTQ is a checklist and a rating scale that clients can use to "train" therapists. An implicit suggestion is that what therapists anticipate—on the basis of their own ideas and on the basis of theory—as most useful, may or may not match clients' experience.

A CASE EXAMPLE USING
THE MSU/FTQ IN SUPERVISION

The therapist, a practicum student in a marital and family therapy program, was a 39-year-old former teacher. A very bright and intellectual woman, she seemed unusually hesitant and fearful when presented with

---

TO BE ADMINISTERED AT THE COMPLETION OF TREATMENT   © 1995 Trustees,
Michigan State University

MSU/FTQ   **FAMILY THERAPY QUESTIONNAIRE***

Please provide the following information about yourself:
( ) Female   ( ) Male   _____ Age

Problem for which your family entered therapy:
( ) Marital Issues   ( ) Parent-child Issues   ( ) Other (brief description):_____

Please help us learn more about (your) family therapy. The following are things therapists sometimes do in family therapy. Please go through the list and indicate (x) if you remember that your therapist did this. (If you don't remember, leave the item blank.) For each action you remember, mark the portion of the line showing its **importance** to YOU.

**Did
This: IMPORTANCE:**
X   None   Great

— — — — — — — —   1. Was both caring and firm.

— — — — — — — —   2. Encouraged humor.

— — — — — — — —   3. Used stories and examples to make a point.

— — — — — — — —   4. Respected silence.

— — — — — — — —   5. Kept his/her personal problems to self.

— — — — — — — —   6. Really knew how to listen.

— — — — — — — —   7. Stayed calm in emotional situations.

— — — — — — — —   8. Appreciated how each of us is different and special, and accepted us as we are.

— — — — — — — —   9. Helped us know and talk about our feelings and ideas no matter how uncomfortable.

— — — — — — — —   10. Identified and reinforced good things about the family and family members.

— — — — — — — —   11. Helped us to rethink our thinking.

— — — — — — — —   12. Helped us define the problem clearly.

— — — — — — — —   13. Asked each person to share his/her view of the problem.

— — — — — — — —   14. Asked what led up to the problem.

— — — — — — — —   15. Asked who had already tried to solve the problem and what he/she had done.

— — — — — — — —   16. Asked about ways we handled other problems.

— — — — — — — —   17. Helped us to understand how the problem was a normal thing and gave us hope it could be solved.

— — — — — — — —   18. Showed us how our problems might actually do good things for us.

Did
This: **IMPORTANCE:**
X   None   **Great**

— — — — — — — —   19. Showed us how everyone's behavior was connected to the problem.

— — — — — — — —   20. Helped us figure out what we could change, and which changes were most important.

— — — — — — — —   21. Helped us figure out specific things to do to make things better.

— — — — — — — —   22. Insisted parents be parents and children be children.

— — — — — — — —   23. Helped us be a more effective family.

— — — — — — — —   24. Helped each of us to sort out our rights and responsibilities.

— — — — — — — —   25. Stopped the shifting of blame to others, and made change the responsibility of every family member.

— — — — — — — —   26. Predicted reactions to change.

— — — — — — — —   27. Gave each person credit for his/her efforts for positive change.

— — — — — — — —   28. Helped us get together or apart (whichever was needed).

— — — — — — — —   29. Told us something concrete we could do to mark the end of something bad, and make a fresh start.

— — — — — — — —   30. Helped us face and handle important losses.

— — — — — — — —   31. Spoke in a way that matched our moods and experience.

— — — — — — — —   32. Checked that we were each understanding what was being said.

— — — — — — — —   33. Explored how we treated each other during therapy and at home.

— — — — — — — —   34. Helped us determine what is typical about us.

— — — — — — — —   35. Interrupted interactions (harmful or otherwise) and explained why.

— — — — — — — —   36. Separated what we said to each other from what we actually did.

— — — — — — — —   37. Explained behaviors differently from how we had understood them.

— — — — — — — —   38. Suggested better ways for us to relate to each other.

— — — — — — — —   39. Helped family members speak only for themselves.

— — — — — — — —   40. Discussed ways in which we might be loyal to our parents and other members of the family in which we grew up.

— — — — — — — —   41. Helped us learn to be more fair toward each other.

— — — — — — — —   42. Helped us to learn from our disagreements.

— — — — — — — —   43. Taught us to "fight fair."

Did
This: **IMPORTANCE:**
X   None   **Great**

— — — — — — — —   44. Encouraged discussion of family secrets.

— — — — — — — —   45. Focused therapy on our lives here and now.

— — — — — — — —   46. Helped us play together.

— — — — — — — —   47. Helped us with our sex life.

— — — — — — — —   48. Helped us be more affectionate.

— — — — — — — —   49. Worked with family members individually and together.

— — — — — — — —   50. Involved in therapy other family members and/or other persons connected to the problem.

— — — — — — — —   51. Insisted family members treat each other with respect.

— — — — — — — —   52. Discussed each member's background including experiences of growing up.

— — — — — — — —   53. Drew a diagram showing three generations of our family.

— — — — — — — —   54. Asked about family beliefs, rules and customs.

— — — — — — — —   55. Discussed future plans of individuals and family.

— — — — — — — —   56. Asked which family members stick up for each other/join together/are allies, and which do not.

— — — — — — — —   57. Described how what we learn as children connects to our problem.

— — — — — — — —   58. Helped us separate our present problems from things that happened in the past.

— — — — — — — —   59. Taught us things to do when we have a problem we need to solve.

— — — — — — — —   60. Used demonstrations, limit-setting and teaching to keep sessions safe, under control, and focused on therapy.

— — — — — — — —   61. Didn't take sides.

— — — — — — — —   62. Took sides with one of us when it was needed.

— — — — — — — —   63. Gave us special things to do during therapy sessions.

— — — — — — — —   64. Had us act out real and imaginary situations during therapy sessions.

— — — — — — — —   65. Made homework an important part of our therapy.

— — — — — — — —   66. Kept us on track from week to week.

— — — — — — — —   67. Discussed our progress and asked our opinions about how therapy was going.

— — — — — — — —   68. Prepared us for the time therapy would end.

— — — — — — — —   69. Was professional, honest, trustworthy and reliable.

— — — — — — — —   70. Worked with other professionals, as appropriate, to help our family.

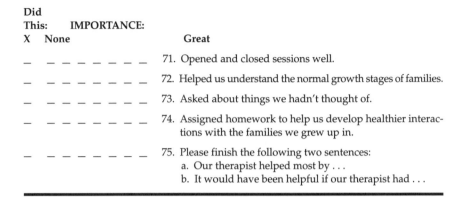

her first family. The "N" family household consisted of Mrs. N. and two daughters, Susan, 17, and Martha, 13. The parents had divorced 5 years earlier, and the girls had no contact with their father. Mrs. N. tearfully presented herself as overwhelmed, martyred, and ready to give up and "run away." (On questioning she also admitted that she could be unorganized and inconsistent.) Mrs. N. reported that Susan, a senior in high school, was an almost perfect daughter, made good grades, helped her mother, and stayed out of trouble. Martha was described as exactly the opposite: sloppy, uncooperative, surly, and underachieving in school.

From behind the mirror the supervisor observed that Susan sat up straighter and smirked slightly at her sister as her mother described the differences between her two daughters. At the same time, Martha slid down in her chair, focused her eyes on the ceiling, and sent a "Here we go again, why bother?" nonverbal message. However, the therapist did not look at the girls, and concentrated on Mrs. N.'s words and tears.

Despite her course work, in the subsequent supervision session the therapist quickly demonstrated that she had accepted the family's diagnosis of its problem. Martha was a "bad" 13-year-old who was causing her mother and her sister trouble. "I need to work with her to get her motivated to do her schoolwork, her chores at home, and to clean up her attitude." When the supervisor cautioned against a hasty decision about "the problem," and suggested a more systemic view, Marilyn nodded hesitantly. However, she met with all three family members the following week rather reluctantly and only after arguing with her supervisor that she needed to work individually with Martha. In the therapy session itself Martha appeared to elicit the "teacher" part of the supervisee's personality more than the therapist part. The therapist bombarded Martha with questions about what she did after school, why she didn't do her homework, why she continued to talk on the phone to friends that her mother had forbidden her to see, and why was she generally making her mother's life miserable. Understandably, all she received from Martha was a look of disgust, accompanied by shrugged shoulders.

Again the supervisor suggested that the system might be as much a part of this family's unhappiness as Martha's alleged misbehavior. She suggested that perhaps the mother and eldest daughter had something to gain from Martha's misbehavior, or perhaps that Martha was demonstrating the dysfunction of all three, while taking all the "heat" on herself. The therapist nodded in apparent comprehension, expressed distress that she had been "all wrong" about the case, and agreed to "think about it." The supervisor assured her that no one was right or wrong, but that it could be helpful to look at things from different perspectives. The following week, the therapist valiantly tried to get Mrs. N. to talk about herself but instead received the usual barrage of complaints about Martha. For her part, Susan interrupted frequently, amplifying her mother's complaints about her sister. The therapist in turn became the "teacher" again. She instructed the mother and Susan about managing unruly children and described a token behavior system whereby Martha could be motivated to do her chores and monitored. All the while, Susan enthusiastically agreed, saying what she would do to "make Martha behave better."

Variations on this dance occurred each week despite the supervisor's remonstrations about linearity and identified patients, the supervisory team's observations, and the therapist's vow to try a different therapeutic role. Mrs. N. spoke of how hard she had to work to feed her two daughters, how little help and respect she received from Martha and how, with Susan leaving her at the end of the year, she would be stuck with this recalcitrant child. Susan would concur sympathetically, Martha would "tune out," and the therapist would take on the role of interrogating teacher.

The semester was ending, and the therapy center closing for the holidays. The family members were each asked to fill out the MSU/FTQ, and then the supervisor went over the questionnaires carefully with the therapist. Mrs. N.'s and Susan's answers often were identical. They continued to express discontent with their family situation, but were happy with the therapist. They thought that the therapist was "both caring and firm" (1), "really knew how to listen" (6), and "helped us to define the problem clearly" (12). They said that she had asked what led up to the problem (14), what solutions had already been tried (15), and "spoke in a way that matched our moods and experience" (31). In contrast, Martha was very unhappy with both the family situation and therapy. She used the MSU/FTQ to state that the therapist, her mother, and her sister did not listen, were not caring, and did not understand the problem. She did not feel that the therapist "appreciated how each of us is different and special, and accepted us as we are" (8). Nor did the therapist show them "how everyone's behavior was connected to the problem" (19), or stop "the shifting of the blame to others," making ". . . change the responsibility of every family member" (25). Indeed, none of the responses of any of the family members indicated that the therapist had focused on the "we-ness" of the family, reframed problematic behavior, or worked to increase the family's adaptive resourcefulness as an ecosystem. In fact, on the basis of all three questionnaires one could reasonably ask whether or not family therapy actually was being done.

Since the therapist had insisted all along on dealing individually with Martha as the identified patient, the supervisor proposed that in one last session before the holidays, Martha be met with alone and asked to elaborate on some of her answers. Martha at first was reluctant to talk at all, just as in previous family sessions. However, the therapist waited patiently, conveying a willingness to listen and to try to understand her perspective. In response, as the therapist later described it, Martha "really unloaded on me!" Martha went directly to the statement regarding therapist's showing of respect for all family members (51). She stated that the therapist definitely had not shown her any respect. "You didn't want to hear anything from me, just like my mom. Your mind was made up, just like hers." She then went to question 22, which asked about the therapist insisting that parents be parents and children be children. Martha declared bitterly that this was not the case in her family. "Mom is out with her boyfriends practically every night after work. She sleeps all day on the weekends, and Susan bosses me around like she was my mom. Mom lets her, and says I have to mind her. It's not fair. She's not my mom. And you're just like them, telling me what to do, and not listening to my side of things." Martha angrily left the therapy room and the therapist was in tears. "I've failed! I'll never be a therapist. I can't do it."

A long supervision session, tempered with lots of tact and positive reframing, enabled the therapist to look more objectively at what had happened. A great many things indicative of systemic family therapy were not taking place. Instead the therapist had been inducted into the family system. The therapist clearly adopted the N. family way: Mother and eldest daughter take no responsibility for the family disharmony and instead focus on Martha, who behaves badly and allows herself to be scapegoated. Upon reflection the therapist admitted that she intellectually comprehended systemic approaches and could correctly describe how and why the diverse theorists would approach various problems. However, when confronted with parents and children, she slipped back into her familiar role as a teacher in a parent-teacher conference, that is, talking with the parents about what was wrong with their child and how to fix it behaviorally. She finally admitted to the supervisor, with amazement, that although she truly understood the major marital and family therapy approaches, she had not "swallowed it to a gut level." The supervisor suggested that, if the family returned following the holidays, this therapist could be assigned to them again. The therapist soberly agreed.

She thought that she might regularly review the MSU/FTQ before and after therapy sessions, as a kind of review guide, to keep herself on track and to resist being inducted by the family system and thereby rendered ineffectual.

Her first session of the new semester with this family began with verbal reassurances to the rebellious Martha that "things are different now. I understand what you said to me. I appreciate your helping me with your excellent insights into your family. I couldn't do it right until you showed me the real problem." This captured Martha's attention and confused her mother and sister. They discovered a "different" therapist who, over the course of several succeeding weeks, helped them discover that Martha's rebellion was neither mysterious nor maliciously intended. Some parts of it were normal for her stage in life. Some parts involved taking on traits expected of her. And some parts were a desperate cry from a lonely child who had "lost" both her parents at a young age. She had been only eight when her parents divorced, her father disappeared, and her mother became deeply involved in her work and her new social life. Concurrently, her mother and older sister had stifled their own grief and anger, accompanied by the parentification of Susan. In therapy Susan began to discover her own resentment and appropriately shifted the focus of her anger from Martha to her mother and father.

Therapy came to a close with the end of the new semester. Susan seemed less interested in Martha and her mother. Instead she split her interests between senior activities, a new boyfriend, and picking a college. Susan also was planning to meet with her father prior to leaving for college in the fall. She wanted to get her own sense of how he felt about them. She speculated about a continuing relationship with him, including a financial one, if that were possible. Mrs. N. was nervous about this initiative, but Martha was curious. For her part, Mrs. N. took more daily time to look into Martha's affairs and to talk with her. However, overall she was more consultative than directive and let Martha make choices and experience consequences. Concurrently, Martha became more available socially to her mother and sister, keeping them company, and being more communicative in a positive way. Her grades began to go up and she was investing in an acceptable group of peers.

To recapitulate, the supervisor and the student practicum group had tried to help the therapist recognize and understand the N. family dynamics. However, the therapist had been inducted into the family system and was trapped until the MSU/FTQ gave her a much needed cognitive lift. With the support of the questionnaire, supervisor, and observation team, she eventually was able to shift from her inducted, didactic teacher role to one of systemic family therapist. She might have reached that point eventually, but use of the questionnaire provided a necessary nudge to that growing edge.

CONCLUSION

The MSU/FTQ is a useful adjunct to family systems therapy and training. Like testing and other questioning instruments, it is an additional opportunity for seeing and hearing. It is a structured way for clients to tell therapists and trainers something about what the therapists are doing and not doing with regard to the major theorists' ideas about how therapy works. That structure is important. With a more open-ended instrument, client feedback well might reflect the problematic family view of its situation, and recapitulate the status quo (Minuchin & Fishman, 1981). In the example, the therapist needed to be reminded about family systemic functioning and that which is said to elicit and maintain problematic situations. By asking the clients specifically about those things, the therapist learned where she was going astray and what she needed to change. Presumably the clients appreciated being asked to guide their own therapy while concurrently having their attention drawn to those things considered influential with regard to behavior maintenance and systemic change.

The MSU/FTQ has passed a series of pilot tests. What remains is systematic and thorough standardization. This can be accomplished if a large number of the questionnaires are administered in conjunction with marital or family therapy, the forms subsequently sent to the developers, and the data compiled and explored statistically. Because the entire training team—supervisor, therapist, and client family—will find the MSU/FTQ to be both emotionally and educationally supportive, trainers and therapists are encouraged to collaborate with the developers; that is, to use the MSU/FTQ freely, and then to mail copies of the form to the senior author. Collaborators will be acknowledged in future presentations.

REFERENCES

Andersen, T. (1993). See and hear, and be seen and heard. In S. Friedman (Ed.), *The new language of change: Constructive collaboration in psychotherapy* (pp. 303–322). New York: Guilford Press.

Anderson, H. (1993). On a roller coaster: A collaborative systems approach to therapy. In S. Friedman (Ed.), *The new language of change: Constructive collaboration in psychotherapy* (pp. 323–344). New York: Guilford Press.

Bailey, C. E. (1996). Editor's introduction: Postmodern practices in marriage and family therapy. *Journal of Marital and Family Therapy, 22,* 287–288.

Bernal, G., Flores-Ortiz, Y., Rodriguez, C., Sorensen, J., & Diamond, G. (1990). Development of a contextual family therapist action index. *Journal of Family Psychology, 3,* 322–331.

Bischoff, R. J., McKeel, A. J., Moon, S., & Sprenkle, D. H. (1996). Therapist-conducted consultation: Using clients as consultants to their own therapy. *Journal of Marital and Family Therapy, 22,* 359–379.

DUMKA, L. E., MARTIN, P., & SPRENKLE, D. H. (1995). Development of brief scales to monitor clients' constructions of change. *Journal of Family Psychology, 9,* 385–401.

FIGLEY, C., & NELSON, T. (1989). Basic family therapy skills, I: Conceptualization and initial findings. *Journal of Marital and Family Therapy, 15,* 349–365.

FIGLEY, C., & NELSON, T. (1990). Basic family therapy skills, II: Structural family therapy. *Journal of Marital and Family Therapy, 16,* 225–239.

HOFFMAN-HENNESSY, L, & DAVIS, J. (1993). Tekka with feathers: Talking about talking (about suicide). In S. Friedman (Ed.), *The new language of change: Constructive collaboration in psychotherapy* (pp. 345–373). New York: Guilford Press.

JENKINS, D., & SMITH, T. E. (1994). Applying Delphi methodology in family therapy research. *Contemporary Family Therapy, 16,* 411–430.

LEE, R. E. (1993). The marital and family therapy examination program. *Contemporary Family Therapy, 15,* 347–368.

MINUCHIN, S., & FISHMAN, H. C. (1981). *Family therapy techniques.* Cambridge, MA: Harvard University Press.

NELSON, T., & FIGLEY, C. (1990). Basic family therapy skills, III: Brief and strategic schools of family therapy. *Journal of Family Psychology, 4,* 49–62.

NELSON, T., HEILBRUN, G., & FIGLEY, C. (1993). Basic family therapy skills, IV: Transgenerational theories of family therapy. *Journal of Marital and Family Therapy, 19,* 253–266.

PASLEY, K., RHODEN, L., VISHER, E. B., & VISHER, J. S. (1996). Successful stepfamily therapy: Client's perspectives. *Journal of Marital and Family Therapy, 22,* 343–357.

QUINN, W. H. (1996). The client speaks out: Three domains of meaning. *Journal of Family Psychotherapy, 7* (2), 71–73.

QUINN, W. H., NAGIRREDDY, C., LAWLESS, J., & BAGLEY, R. (1996). Utilizing clients' voices in clinical supervision. *The Supervision Bulletin, 9* (1), 4–8.

SELLS, S. P., SMITH, T. E., & MOON, S. (1996). An ethnographic study of client and therapist perceptions of therapy effectiveness in a university-based training clinic. *Journal of Marital and Family Therapy, 22,* 321–342.

SELLS, S. P., SMITH, T. E., & SPRENKLE, D. H. (1995). Integrating qualitative and quantitative research methods: A research model. *Family Process, 34,* 199–218.

CHAPTER 11

Utilizing Clients' Voices in Clinical Supervision

The Interpersonal Process Recall Method

WILLIAM H. QUINN
CHANDRA NAGIRREDDY

Supervisee: I wish I could be a fly on the wall and listen to what my clients say to others about their therapy.
Supervisor: Oh, but you can!
Supervisee: I couldn't sneak in and hide in the house.
Supervisor: No, but we could invite the client to do an IPR.

This chapter will provide a description of a very useful supervision model, Interpersonal Process Recall (IPR), which is based on client feedback. It is a structured way for therapists to learn about their therapy because they are given the opportunity to view it through the eyes of their clients. With IPR, clients help train therapists at the same time that clients are given an explicit role in the design and delivery of their treatment.

ORIGIN OF A CLIENT VOICES MODEL

This model of client feedback-centered supervision has evolved from several previous projects at the University of Georgia. Each impressed us with the importance of asking clients to help us learn how to be better therapists. The first project (Quinn, 1996) asked clients to share the story of their therapies. Ethnographic analysis demonstrated that three things were very important to clients concerning the process of their therapy. The first was affirmation, or the sense that the therapist provided validation and a sense of acceptance. The second was congruence. The therapy process had to have meaning and relevance for the client. The third highlighted the therapeutic climate of discovery.

A second investigation (Gale, Odell, & Nagirreddy, 1995) asked couples to observe and comment on videos of their own therapy sessions—IPR—and, in so doing, provided meaningful data about the process of marital therapy undetected by other approaches. Finally, a third project was undertaken (Quinn, Nagirreddy, Lawless, & Bagley, 1996) in which IPR was incorporated into marital and family therapy supervision. A therapy session was videotaped. The client watched that videotape with a trained interviewer, and this session itself was taped. Finally, the therapist and the supervisor would sit together and watch the tape of that interview. This provided the therapist with a "fly on the wall" experience as his or her client talked about how therapy was going. This project was so powerful that it provided the impetus for what has become an entirely new approach to training therapists.

IPR is not meant to replace more traditional forms of supervision such as case report, videotape review, and live consultation. Rather, it is an additional supervisory tool that uniquely elicits and amplifies clients' voices and in so doing sheds light on their experience of treatment. The clients' voices provide much original material for discussion in supervision. IPR is a vital, innovative, and enriching method of training.

POTENTIAL GAINS FROM USING CLIENT VOICES IN SUPERVISION

The supervisee may gain the following benefits from client feedback:

- The opportunity to be the recipient of raw data in the form of what the client directly reports about the therapy and therapist. This minimizes the political overtones and theoretical biases that exist when a supervisor sifts all data through his or her theoretical lens.
- The immediate opportunity to translate the client voice into revisions of therapeutic goals and action. ("What should I do based on what I am hearing?") In this way, supervision (and thus therapy) is timely, relevant, and energized.
- The immediate opportunity to help the client subsequent to supervision. This does not always happen in supervision in which session analysis has not been linked to future sessions, or in which little overlap exists in the thinking of the supervisor and therapist about the management of the case or the therapy process.
- The opportunity to learn about the importance of client description and to incorporate activity that calls on the client as an ongoing element of case management. (Unlike supervisor dominated supervision and therapy, this is consumer-driven.)

In this context of observing therapy process, both the supervisor and the supervisee may have their own unique observations of therapy events depending on their theoretical perspectives and subjectivity. In the absence of the client's feedback, there may be a struggle for legitimacy of perspectives when the supervisor and supervisee have competing views. When the client is a couple or a family, different members of the client system may have divergent goals for therapy and may react differently to a therapy event. In working with couples and families, both the supervisor and the supervisee face a greater challenge in rendering therapy responsive to the competing needs and goals of the family members. This problem can be addressed by directly obtaining feedback from the clients about their experience of the therapy events and therapist actions. Supervision dialogue then is based on that client feedback.

In supervision dialogue, both the supervisor and the therapist bring their own agenda into play. The therapist and the supervisor may envision certain outcomes for the client system, may prefer certain interventions, and may accord differing importance to the mastery of certain skills and competencies. When the supervisor and the supervisee differ in their agenda for supervision, struggle for dominance may become a theme in supervision. Often the supervisor and supervisee in time work through these dilemmas to arrive at a mutually agreed on place where the conditions of effective interaction are built. However, in some circumstances, the agenda of the supervisor may prevail but often at the cost of the supervisee's motivation and agency.

When the supervisor and the supervisee have the benefit of feedback from clients about their priorities and needs, reactions, and interpretations, the supervision process can become focused on clients' concerns. The supervisee's learning goals and the supervisor's instructional goals now can be in the service of explicit goals for the client, thus rendering the supervision process responsive to the clients' needs. When the therapist's developmental goals emerge in the context of stated needs of his or her clients, learning can be more exciting.

INTERPERSONAL PROCESS RECALL IN SUPERVISION

Over the years, the method of IPR primarily has been used for psychotherapy process research (Elliot, 1984, 1986). It is an opportunity to comprehend the person or subject under study within his or her own experiential world. Adapted for supervision, it is a method for tapping into the world of a client for the benefit of the supervisor and therapist without regard to the theories mapped onto such client perceptions by therapists or supervisors. This information would be unlikely to be revealed otherwise. A case example illustrates this point.

Client (as Listened to by the Therapist and Supervisor)

A therapist and supervisor were listening to the videotape of the supervisor's interview with the client using the IPR method. The client stopped the video of the therapy session and stated that this segment reminded her of how frustrated she was with the therapist. They had been discussing child care for her toddler. She felt that the therapist was in a rush to solve her problem to find quality child care with which she could be comfortable. She herself was not certain that she was ready to leave her daughter for long periods of time. For her the issue was whether to "give up" her young daughter to a child care facility at all. The therapist, however, wasn't picking up on that and seemed intent on locating a site that his client could accept. The client was not ready for that yet. She stated that she felt misunderstood and frustrated. Her needs were not being met.

Therapist (as Written to the Supervisor)

"As I watched the videotape of my client and my supervisor discussing the therapy, I thought that my client's desire to stay home to raise her daughter is a very valuable worthwhile activity. It is as important as or more important than working outside the home. However, as I listened to my client talk with the IPR interviewer I realized that she felt that I didn't value her parenting of her daughter and thought that she should be out working instead. This misunderstanding occurred in a session in which my client was complaining about the fact that her husband could not be depended on to provide for the family and she needed to go out and get a job. However, she could not put her daughter in headstart until she was three years old. She then talked about good paying jobs that she was interested in pursuing. I told her that if she felt it was important to get a job to provide for her family then there may be a way to arrange child care before her daughter was three. I knew of a quality site and I began to problem-solve ways that she could arrange day care. Because I thought this was a goal of hers I was confused. When I watched the IPR interview I learned that she felt that I was eager for her to get her kids into day care so that she could get out and do more important things like get a job. As I reflected about this misunderstanding it occurred to me that there was an interactional pattern that was being repeated in our sessions. My client would complain about some problem she was having and I would offer suggestions about possible solutions to the problem. She would offer what I considered excuses for why the solutions would not work and go back to talking about her problem. I began to realize that she did not want someone to always offer her solutions to her problems. What she really wanted was an empathic ear. I was reminded of a book that claims that when men hear about a problem they usually try to offer a solution to the problem. When women share a problem they are looking for empathic listening. In fact, a female listening might share a similar problem she herself has experienced. Once I realized this pattern, and better understood what my client was looking for in therapy, I was better able to notice when my client was not at the moment interested in problem-solving, and realize that what she really wanted in those situations was more empathy. I know I'll have to be more vigilant about this tendency with my cases."

The IPR process has four steps. Step 1: A therapy session is videotaped. If therapy sessions are routinely videotaped for supervision, the one used for IPR can be selected by the therapist in consultation with his or her clients. The session chosen may involve a significant positive shift, an impasse, or a negative experience for either the clients or the therapist. However, one might begin with a noneventful session with the goal of gaining comfort with this supervision process. Step 2: An interviewer and the client watch this videotape, or a selected part of it, and this process—interviewer and client reviewing the therapy session—is itself videotaped. The client has control of the videocassette recorder and is encouraged to stop as often as possible to share any thoughts and feelings about the events reviewed. The interviewer also can ask the client to pause the therapy tape if the interviewer becomes intrigued by events in the session. The interviewer then would make an open-ended request for the client's comments. Step 3: The supervisor and the therapist in turn watch the videotape of the interviewer and client (watching the videotape of the therapy session!). Alternatively, they may choose to review a particular event in a session on which the client wants to focus. This time the therapist has control of the playback unit and is encouraged to stop the videotape frequently and to react to it. Step 4: The therapist uses the insights gained to inform the next therapy session.

IPR as a supervisory tool not only situates the therapy within the needs of clients, but it also accommodates the developmental needs of therapists-in-training. The therapists-in-training are encouraged to stop IPR tapes wherever they have a reaction, be that curiosity, bewilderment, or something else. This active participation of therapists in their own learning locates the supervisory conversation within the parameters of the therapists' intellectual and emotional processes. This makes it unlikely that supervisory conversations will be experienced as irrelevant or power-based. When IPR is used, the supervisor is not viewed to be the origin of clinical observation, insight, and supervision agenda. Instead, the clients' needs, priorities, problems, and frustrations as revealed through feedback interviews provide the context and the goals for the supervision process. The supervisor's role is to enable therapists to respond to their clients in a way that best challenges their clinical competencies and meets the clients' goals most effectively. We think IPR enables the supervisor to do this best by providing an effective way to obtain feedback from clients and a safe climate so that therapists will be open to that feedback. The supervisor then serves as a resource person willing to assist the therapist when such help is solicited. However, feedback-centered supervision may work best when it is situated within the context of a broader contract between the supervisor and the supervisee. The contract may involve a focus on a particular model of therapy, a specific set of skills and competencies, a particular problem condition, or a supervisee's need to articulate his or her theory of therapy.

GUIDING PRINCIPLES FOR GENERATING FEEDBACK FROM CLIENTS FOR SUPERVISION

It is the responsibility of the therapist to seek the cooperation of his or her clients by informing them about the purpose of the feedback interviews, how the information will be processed, and how it might impact their therapy. When the clients sense that their therapist is genuinely interested in what they have to say and they understand how their feedback can help their therapy, they usually consent to provide it. If the client is a couple or a family, it may be important to interview the members separately and assure them that any information revealed about the other family members will be used with discretion in future sessions. The therapist subsequently asks the supervisor or a peer trained in this qualitative interviewing approach to interview the clients.

In so doing, it is crucial that the interviewers do not jeopardize therapist-client alliances. Interviewers must demonstrate respect and regard for therapists in their clients' presence. Ideally, the interviewers will assume the role of researchers who are solely concerned with eliciting the clients' experiences of their therapy.

Avoiding Evaluative Labels

Typically the intent of the IPR is not to overtly focus on generating the client's evaluation of the therapist or the therapy process. Rather, it is hoped that by eliciting a client's narrative of significant therapy events, the therapist can better comprehend the client's perspective of therapy, evaluate one's hypotheses, assumptions, and interventions in light of the evidence, and respond more appropriately to the client's concerns. Thus, questions that are tempting to ask are usually one-sided, such as: "How was your therapy so far?" "What has been accomplished so far?" "What has been helpful to you in therapy?" "Is there anything you wish were different in therapy?" "Has your therapist understood your problems? To your satisfaction?" "Is there anything your therapist can do to make therapy more helpful to you?" These questions elicit global descriptions of the usefulness of therapy or the general qualities of therapists. It may provide a richer learning experience for the supervisee if he or she can learn about specific behaviors, emotions, and cognitions that arise.

Interviewer Premises

The interviewer's role should be guided by the following:

- The spirit of the interview is investigative and not interpretive.
- The interviewer is the supervisee's representative, and is not present to make judgments.
- The goal is to help the supervisee gain access into the client's experience of therapy.
- The primary role is to generate feedback from the clients about the therapy events.
- The interviewer should not act in any manner that may undermine the therapist's credibility or the client-therapy alliance.

Regarding this last premise, some elaboration is necessary. The client is in effect permitting another person, albeit a qualified therapist or a supervisee, to peer into the therapy to conduct the interview. While examining therapy process via videotape collaboratively, a client may feel tempted to explain the content of what is discussed on video to the interviewer who has not heretofore been privy to these matters. As a result, the interview may turn into a therapy conversation in which the client looks to the interviewer for suggestions or comments that might help alleviate the discomfort or confusion that the client is experiencing and sharing with the therapist.

It is absolutely essential that the interviewer avoid this circumstance of sliding into the therapist role for two reasons. First, the interviewer does not know what has transpired across the therapy sessions and therefore is operating from an insufficient amount of information to help the client. Second, by permitting such a therapy conversation, the interviewer is violating a boundary with a peer (in the case of a cosupervisee) or student (in the case of a supervisor) with whom he or she has a relationship. The therapist may feel exploited because the interviewer is positioned to become the confidante of the client. The net result is that the therapist's position with the client for future sessions is compromised, as is the supervision in the future. The interviewer should avoid the following:

- Playing therapist.
- Offering interpretations or suggestions to clients.
- Pointing out what the therapist could or should have done.
- Criticizing the therapist's actions and interventions.
- Making any promises to clients on behalf of the therapist. ("I can let the therapist know of this. I'll make sure the therapist follows up on this.")

Recruiting the Client

The choice of client to interview should be left up to the therapist who is in supervision. This is particularly important if this is a one time only event. The therapist will be more confident in the process of IPR if the therapist believes that the client can provide meaningful data. In addition, the therapist will want to select a client who is perceived to be open-minded about the request for an interview and has the choice to respectfully decline. If the supervisor selects the client, the therapist may feel a loss of control of the client. This can breed resentment and feelings of intrusiveness. Therapists can be very protective of their clients because of the desire to preserve the therapeutic relationship.

This does not mean the supervisor does not have an opportunity to discuss the possible choice of client to be interviewed. The supervisor might suggest a particular client based on judgments about the most optimal learning situation for the therapist. For example, the supervisor might choose a client system that has been very challenging for the therapist, such as one involving young children, cultural differences, or certain marital dynamics, which previously has elicited certain emotional reactions in the therapist. Another indication for IPR might be when supervision includes discussion about being "stuck," or where alliances appear to be skewed or unclear. The most important ingredient in selecting a client for the IPR is that the therapist believes that a legitimate educational reason exists for the choice of that client and that session.

Therapist Recruitment of the Client

The therapist should approach a chosen client with the intent of informing the client of the therapist's desire to learn. It is better not to be very specific about what the therapist is most interested in learning because it can influence how a client thinks about the therapy and could affect what the client chooses to comment on while watching the videotape of the session. For instance, if a therapist is interested in knowing whether the client believes that the therapist is accepting or caring, the IPR remarks will center on this dimension to the potential exclusion of many other dimensions. What is valuable about IPR is that the client selects the data from the videotape that are meaningful, thereby giving the therapist an opportunity to enter some unexplored areas.

The therapist selecting the client for IPR considers the following matters:

1. Have I been directly involved in the choice of client being interviewed?
2. Have I communicated the genuineness and rationale for this request to my client?
3. Have I shared with my client the goals for feedback interviews?
4. Have I shared with my client how feedback will be used for future sessions?

Guidelines for the IPR Interviewer

The single objective of the interview is to generate information that may help the therapist to be more effective and responsive to the client's needs. During the IPR, the interviewer attempts to elicit as much data as possible from the client once the client has stopped the tape to discuss an issue. The interviewer should try to engage the client in a dialogue that makes the issue as transparent (minimal interpretation necessary) as possible. This reduces the need for second-guessing either by the supervisor or supervisee when they in turn examine the IPR video interview (see step 3, discussed previously). It is important for the two of them to feel secure about ". . . what the client really meant." The interviewer is an investigator who wants to unravel the mystery of therapy events. However, the interviewer's role is solely in the service of the therapist's objectives of rendering therapy more effective.

On occasion the client may be so caught up in the video of his or her therapy that the instructions to pause the video are forgotten. The client in effect becomes inducted into the therapy a second time. If such occurs, the IPR interviewer may need to interrupt the "trance" that the client is in and ask a question. Examples include the following:

- Is there anything in this segment that you might want to discuss?
- What were your feelings or thoughts at this point?
- What was your internal reaction to that?
- What do you think the therapist is focused on here?
- Was this part of the session helpful or harmful to you? If so, why?

A Supervisor-in-Training as Interviewer

The following description is a verbatim report by a supervisor-in-training who conducted an IPR with the therapist-supervisee and submitted it to the supervision course instructor.

"The client I interviewed has had a highly positive experience in therapy. Upon hearing her positive comments, my supervisee began to see just how powerful therapy has been in this client's life. For example, she likes how he can condense her thoughts to make things seem clearer and more manageable. In addition, she appreciates how he keeps an upbeat, positive attitude. Hearing these comments directly from the client gave my supervisee an increased awareness of some of the things that he does in therapy. The client stated that he has a genuine desire to help people. Therefore, hearing about how he has been helpful to his client was a rewarding experience. The supervisee said that viewing the videotape really 'made his day.'

"During the IPR interview the client said that it is very rare to find a therapist as caring as her therapist. She 'joked' that she would have to move to the same city as her therapist so he could be her therapist forever. This comment provided the supervisee with useful information about the client's attachment to therapy and to him. Since my supervisee would be leaving the clinic in two months, termination issues had become relevant. We therefore explored dependency issues that clients can sometimes develop. We talked about the need to process issues of separation with clients and talk about their future plans. As the therapist heard the client's comments he became more sensitive to her ambivalence about making progress in therapy, and he thought he might need to give the client an opportunity to convey these feelings. As a supervisor, this interview gave me a greater appreciation of the strengths of my supervisee. It also provided me with an opportunity to discuss client dependency issues that I might not have had the opportunity to observe since the client herself raised the issue somewhat unintentionally."

Processing of Clients' Feedback in Supervision

The goal of this session (step 3) is to help the supervisee review and respond to clients' feedback about therapy sessions. The supervision session is parallel to the IPR interview with the clients. That is, the supervisee-therapist maintains control of the remote and punctuates the tape by stopping it when something on the tape prompts a response or comment. The supervisor's role is to facilitate the supervisee's articulation of his or her reactions, thoughts, and feelings in response to the clients' feedback. The supervisee plays back the video record of the feedback interview and stops at points to articulate thoughts, feelings, interpretations, and inferences. This could lead to typical supervision dialogue. However, the supervisor is not responsible for selecting the data to be considered in the supervision discussion. Such a dialogue now occurs in the context of the feedback data from the clients and the supervisee's reactions to the feedback, and his or her perspective of therapy events. Supervision dialogue may focus on making sense of the feedback data, integration of perspectives, challenging previous conclusions, reviewing intervention strategies and, ultimately, arriving at a new understanding of the therapy processes and events in the case. Feedback-centered supervision may lead to new learning goals for the therapist and new instructional tasks for the supervisor, while introducing a new twist into all of the relationships in the arena.

The following guidelines are useful in managing the client feedback video interview between the supervisor and therapist:

- The therapist should control the session by selecting video segments to stop and discuss.
- The therapist should identify meaningful data.

- The supervisor should present hypotheses, interpretations and competing alternatives based only on the data available.
- The supervisor should facilitate the therapist's expression of thoughts and feelings.
- The supervisor should facilitate discussion of the consequences of client data and supervision discussion for future sessions.

Two Case Examples of Benefits to Supervisees

Supervisee 1

"The supervisor explained the IPR process and it sounded exciting and scary. It was exciting because the clients were sharing information that most therapists do not hear, like 'what do they think about me, is he understanding my view, what happened that made a difference.' It was also scary. The clients say things about the process of therapy that I do not agree with. I needed to prepare myself for this. I did this by first realizing that this must be a scary process for them too. I may not agree with them but I need to respect the fact that they took an enormous risk, too, first by coming for therapy, second by agreeing to describe their experience. For example, Joe stated during the IPR interview that he thought I had a better relationship with Carol and that he was somewhat distressed by that. I was aware that I could talk to Carol easier and made a conscious effort to connect with Joe. I thought that this was happening because Joe was becoming more involved and sharing his thoughts and feelings more during the therapeutic process. We used this experience to strengthen the therapeutic relationship as well as using it to strengthen Joe and Carol's relationship. Joe was afraid of taking risks in the relationship, particularly with Carol. We used this experience as a way of highlighting to Joe that he can take risks. I realized too that I needed to take risks with Joe by trying to connect with him more."

Supervisee 2

"At first I thought the supervisor was interfering with my therapy by conducting an IPR interview with my client, and it bothered me. But probably because I was an inexperienced therapist I found that it helped because I don't always have a real clear sense of what my goals are with clients. The IPR provided a rare opportunity to listen to what my clients thought about me as a therapist and what they thought about their therapy experience. It was almost like following them home and listening to them describe to a close friend what they liked and what they weren't keen on. Something about being interviewed by a third person seems to provide a level of feedback from your client that in some ways is richer and more credible than when the therapist asks the client personally about it. One interesting thing I learned: The client interviewed was one who canceled sometimes and I thought it was because she was not motivated and didn't take this seriously. But I found out in the IPR that she didn't come sometimes because she thought she was helping me out. I had told her earlier that I was a graduate student with many different roles and responsibilities. She thought she would be helping me by freeing me up a little. It was amazing how something so basic could be so misunderstood. This told me that we should be careful about what we assume as therapists."

CONCLUSION

The feedback-centered model of supervision can be utilized as the mode of supervision or can be integrated with the ongoing supervision process, whether it is video assisted supervision or live supervision. However, learning is most facilitated when the relationship between the supervisor and supervisee is open and supportive. This supervision model also can be instituted where the goal for the supervisor is to move away from authority oriented supervision to a more collaborative supervision.

In our training center, IPR has become a regular and ongoing component of supervision. Each supervisee must participate in a minimum of one IPR in which a client is requested to meet with an interviewer. Often that interviewer is another supervisee. The value of this method is that this format conserves supervisor time by limiting the number of interviews a supervisor must conduct at step 2, and provides the cosupervisee with a unique perspective on the world of a client's experience with another therapist.

The structure provided by this model facilitates the supervisor's sensitivity to the unique distinctions and interpretations a supervisee may bring to his or her role as a therapist, such as a function of one's gender or ethnicity. This model of supervision can also be used to gain insight into therapy events and processes which are opaque. That is, the method is timely when neither the supervisor nor supervisee can offer a coherent analysis of what is happening with the client in the treatment or a given session. Then, the IPR method is extremely helpful in providing new insight and perspective. In addition, this method is very valuable in understanding how certain changes occur in therapy or why the therapy process is stuck. It also produces therapy that is responsive to the client's well-being. The penetrating voice of a client can serve to engage the learning process.

REFERENCES

ELLIOT, R. (1984). A discovery-oriented approach to significant events in psychotherapy: Interpersonal process recall and comprehensive process analysis. In L. Ricks & L. Greenberg (Eds.), *Change episode* (pp. 249–286). New York: Guilford Press.

ELLIOT, R. (1986). Interpersonal process recall (IPR) as a psychotherapy process research method. In L. Greenberg & W. Pinsof (Eds.), *The psychotherapy process: A research handbook* (pp. 503–527). New York: Guilford Press.

GALE, J., ODELL, M., & NAGIRREDDY, C. (1995). Marital therapy and self-reflexive research: Research and/as intervention. In G. H. Morris & R. J. Chenail (Eds.), *The talk of the clinic* (pp. 105–129). Hillsdale, NJ: Lawrence Erlbaum Associates.

QUINN, W. H. (1996). The client speaks out: Three domains of meaning. *Journal of Family Psychotherapy, 7*(2),71–83.

QUINN, W. H., NAGIRREDDY, C., LAWLESS, J., & BAGLEY, R. (1996). Utilizing clients' voices in clinical supervision. *The Supervision Bulletin, 9* (1), 4–8.

CHAPTER 12

Barging In

TIMOTHY F. DWYER

A WORD ABOUT THE TITLE

I imagine the reader could experience some dissonance with the title of this chapter. "Barging in" implies intrusion, interruption, and hegemony. In a therapeutic context it suggests an external dominating force, the supervisor, imposing its will upon the players, the trainee and client, and invading the sacred space of therapy. Indeed, the word generally means "to enter rudely and abruptly" and "to move about clumsily" (Webster's II, 1988, p. 153).

Please suspend those violent images for the time being. Barging in elicits surprises that in turn generate useful and clarifying information. I have found that these surprises most often involve the discovery of untapped themes, revelations of commitment, strength, humor, and new meaning for one's pain and struggle. All of these typically produce both new resolve and growth in trainees and supervisors, and in clients as well.

Admittedly, entering into a therapist's session is an invasion into the ongoing process between the therapist and the client/family. This invasion can raise anxiety for all parties. But is this necessarily a bad thing? As a consultant to an ongoing trainee's therapy session, our invasion may heighten the awareness that someone has been adopted in this therapeutic system. That is, either the family has adopted the therapist or the therapist has adopted the client. Whitaker (1986) aptly noted that consultants in family therapy can intrusively disrupt the power that families have to co-opt therapists by making them members of the family or by excluding them. Furthermore, he notes that if the therapist can dare to be vulnerable enough to invite a consultant in, they may give the family the idea that they too can be vulnerable without being destroyed.

REQUISITE PROVISO

The foregoing is predicated on the condition that the supervisor and supervisee have negotiated a workable supervision contract. It presumes that supervisor and trainee are operating from ethical stances, from positions of mutual respect, and keen awareness of the context and multiple perspectives inherent in the work of their relationship. Moreover, the following ideas presuppose that the supervisor and trainee are mindful of each other's therapeutic philosophy, values, and beliefs, and that they share requisite agreement for the manner in which they will work, share ideas, solve problems, and negotiate change together. These ideas are not about supervisors imposing their will and presence in therapy without explicit agreement and shared understanding with the trainee. Indeed, barging in is a carefully crafted partnership between supervisor and trainee.

Therefore, what follows is an invitation to consider how entering into the therapy session can serve both as an empowering and collaborative teaching model, as well as a constructive stance for a variety of clinical interventions. Several clinical examples will be described, along with consideration of specific techniques, which can open avenues of growth for all members of the training system.

MY FIRST TIME

When I was completing my training at Purdue, two of my colleagues, Rich Bischoff and Jay McKeel, initiated a consultation study in our marriage and family therapy clinic. The idea was a simple one: "What if we asked clients and their therapist about their impressions of therapy?" Specifically, from their spirit of solution-oriented leanings, Rich and Jay asked "What have you found helpful in therapy, and how could therapy better meet your goals?" I was one of the first trainees to relish this experiment because I saw a definite fit with the narrative framework that I was cultivating. I invited my own supervisor, Lee Williams (a supervisor-in-training at the time) to barge in for me during a couple session. This was not planned, in the sense of knowing what direction we (he) would pursue. I had expressed that I was feeling stuck with the couple, and I had my doubts about this couple's commitment to therapy. Lee asked if I would be willing to have him come in and interview us all about our thoughts about therapy. He also asked if I was willing to discover how this couple viewed me. Taking a deep breath, I said "Sure."

For this couple, it was a pivotal session in their treatment. I felt empowered as a trainee. I learned new ways to risk asking "How is therapy going for you?" and also how to utilize a supervisor's presence in order to develop new therapeutic conversations. This was my first experience with barging in. As a therapist I request it. As a supervisor I offer it. I have experienced these types of consultations countless times from both chairs. I see it as a way to teach trainees a certain respect for clients' strengths, to cultivate a method for validating resources (both the clients' and the trainees'), and open up space for clients themselves to be teachers. Through barging in I have learned a great deal from my clients about their theories of change, how to court their positive experiences of therapy (Duncan, 1997), and how to model for trainees the exploration of client narratives of treatment.

A BRIEF THEORETICAL BACKGROUND

Of course, there are a number of clinical models and theoretical approaches that include inviting outside team members or consultants into the therapy session (e.g., Andersen, 1991; Boscolo, Cecchin, Hoffman, & Penn, 1987; White & Epston, 1990). The role and territory of consultant were wonderfully mapped out in Wynne, McDaniel, and Weber's (1986) text on systems consultation. They pointed out that a systems consultant—unlike others—takes a comprehensive, meta view of the trainee's concern, and that the distinctive feature of systems consultation is the explicit attempt to consider the multiple contexts or systems of a presenting problem. Barging in takes a similar frame. The supervisor is ever mindful of his or her role as a consultant, not therapist. He or she remains focused on the trainee's needs and concerns, in the context of therapy with a specific client. Thus it remains supervision. The notion of supervisor as consultant challenges the traditional complementary teaching role because the consultees (trainee and client) each may perceive and use the information differently. However, barging in is not consultation. The information becomes material for further hypothesizing, clarifying direction, strengthening alliance, generating narratives, and formulating interventions.

Bateson (1972) referred to impasses in family therapy as double description in that more than one component is essential to understanding an integral whole. Or, in other words, "How can we appreciate both sides of a coin at the same time?" The process of barging in invites all members of the therapeutic system to consider the wider whole. The current discussion presents barging in as a specific supervision method which allows trainees to gain a fresh, new window into their therapeutic role and the experience of their clients. Moreover, it offers an opportunity to learn from clients themselves what they do that is helpful.

HOW IT IS DONE

In barging in the trainee prearranges to have the supervisor enter directly into a therapy session in order to engage the therapeutic system in a discussion about therapy. The general aim may be described to clients as a way to help assess how therapy is going, although the overarching purpose of this set of techniques is to create new knowledge about what is taking place in the session, and to open up space for clearer understanding in the client-therapist relationship for the trainee and client. Patterns of expectancies and interactions can be examined, new information developed, goals clarified, successes highlighted, contradictions challenged, and ultimately the work of therapy accelerated.

There can be several different approaches to barging in, depending on the learning needs and goals of the trainee, clinical needs of clients, and the context of the clinical training setting. As supervisors, there are a few ground rules you should adhere to when barging in. You are advised to discuss and negotiate these and other points with your trainees, and to clarify for each case what the goals and needs are for the session. First of all, you are not out to correct or change anything. You are like an anthropologist, trying to understand the culture of the session. If new thoughts, ideas, and interventions are revealed, the trainee should refrain from responding to those and should not discuss those with you—until after the barging in session. A second and equally important point is to not allow barging in to become a "gripe session." That is, the primary task of the supervisor is to facilitate the conversation so that it remains safe, nonblaming, and informative. The trainee is put in a very vulnerable position, so every effort should be made not only to recognize that risk but to direct the conversation in a way that protects the trainee when necessary.

In the next few pages a variety of approaches and defined purposes for barging in will be described. The first approach, taking stock, describes a way to introduce this method to clients. I encourage a certain anticipation about the conversation, though this cannot always occur. At the outset of therapy, and as a socializing aspect to the treatment context, trainees should inform their clients of the possibility that a consultant may barge in, or be invited to sit in on a session.

Taking Stock

The simplest, more straightforward purpose and approach for barging in is taking stock. This can occur after about the third or fourth session simply to determine how things seem to be going and whether the therapist and client are "on the same page" with regard to understanding the problem and goals. This is a good time to clarify whether the clients feel like they are being heard and understood. The outcome of this sort of consultation is that it can strengthen the therapeutic alliance. By using the supervisor, an outside person, the session is kept from slipping into therapy. In fact, through barging in, both trainees and clients may get a different experience of themselves (and each other) that can liberate the therapy to proceed with great openness and trust.

Prior to taking stock the trainee can assign a homework task inviting the clients to consider how therapy is going. Specifically, the trainee could ask them to think about what seems to be going well for them; how therapy is or isn't giving them hope that their problem can be resolved; what, if anything, could be done differently in therapy. The trainee should let the client know that he or she plans to invite the supervisor into the next session. (Some trainees prefer to refer to their supervisor as a teammate, a consultant, or simply another therapist.)

By asking the clients to give some thought to how therapy is going we can underscore the difference between doing therapy, and talking about therapy. It helps to make the point by saying, "We're going to step back from therapy, and take a look at how it's going for everyone." Taking stock is explicitly framed as a conversation. The presence of the supervisor is to help guide and facilitate that conversation. Sometimes clients think that this is some kind of evaluation for their therapist, and they want to make a good impression. Thus, it is important to note that this taking stock is not being conducted to assess how the therapist is doing, but more generally how therapy is going. It is helpful to point out that "We encourage this sort of 'taking stock' in all important endeavors of life: work, marriage, parenting, or rituals and routines such as holidays, mealtimes, and events such as vacations."

Specific questions you may wish to ask clients in taking stock include:

- What are your impressions of therapy so far?
- What has been most helpful about therapy?
- What has your therapist done or said that has been most helpful?
- How could therapy be changed in some way to better meet your needs?
- If you could change one thing about therapy to better meet your needs, what would it be?

Questions to the trainee-therapist you may consider asking invite the trainee to identify particular client strengths, to simply reflect in a candid and genuine way how the trainee experiences the clients, or to voice some question they have had about the direction, content, or process of therapy. These questions may take the form of the following:

- What are your impressions of therapy with this client(s)?
- Are there some things you have been particularly impressed with about this client(s)?

- What do you find enjoyable or challenging about working with this client(s)?
- What thoughts or images do you get when you are preparing for a session with this client(s)?

It is important to give permission for the clients to disagree, or to voice their disagreement. Therefore, you might ask them "Do you feel comfortable saying if you disagree with a suggestion from your therapist?" Or, "What would you do if you did not like a suggestion from your therapist?" Similarly, you could clarify with the trainee, "How do you know if this client does not agree with you, or does not like your suggestions?" Wrapping up a "taking stock" session can be as simple as asking, "Is there anything else about therapy you would like to mention before I leave?" The session can be as brief as 10 to 15 minutes, or it can take longer, depending on the number of family members in the session and the openness of all members to disclose.

Again, the task of the supervisor is to keep the session from slipping into therapy, to keep it safe, nonblaming, and to facilitate a meta-dialogue about therapy. Other goals and tasks (to be discussed later) can be embedded in the questions posed, and should be discussed with the trainee in a presession.

This frame of taking stock should be present for each barging in session, although the goals and questions will obviously differ. The questions in the following section will drive the session for each stated purpose.

Reviewing Goals

In reviewing goals, it is not uncommon to discover that individuals, including the therapist, each take a slightly different view of what they consider the goals for therapy. Often goals change, become modified and clarified slightly as therapy continues. Therefore, asking clients for their perception of how their goals have changed highlights the process nature of the therapy. Moreover, barging in on the review of goals allows the therapeutic system to reorient in a concerted manner and in a unified direction.

You might ask the clients the following questions:

- What were your goals when you first came in to therapy?
- How have your goals changed since you have been in treatment?
- How can you tell that the therapist has the same goal as you?
- How will your therapist know when you've achieved your goals?

You might ask the trainee the following questions:

- How have you noticed the client's goals change over the course of therapy?

- Are there goals you have for the clients that they may not specifically identify?
- What are your own goals in therapy, in addition to theirs?
- What are the signs that will tell you they are making clear headway in reaching their goals?
- What are the major obstacles for them in reaching their goals?
- How will you know when they have reached their goals?

Clarifying Communication

Many times clients will say "We have communication problems." Others will note, "We just don't communicate very well." Sometimes we even hear our trainees say, "It gets confusing with them because they say one thing but do another." Barging in to clarify communication is a useful purpose for this technique. Again, you will want to explore the specific points of confusion with the trainee and make a plan for addressing the communication issues. Clients may be operating with different assumptions and expectations about therapy, and so taking stock may already have helped illuminate those issues. However, clarifying communication will highlight the different data to which clients and trainees are attending, and help engender both a more unified lexicon for treatment, and a common frame of expectancy.

For example, I worked with a couple where each had a different orientation to the problem. The husband wanted to underscore what had gone well over their 16 years of marriage, and try to build on their strengths. The wife, on the other hand, would get furious when he would want to be so solution focused, because she felt that he minimized her frustration and perception of the extent of the "problems." During a barging in session, my supervisor helped to punctuate this point and, since it wasn't coming from me directly, they saw more clearly the dilemma their positions imposed on me as their therapist. Clarifying the communication allowed us each a greater flexibility, observational skill, and even more humor in the sessions. We were able to make a little game of identifying when each of them was being more problem oriented or solution focused, and created tasks that allowed each of them to try on the position of the other party.

Some suggested questions to clients for clarifying communications include:

- What is your theory about communication? What are the critical aspects?
- How can you tell when someone is not communicating?
- What do you think about the phrase, "one cannot not communicate"?

Since what we think and do informs what and how we communicate, it is important to assess clients' expectations about therapy. The following questions may be useful in that attempt:

- What did you think therapy would be like for you?
- How long did you think it would take, and what would it entail?
- How does your current experience of therapy match your earlier expectations?
- How do you know your therapist understands your concerns?
- Are there aspects of treatment that you would like to know more about?
- Are there questions you would like to ask your therapist that you have not yet found a way to ask?

Barging in questions to clarify communication also may be tailor made to suit the trainee and the situation. I had a supervisor barge in and put a chair between the clients to represent me. The supervisor then asked each of the clients to move the chair in a way that reflected their perception of my alignment. The clients each chronicled the history of our work in therapy with every movement of the chair. Furthermore, they expressed how they had changed with respect to my alignment, beautifully illustrating the interactional quality of client-therapist movement. Some suggestions to highlight the therapists' tasks and open up space for dialogue about communication might include:

- Have you told your clients about your theory of communication?
- How do you know your clients are following what you're saying?
- How is it that you can hear both (all) of their stories and not take sides?
- Do you think your clients each speak the same language?
- What do they need to do to become multi-lingual?
- How do you do it?
- How do you know when you've 'lost' them?
- Do you think they can tell when they've 'lost' you?

Challenging a Dominant Story

In our efforts toward therapeutic change, regardless of how we go about it we are usually looking to discover a new story, edit an old one, uncover and clean up a dusty, forgotten one, or complete an unfinished one. Sometimes a dominant story keeps us from developing a new one. We can become bound and constrained by the narratives, symbols, and metaphors of the dominant story. Barging in to challenge the dominant story can allow clients and trainees a chance to participate in the deconstruction of that story and the unfolding of a new one.

I worked with a couple who in the first session said to me, "We have about 33 years of pain and bitterness we wish to resolve so we might have a chance to enjoy the golden years of our retirement." After about 15 sessions and admittedly very modest gain toward that heroic goal, my supervisor, Carlos, noted how hard I was working. He said to me, "It seems to me you think this couple's golden years are largely dependent upon your clinical skill and wisdom." I admitted, "Yes, I do feel that responsibility." He responded, "And what about them? Do you think they see it that way?" I wasn't sure, but in my guts I believed it was quite likely they did bestow that power onto me. I invited him to barge in and check out this story with me. (Note: This was a couple with whom I had previously done a session of taking stock by myself—without a consultant—and had found it very difficult not to take the bait to do therapy.) He said he would, and we made a plan to have him challenge the "dominant story."

Carlos explored with them what it was that held them together as a couple. (Of course, he got different information than I had received when I had asked that question some time earlier. He asked what some of the rough times were that they had endured and gotten through. And then came the clincher; "What would happen if you didn't make it through together for your golden years?" They were astounded! They looked to me with a mix of fear and sympathy. That look to me said, "We believe you can do it, Tim. Don't despair in those doubtful words."

Carlos turned to me. "Tim, you are not the cause of this marriage, and you know, you will not be the cause of their divorce. It is, has been, and always will be their choice, you know. They can divorce, if they wish. People do it all the time." He spoke the unspeakable. There was a deafening silence in the room, and a huge sigh of relief escaped from me! This experience was a revelation. He could have said this in our individual supervision, or at the postsession. I could have tried to figure out a way to communicate this message to my couple. Nothing would have been as potent or as palpable as that moment. The shift happened, and there was no return to my overfunctioning. I had been seduced. I was successfully recruited to be the savior of that troubled marriage. That was the dominant story, and I was flattered.

This example illustrates the hold that a dominant story can have on a trainee. The consultant may be able to deftly peel back the mythology and reveal a different, ultimately more useful story. The questions to guide this process are found in revisiting the given history of the client, and the history of the therapy. It originates in supervision with the trainees, soliciting the stories they have to tell about their own experiences with their clients, and the ones they embrace that the client relates to them. Of course, not all stories need to be challenged. Sometimes by revisiting them we can validate and affirm them "Yes, this story is useful and productive." So, in barging in we have an opportunity to reveal further narrative passages, and punctuate the fact that a goal of therapy may be to continue to explore and cultivate the themes of resource, resilience, flexibility, humor, insight, caring, and love.

Split Messages—Or "Good Cop/Bad Cop"

Sometimes we might like to throw a dash of our strategic roots into the supervision mix. We can use paradox without being devious. Since life is full of paradox, I believe we would do well to educate our trainees and clients to this simple fact, and help them to observe paradox in nature more clearly and with less dissonance. Punctuating choices, entertaining extremes, exploding fantasies, and wrestling with angels all have an element of paradox. Barging in to assist our trainees with these sorts of elements can be illuminating. In the example above, Carlos was expressing the fact that the couple could divorce. That was simply one of several options. If I had proposed that, it may have seemed like a heresy.

Barging in can allow you to say what trainees would like to say, when they, or you, may not see it as prudent. Supervisors can and should offer themselves as messengers for therapeutic messages that perhaps need to come from an outside source. As a novel way to barge in, I once invited a trainee to play a videotaped supervision session for her clients. The trainee had felt like she was being run off the road in her sessions with these clients, and rarely got a chance to complete her statements—whether they were compliments, challenges, or homework tasks. On the videotape, I interviewed her about how she felt things were going with the case. We were taking stock without the clients.

It was an extremely effective method. The couple was more interested in hearing the therapist's ideas when she was talking about them than when she was talking with them. As the supervisor, I posed some strong hypothetical questions that challenged their commitment to therapy, relational change, and the necessary therapeutic work. The trainee then was in a position to respond to my hypothesizing in a way that supported them in their efforts and complimented them for the hard work they had been doing—while echoing my strong challenges softened by her voice of experience with them. Accordingly, the couple had a negative response to the tone of my questions (they were rather flip and sarcastic), and they questioned my clinical judgment and competence. But they endorsed and validated the skill and wisdom of the trainee.

Building Bridges to Stronger Therapeutic Alliances

As the preceding example illustrates, stepping back from therapy to discuss its process and reflect on the moments that have been successful, or tension filled, awkward or humorous, confusing or irritating can serve to strengthen the alliance in therapy and create more solid bridges of trust. Whether conducting a sort of self-consultation with your own clients, or barging in with your trainees' permission, hosting conversations and modeling reflective dialogue in a therapeutic context has "trust building" written all over it. The process of talking about therapy in a therapy setting underscores the humanity of all participants and validates the risk that everyone takes in therapy. As a training technique, it can provide the trainee with a new experience of their supervisor, their clients, and themselves in relation to the therapeutic system. Not only can new information be gleaned from the conversation, but relationships can be enriched. The barging in method and techniques can effectively demonstrate a capacity for trust and care that will further open up space for growth in the supervisory relationship. It also can expand the trainees' ability to think flexibly in relation to the messages they send and receive, and consider novel and creative ways to utilize live supervision.

REFERENCES

ANDERSEN, T. (1991). *The reflecting team.* New York: Norton.

BATESON, G. (1972). *Steps to an ecology of mind.* New York: Ballantine.

BOSCOLO, L., CECCHIN, G., HOFFMAN, L., & PENN, P. (1987). *Milan systemic family therapy.* New York: Basic Books.

DUNCAN, B. L. (1997, July/August). Stepping off the throne. *Family Therapy Networker,* 22–33.

WEBSTER'S II. (1988). *New Riverside University Dictionary.* New York: Houghton Mifflin.

WHITAKER, C. A. (1986). Family therapy consultation as invasion. In L. C. Wynne, S. H. McDaniel, & T. T. Weber (Eds.), *Systems consultation: A new perspective for family therapy* (pp. 80–86). New York: Guilford Press.

WHITE, M., & EPSTON, D. (1990). *Narrative means to therapeutic ends.* New York: Norton.

WYNNE, L. C., McDANIEL, S. H., & WEBER, T. T. (Eds.). (1986). *Systems consultation: A new perspective for family therapy.* New York: Guilford Press.

PART FOUR

Attending to Contextual Influences

CHAPTER 13

Everyone Has a Culture

MARJORIE J. KOSTELNIK

Most people take their culture for granted. It is learned so early in life that we come to feel that it is the natural way of thinking, acting and viewing the world.

—LEAF, 1975, p. 19

The instructor thought she was asking the class to participate in a simple exercise. The students, who had come to know one another fairly well after several days of class meetings, were divided into small groups and then asked to describe their cultural identity. This conversation was meant to be an icebreaker, with the real meat of the class focused on the sensitivities needed for working effectively with culturally diverse families. As the instructor moved through the room she heard the following comments:

- Our family has no culture. We're just regular Americans.
- I must be a member of the lacking culture. I can't think of one thing in my life that relates to any kind of cultural identity.
- I wish I had a rich cultural heritage like yours (White student speaking to a Korean student).
- I don 't know what kind of culture I have. None of my relatives lives any place outside of Michigan. I don 't know where we started, I just know we've always lived here.
- We don 't do anything different than anyone else. We don 't carry out any dramatic customs or rituals. I guess we 've lost our culture.
- I don't see you as a Black person, I just see you as a member of the human race. Aren't we all the same underneath?
- I guess you can call me a product of the [Name Brand] Bread culture. Just white bread, nothing much interesting.

Each of the speakers was a member of the dominant culture. None had much knowledge of their cultural backgrounds or the cultural beliefs that permeated their interactions with others. They treated culture as a given, presuming a sameness of experience and perception that was not true for everyone in the class. Black students, especially, voiced a real sense of cultural distinctiveness and keen awareness of the salient features of the dominant culture. They were surprised, exasperated, and sometimes suspicious of their classmates' cultural ignorance. Although most all the students had created genograms in previous classes and had participated in values clarification workshops, these exercises seem to have occurred in the absence of any cultural considerations. As we discussed the issues, it was clear that a lack of self-understanding among many of the students was a barrier to the cross-cultural competence I hoped they would ultimately achieve. Thus began this author's exploration of how to help students develop an awareness that all people have culture and that understanding one's own culture is the first step toward respecting the culture of others.

CULTURAL MISPERCEPTIONS

Whether aware of it or not, everybody has a culture.

—NIETO, 1992, p. 16.

The student comments previously cited highlight a variety of misunderstandings about what culture is and how it functions in people's lives. Such misperceptions permeate our society, hindering people's understanding of themselves and others (Green, 1995). Here are some examples of cultural misperceptions.

Culture Is Foreign

This misinterpretation is based on the belief that culture is derived from another country or society. According to this way of thinking, culture is imported from someplace else. People who possess culture do so because their national origins are clearly outside the United States. Thus, culture refers to something French or Bolivian or Latvian or South African. This definition implies that there is no discernible American culture, which is untrue. The United States has a dominant culture that is quite clear to outsiders. In addition, this country has a wide array of subcultures with which people identify (Kohls & Knight, 1994).

Culture Belongs to Someone Else

There is evidence that many White Americans attribute culture to others in the society, but not to themselves (O'Connor, 1993). "We're just regular Americans. Ethnics are people different from you" (Derman-Sparks & Phillips, 1997, p. 52). Because United States culture is centered around White norms, White people rarely have to come to terms with this part of their identity. As a result, White people often do not see themselves as being white (Katz, 1978). In point of fact, in the United States, the dominant society is rooted in a Northern European, White, Christian experience. According to Lynch and Hanson (1992) and Dundes (1975), values that characterize the dominant culture include:

1. The importance of individualism and privacy
2. A belief in the equality of individuals
3. Informality in interactions with others
4. An emphasis on the future, change, and progress
5. Belief in the general goodness of humanity
6. An emphasis on time and punctuality
7. High regard for achievement, action, work, and materials
8. Pride in being direct and assertive
9. Right of freedom of speech
10. Belief in meritocracy—those with ability will rise to the top
11. A belief in humans' ability to control nature
12. A belief in the value of empiricism

While some of these values are shared to varying degrees by subcultures in the United States, they are not universally accepted. Even when values are basically harmonious, culture groups may realize them through different behaviors and practices. For example, education may be prized by many groups, but some cultures believe students should question and develop their own thinking to be truly educated, and others believe that the teacher is never to be questioned (Chang, Muckelroy, & Pulido-Tobiassen, 1996).

Culture Is Exotic

Many individuals believe that culture encompasses only the unusual. Culture is not mundane, it is strange. Based on this perspective, the county fair, Sesame Street, local voting practices, and inner-city playgrounds lack cultural significance. On the other hand body painting in India, a game of cricket, and Boys' Day in Japan are perceived as culturally significant because they are not common happenings for many people in the United States. However, the truth of the matter is that culture represents the day to day patterns of behavior that characterize people's lives and that contribute to each person's cultural identity.

Culture and Ethnicity Are Synonymous

According to Allport (1958), ethnicity is characterized by three factors: (a) nationality, (b) ancestry, and (c) religious affiliation. Other authors have also included language as an emblem of ethnic group membership (Henderson & Bergan, 1976). On a personal level, ethnicity is the sense a person has of being part of a community. That sense of community is derived from family experiences passed down from one generation to another. The impact of ethnicity on people is that it may be used by oneself or others to identify individuals within a spectrum of the overall society (Robles de Melendez & Osterag, 1997). Ask White Americans about their culture and among the first things they are likely to talk about are their ethnic roots. "I'm part Scottish, part Irish, part Polish, with a little French thrown in too." Not knowing their ethnic origins may cause them to believe they have no culture (Green, 1995; Derman-Sparks & Phillips, 1997). In reality, ethnicity is only a part of one's cultural identity. It is not the whole of it. Thus, culture is a multidimensional construct that includes additional identifiers besides ethnicity, such as social class, gender, and geographic location.

Culture Is Color Blind

A common approach to the notion of culture is to emphasize similarities among people while ignoring their differences. This is described as being color blind. Color blindness ignores cultural strengths by assuming that all people are the same (Cross, Bazron, Dennis, & Isaacs, 1989). Unfortunately, not noticing that someone is Black, for instance, denies that person's history and culture, just as only noticing that someone is Black denies individuality (Derman-Sparks & Phillips, 1997). The same is true when White students fail to acknowledge that they are White, and that being White influences their own experiences as well as the experiences of others who live in the United States.

Culture Is Primarily External

Many people believe that culture consists simply of the artifacts or outward behaviors one associates with a particular group. This involves a preoccupation with the surface features of culture. Surface features include clothing preferences, speech patterns, behavioral styles, physical characteristics, housing locations and types, living arrangements, and decor, food items, as well as family and community rituals and celebrations (Green, 1995). Such external cues serve as identifiers or badges linking people or differentiating one person from another. They are the superficialities people commonly think of when they comment on culture. African Americans rap, Native Americans have powwows, Mexican Americans eat beans, and White Americans drive pickup trucks. Preoccupation with surface features, either in praise or derision, results in what Clifford Geertz (1977) describes as a "thin" understanding of culture. The danger of such an approach is that one is susceptible to stereotyping people rather than accurately understanding their worldview. In addition, surface features may be trivialized, making it less likely that true cross-cultural understanding will occur. Some authors have termed this a "tourist approach" to culture, meaning that one has little awareness of cultural identifiers beyond food, holiday rituals, and traditional costumes (Derman-Sparks & ABC Task Force, 1989). Such visible signs are often part of one's cultural affiliation, but they do not wholly represent the deeper or "thicker" aspects of culture that in fact, are its essence.

A "THICK" DEFINITION OF CULTURE

There is not one aspect of life that is not touched and altered by culture.
—HALL, 1976, p. 16

There are literally hundreds of definitions of culture in the professional literature. Sociologists, anthropologists, psychologists, economists, and educators all have varying versions. Some of these definitions focus on the behavioral dimensions of culture, emphasizing patterns of action or customs that bind people together in groups. Others emphasize the historical dimensions of culture and how cultural behaviors and attitudes are transmitted from one generation to the next. A third perspective focuses on the cognitive aspects of culture, stressing what people know and how they interpret the world. Within this definition, culture is something that is shared among persons who possess a common cognitive map (Green, 1995). Most recently, definitions of culture have encompassed all of these perspectives in a more comprehensive fashion (O'Connor, 1993). Such "thick" cultural definitions include both surface features as well as the underlying assumptions, ideas, behavior patterns, symbols, values, ethics, and institutions of a culture group (Katz, 1994). With this definition in mind, we recognize that people may come to share certain material dimensions of culture as well as values, traditions, and beliefs as follows:

- They are Mexican American.
- They can trace their roots to Ireland.
- They live in the back hollows of Appalachia.
- They speak Italian.
- They consider themselves middle class.
- They see themselves as part of the baby boomer generation.
- They are family members of a child with a disability.
- They grew up in a single-parent home.
- They are gay or lesbian.

In every case, culture is more than a singular experience (i.e., ethnicity) but rather the outcome of several key elements (ethnicity, gender, and religion) that are pertinent to an individual's identity (O'Connor, 1993). Consequently, individuals may be embedded in their cultures to different degrees. Thus, most of the time this author perceives herself as a middle-class, female professional, living in the Midwest and feels a sense of kinship with others who share these cultural identifiers. Yet on certain occasions, being a baby boomer might become more or less important, as is being a dog lover, a person of Slovakian descent, a nonpracticing Catholic, and so forth. In this way cultural dimensions take on greater or lesser import depending on the circumstance and the individual. Finally, culture may be viewed as something very individual as well as something more pervasive that affects whole groups of people. It is this working definition of culture that students benefit from exploring prior to considering the function culture plays in the human experience.

THE FUNCTION OF CULTURE

Culture provides a framework for our lives. It is the paradigm humans use to guide their behavior, find meaning in events, interpret the past, and set aspirations.
—ROBLES DE MELENDEZ & OSTERAG, 1997, p. 44

Nothing escapes the power of culture. How people dress, what they eat, what they do for fun, how they spend their waking hours, what they believe is true, right, or wrong all comes about as the result of cultural influences. Thus, culture serves two important functions in human societies.

First, culture defines the accepted behaviors, roles, interpretations, and expectations of a social group (Robles de Melendez & Osterag, 1997). Cultural beliefs vary from society to society and within societies among various subcultures. Such variations include the way human beings relate to one another, the significance of time, what personality traits are highly prized, and fundamental notions of whether human beings are naturally good or bad (Berns, 1996). As a result of how different groups approach these issues, group members learn different things. For instance, some learn that competition is good, others learn to value cooperation more highly. One culture group might interpret a child's loud behavior as a positive sign of independence, another might translate that same action as disrespectful. In this way, cultural beliefs broadly define how people believe individuals should be treated, what people should learn, how people should conduct themselves, and what goals they should strive to achieve (Shaffer, 1994).

Second, culture gives people a sense of identity (Robles de Melendez & Osterag, 1997). The sharing of surface features and essential cultural dimensions such as values, beliefs, and attitudes gives human beings a feeling of connectedness with one another. These same cultural dimensions also provide a sense of distinctiveness within each group. Having a gender, age, religion, history, and certain material possessions provide the tools through which self-identity is forged.

HOW CULTURE IS ACQUIRED AND HOW IT EVOLVES

> Growing up as members of a family and community, children learn the rules of their culture—explicitly through direct teaching and implicitly through the behavior of those around them. Among the rules they learn are how to show respect, how to interact with people they know well as compared to those they just met, how to organize time and personal space, how to dress, what and when to eat, how to respond to major life transitions and celebrations, how to worship, and countless other behaviors that humans perform with little apparent thought every day.
> —BREDEKAMP & COPPLE, 1997, p. 42

Students first need to recognize that culture is a social construct. James Spradley and Michael Rynkiewich (1975) point out the following:

- Culture is learned. It is not an innate characteristic of the individual. As already described, people begin learning the patterns and shared meanings of the groups they belong to from the moment they are born. This knowledge increases and changes as people grow and develop (Robles de Melendez & Osterag, 1997).
- Culture is shared. Members of the same society come to share certain customs and tend to agree on the basic characteristics of reality. Although they may disagree about some of the fine points, many points of agreement are strong enough to be considered unquestionable.
- Culture is adaptive. Just as is true for individuals, the culture of groups is not static. It is constantly evolving. Cultures do not arise fortuitously. They develop as ways to understand particular environments and to cope with the problems environments present. For instance, the culture that develops in a densely peopled urban locale will necessarily vary from the culture that comes about in a sparsely populated rural region. Culture defines the situation for both groups of people and provides economic and social solutions. The environment, social and economic organization, and culture affect and influence one another. In addition, cultures adapt and change as a result of how groups are treated—positively or negatively—within the larger society and through exposure to values, practices, and traditions of other culture groups (Chang, Muckelroy, & Pulido-Tobiassen, 1996).
- There are variations among people of the same culture group. Not everyone who lives in a rural area believes all the same things as his or her neighbors. Mexican Americans are individuals who share certain cultural beliefs and values, but who also differ from one another.

Not all people of Asian descent are alike, neither are all Whites. Single parents may share many similar life experiences, but one cannot assume that one knows exactly how a person will react simply by knowing that he or she is raising a child without a spouse at home.

Having developed a common idea of how cultures operate, students next find it useful to examine the concept of cultural competence.

CULTURAL COMPETENCE: OUR ULTIMATE AIM

As American society becomes increasingly diverse, therapists, social workers, educators, and other helping professionals must become more adept at working with culturally diverse families. For instance, ethnic and racial diversity has increased substantially in the United States over the past 20 years, and is projected to increase even more as we move into the twenty-first century. The U.S. Bureau of the Census expects the proportion of White families to decline steadily from 69% in 1990 to about 50% in 2030. Conversely, the proportion of all families who are Hispanic or who are African American or of another minority group in the United States is expected to grow from 31% to 50% (Kostelnik, Soderman, & Whiren, 1998). Unfortunately, the number of marital and family therapists from nondominant culture groups is not keeping pace with this demographic trend. The field continues to be dominated by White middle-class professionals (Lee, 1998). Although recruiting potential therapists of all groups is a critical task, we also must find ways to increase the cultural competence of members of the dominant culture, who will find themselves working with clients whose cultures vary significantly from their own. These circumstances have resulted in a call for greater cultural competence among helping professionals in all fields (Bredekamp & Copple, 1997; Green, 1995).

Cultural competence associated with individuals includes the following (Isaacs & Benjamin, 1991):

- Acceptance and respect for cultural differences
- Possession of cultural knowledge
- Demonstration of continuous self-assessment
- Attention to the dynamics of cultural differences to better meet client needs
- Adaptation of service models to match sociocultural contexts
- Solicitation of advice and consultation from culturally diverse groups
- Personal commitment to policies that enhance services to diverse clients

The culturally competent organization or program incorporates behaviors, attitudes, policies, and practices for effective work in cross-cultural situations (Weiss & Minsky, 1996).

The classic description of the culturally skilled clinician put forward by Corey, Corey, and Callanan (1988) offers valuable insights for both individuals and organizations who wish to increase their cultural competence.

Beliefs and Attitudes of Culturally Skilled Clinicians

- They are aware of their own values, attitudes and biases and of how they are likely to affect clients who are not of the dominant culture. They monitor their functioning through consultation, supervision, and continuing education.
- They appreciate diverse cultures, and they feel comfortable with differences between themselves and their clients in terms of culture and beliefs.
- They believe that there can be a unique integration of different value systems that can contribute to both therapist and client growth. If necessary, they are willing to refer a client because of their limitations in cross-cultural therapy.

Knowledge of Culturally Skilled Clinicians

- They understand the impact of oppression and racist concepts on the mental health professions and on their personal and professional lives.
- They are aware of institutional barriers that prevent people in non-dominant culture groups from making full use of marriage and family therapy services in the community.
- They understand how the value assumptions of the major theories of therapy may interact with the values of different culture groups.
- They possess specific knowledge about the historical background, traditions, and values of members of groups with whom they are working.

Skills of Culturally Skilled Therapists

- They are able to use therapy styles that are congruent with the value systems of different culture groups.
- They are able to modify and adapt conventional approaches to therapy to accommodate cultural differences.
- They are able to send and receive both verbal and nonverbal messages accurately and appropriately.

- They are able to employ institutional intervention skills on behalf of their clients when necessary or appropriate.
- They are able to make out-of-office interventions when necessary by assuming the role of consultant and agent for change.

Regardless of whose definition of cultural competence is used, all begin with an assumption that practitioners will demonstrate an accurate understanding of their own cultural identity and the values and biases they bring to the profession. However, as we have already established, self-understanding is not automatic. Instead it is the place where training in cultural competence must begin.

THE IMPORTANCE OF CULTURAL SELF-AWARENESS

Knowing who you are is important for attaining an education, because knowing who you are gives you a base for learning everything.
   —ANTHONY BEHILL, CITED IN CHANG, MUCKELROY, & PULIDO-TOBIASSEN, 1996, p. 27

It is important to be clear, knowledgeable and critical of one's specific cultural identity, whether it is historic, adopted or multiple. This form of self-knowledge and clarity is important not only for academic or ethical reasons, but also because it is the basis of defining and discovering our unique and individual contributions, interests and purposes.
   —BOWSER, AULETTA, & JONES, 1993, p . 83

Students who do not recognize their cultural identity fail to see culture as a relevant attribute of their perspective on the world (Derman-Sparks & Phillips, 1997). This is especially true for White students who see their personal perspectives as the norm, rather than variations on the equally legitimate perspectives of members of nondominant culture groups. Lack of understanding of self owing to a poor sense of cultural identity has also been found to cause Whites to develop negative attitudes toward nondominant culture groups both consciously and subconsciously (Katz, 1978). White students are most likely to fall prey to the cultural misperceptions described earlier in this paper and to treat people of other cultures in ways that subtly or blatantly denigrate their cultural backgrounds. This often is done from the best of intentions (Lally, 1995; Green, 1995). However, such perceptions obviously interfere with therapists' and other helping professionals' abilities to interact effectively with clients of nondominant culture groups.

Understanding the dimensions of White culture in the United States involves not only recognizing the cultural values described earlier, but also dealing with issues of power, racism, sexism, and classism. These concepts are best examined personally as well as at an institutional level. Such issues are central to how Whites are perceived by other groups and how Whites perceive themselves. This can be a painful process for students to encounter. However, it also can be a liberating one in which students emerge with greater self-appreciation, as well as better understanding of diversity. Readers are referred to Louise Derman-Sparks and Carol Brunson Phillips' book titled *Teaching/Learning Anti-Racism* (1997) as an excellent example of how such a process can be structured constructively. Judith Katz's volume titled *White Awareness* (1978) is also very useful. In each case, the authors describe ways to help students move from denial of cultural differences to the development of perspectives and skills that enhance intercultural communication. Such far-reaching efforts are beyond the scope of this chapter. However, we will examine some effective strategies that prompt students to reflect on the meaning of culture in their own lives. One of the best ways to promote this kind of reflection is to place students in situations in which they "bump" into cultural awareness.

Bumping into Cultural Awareness

Everyone, at one time or another, has found out more about their own culture by experiencing a challenge to their basic assumptions of how life works. Following are two examples:

- On a recent trip to Great Britain, my husband and I found that in each restaurant we visited we had to consciously work at deciphering how to pay the bill. In some establishments, the check was only presented after coffee. Not being coffee drinkers, we had a problem more than once. In other restaurants, it was impolite to request the bill in the main dining room. Diners were expected to withdraw to a lounge, where after-dinner beverages were served along with chocolates. Only then would a bill be offered. In some places, it was considered gauche to ask for the dinner check at all (one was to wait until it was presented) and, in still other locales, the bill was never offered unless the diner asked for it specifically. More than once, we remarked on how different this all was from what we were used to at home.
- Traveling to Asia and Europe, where smoking is widespread, and nonsmoking areas in restaurants and theaters are generally not available, we became aware of how much has changed in the United States regarding smoking over the past 20 years. The advent of nonsmoking sections in restaurants and smoke-free work and entertainment environments have given American nonsmokers opportunities that are simply unavailable in many other countries.

Both of these incidents highlight examples of bumping into one's own culture in the face of cultural variations. Often, such variables only become evident when one is confronted with a situation in which one's assumptions are no longer valid.

> James W. Green, in Cultural Awareness in the Human Services, explains: Someone else's culture is most evident when I contrast what I see in that person with what I know about myself. The presence of an 'other' makes me self-conscious of my own cultural distinctiveness. The experience of contrast, the presence of an apparent cultural boundary, is certainly stimulating, perhaps even discomforting. When I confront someone I perceive as different from myself, that person's culture might be any number of things—what I believe his or her values or family life to be, what I am thinking about the religious beliefs I presume that person holds, my previous experiences with 'people like that' when they are in contact with people "like me." (1995, p. 14)

The following activities have been designed to prompt students to "bump" into greater cultural awareness through interactions with classmates and the instructor.

Sample Activities Aimed at Increasing Students' Awareness of Their Cultural Identity

The following activities are samples of ones that can be used to help students explore their cultural identity. These are followed by selected resources instructors may use to create their own exercises and experiences for student use. The author has focused on the self-awareness aspects of these materials. However, readers will note that many of the same materials can be used to promote intercultural awareness as well.

Exercise 1. Ask the students to divide themselves into groups according to their perceived cultural similarities. (These groups should be entirely self-selected.) Provide each group with large pieces of poster paper on which the following three headings appear: (a) cultural objects—things, (b) customs—how people live, and (c) values—beliefs and reasons for actions. Ask each group to list (under the appropriate headings) items, actions, or beliefs representative of their group. Come together as a whole group to discuss the results.

Exercise 2. Examine your life and that of your family for indications of how culture, cultural traditions, and rituals affect you daily, monthly, and yearly.

Exercise 3. If you were describing yourself to another person, what would you say about yourself in terms of the cultural group identifiers presented in this class (race, ethnicity, religion, age, gender, geographic orientation, national origin, socioeconomic status, sexual preference, or marital status, physical development, or handicapping condition, interests due to a historical perspective)? Select 10 descriptive words (e.g., female, middle-aged, Hungarian descent, and Catholic). Next, rank these words in order of their importance to you.

Exercise 4. Lucinda Lee Katz, a researcher at the University of Chicago, maintains that people who are members of particular cultural groups have a common understanding of the occurrence of certain behaviors and practice those behaviors with the frequency and intensity expected of group members (Katz, 1994). Examine the following three ideas in terms of your cultural identity as expressed within your family:

- *Occurrence.* This is a behavior you absolutely have to display in your family to demonstrate that you are a good group member. It may seem insignificant to you, but if someone outside your family came to your home and wanted to show that he or she belonged to your family, he or she would have to display this behavior. What is it?
- *Frequency.* Some activities are very ordinary, but occur with such frequency that they typify the lives of group members. What actions, words, or behaviors are frequently displayed in your family? List them here.
- *Intensity.* There are a number of occasions that are extremely significant in some families. The importance of such events is signified by the length of time in the preparation, the number of people involved, or the amount of emotional energy expended. They are often focused around holidays, family gatherings, or rituals. Describe one or two such events in your family.

Exercise 5. Repeat Exercise 4, using the broader culture group with whom you identify as a frame of reference.

Exercise 6. Select one of the following films about family life. As you watch the film, identify instances "like you and your personal experience" and "not like you and your personal experience." What insights did you gain regarding your own cultural identity? Films: *Avalon, The Brothers Mc-Mullen, Joy Luck Club, Rosewood,* and *Like Water for Chocolate.*

Exercise 7. Read the article, "Learning to See Across a Cultural Gap," by Janet Gonzalez Mena (1994) published in *Child Care Information Exchange,* or the two clinical case studies described by J. T. Gibbs and L. N. Huang (1989) in the book, *Children of Color: Psychological Interventions with Minority Youth.* These resources will cause you to "bump into" a variety of cultural assumptions. What are they? Next, reflect on how you might consider each case from different cultural points of view.

Exercise 8. What follows is a list of cultural "truths" which lie so deep in our culture that they are rarely stated, never questioned, and sometimes produce surprise in persons called on to defend them (Kohls & Knight, 1994). They are simply taken as givens, which any intelligent, cultured individual anywhere would accept. Obviously, every intelligent, cultured individual in the world doesn't accept all of our cultural truths. In fact, many, even most, of the world's people operate on their own cultural truths, which may be at complete variance with ours as shown in the following list:

- People control their lives and their environments and should reject the idea of fate.
- Change is inevitable and desirable.
- Equality and egalitarianism are social ideals.
- The individual is more important than the group.
- Self-help is preferable to dependence or interdependence.
- Competition and free enterprise are best for economic development.
- The future is more important than the past.
- Action is better than contemplation.
- Informality is desirable in social interactions.
- Directness and openness are virtues.
- The practical is more important to deal with than the abstract, ideal, or intellectual.
- Improving material existence benefits human beings more than spiritual improvement.
- Problem solving is the best approach to dealing with reality.

You will have 15 to 25 minutes to work in a small group to select the cultural truths that apply to your region or subculture. Write down the ones you select and provide examples of each. (Note that you may value a truth such as equality, yet fail to put this belief into everyday practice.) Share your lists. What do your reports have in common? What is unique about each one?

Exercise 9. Read the exercise "Observations of Foreign Visitors about American Behavior" on pages 43 to 49 of Robert Kohls' and John Knight's book, *Developing Intercultural Awareness.* The instructor will select five of the foreign visitor quotations for your small group to discuss. For instance, a visitor from India remarked: "Americans seem to be in a perpetual hurry. Just watch the way they walk down the street. They never allow themselves the leisure to enjoy life; there are too many things to do." A visitor from Japan said, "Family life in the US seems harsh and unfeeling compared to the close ties in our country. Americans don't seem to care for their elderly parents." A visitor from Colombia said, "The tendency in the US to believe that life is only work hits you in the face. Work seems to be the one motivation." A visitor from Australia said, "I am impressed by the fact that American teachers never seem to stop going to school themselves." A visitor from Lesotho said, "Some Americans I have met seem to like to live with animals, more than with people, and they treat their pets like human beings, even kissing them and holding them on their laps."

After reading the five quotations you have received, answer the following questions, and listen to each subgroup as it reports its reactions:

1. What is the issue?
2. Is the criticism true? Fair?
3. What underlies it? What is the logic behind it?
4. How would you explain or defend it?

Exercise 10.   Read the article "White Privilege and Male Privilege" by Peggy Macintosh (1988). Ask yourself, "How closely does this article match my experience? Is this true for me, for my family? Why or why not? What does this tell me about my cultural identity?" Next, develop a list of "privileges" you may experience in your job or in your family life due to your skin color or gender. Here is an example of the privileges that became evident to one individual as she considered her cultural identity.

I don't often think of myself as having privilege. I work in one of the most underpaid, unacknowledged professions in the country. I struggle as a parent with lack of support, lack of recognition, isolation. But after reading Peggy Macintosh's articles on white privilege, I realize, as a white woman, raising white children, there are many privileges I have just taken for granted. Here are just a few that have become visible to me.

I can assume if I am called into the principal's office to discuss my child, chances are pretty good that s/he will be the same color as I am.

If my kids excel at school or activities, they are unlikely to be called a credit to their race and expected to speak for white children everywhere.

If my kids get into trouble, their behavior is unlikely to be counted as due to their skin color, and my parenting is unlikely to be called into question due to my skin color.

I can generally assume the books, history stories, films, etc., that my children will be exposed to in school will mainly reflect the lives of people with my children's skin color.

If I go to a therapist or counselor to seek help with my children, marriage or work relationship, I can assume the therapist will speak my language and share my skin color, and furthermore, s/he will not assume my struggles are due to my race.

If I am hired at a new center or receive a promotion, I do not have to wonder if other people presume I got the job only because of my skin color.

If the Fire Marshall or Licensing officer come to visit my center, I can presume s/he will share my skin color, and if they find something wrong I can be fairly sure they will not presume the problem is due to my racial background.

If I mess up at work, it is unlikely people will presume it is the nature of my entire racial group to make that error.

If I speak up at work, chances are people will credit my ideas to the quality of my experience and intelligence, rather than presuming I am a spokesperson for white folks in general.

In general, I can presume that most of the time in my dealings with the world, my children and I stand a good chance of being responded to as individuals, not as representatives of a racial group, and people in positions of authority and power in my life will most likely share my skin color and perceive me as a member of their particular human group. (Reprinted with permission from Chang, H. N., Muckelroy, A., & Pulido-Tobiassen, D., 1996)

REFERENCES

ALLPORT, G. (1958). *The nature of prejudice.* Garden City, NJ: Doubleday.

BERNS, R. M. (1996). *Child, family, community.* New York: Holt, Rinehart & Winston.

BOWSER, B. P., AULETTA, G. S., & JONES, T. (1993). *Confronting diversity issues on campus.* Newbury Park, CA: Sage Publications.

BREDEKAMP, S., & COPPLE, C. (1997). *Developmentally appropriate practice in early childhood programs.* Washington, DC: National Association for the Education of Young Children.

CHANG, H. N., MUCKELROY, A., & PULIDO-TOBIASSEN, D. (1996). *Looking in, looking out: Redefining child care and early education in a diverse society.* San Francisco: California Tomorrow.

COREY, G., COREY, M., & CALLANAN, P. (1988). *Issues and ethics in the helping professions.* Pacific Grove, CA. Brooks/Cole.

CROSS, T. L., BAZRON, B. J., DENNIS, K. W., & ISAACS, M. R. (1989). *Towards a culturally competent system of care.* Washington, DC: CASSP Technical Assistance Center, Georgetown University.

DERMAN-SPARKS, L., & THE ABC TASK FORCE (1989). *Anti-bias curriculum: Tools for empowering young children.* Washington, DC: National Association for the Education of Young Children.

DERMAN-SPARKS, L., & PHILLIPS, C. B. (1997). *Teaching/learning anti-racism: A developmental approach.* New York: Teachers College Press.

DIRLIK, A. (1987). Culturalism as hegemonic ideology and liberating practice. *Cultural Critique, 6,* 13–50.

DUNDES., A. (1975). Seeing is believing. In J. P. Spradley & M. A. Rynkiewich (Eds.),*The nacirema: Readings on American culture* (pp. 14–19). Boston: Little, Brown.

GEERTZ, C. (1977). *Interpretation of cultures.* New York: Basic Books.

GIBBS, J. T., & HUANG, L. N. (1989). *Children of color: Psychological interventions with minority youth.* (pp. 371–374). San Francisco: Jossey-Bass.

GREEN, J. W. (1995). *Cultural awareness in the human services: A multi-ethnic approach.* Boston: Allyn & Bacon.

HALL, E. T. (1980). *The silent language.* Westport, CT.: Greenwood Press.

HENDERSON, R. W., & BERGAN, J. R. (1976). *The cultural context of childhood.* Columbus, OH: Merrill Publishing.

ISAACS, M. R., & BENJAMIN, M. P. (1991). *Towards a culturally competent system of care.* Washington, DC: CASSP Technical Assistance Center, Georgetown University.

KATZ, J. (1978). *White awareness.* Norman, OK: University of Oklahoma Press.

KATZ, L. L. (1994, November). *Family and culture.* Paper presented at the National Conference of the National Association for the Education of Young Children, Washington, DC.

KOHLS, L. R., & KNIGHT, J. M. (1994). *Developing intercultural awareness: A cross-cultural training handbook.* Yarmouth, ME: Intercultural Press.

KOSTELNIK, M. J., SODERMAN, A. K., & WHIREN, A. P. (1998). *Developmentally appropriate curriculum: Best practices in early childhood education,* 2nd ed. Columbus, OH: Merrill-Prentice Hall.

LALLY, R. J. (1995). The impact of child care policies and practices on infant/toddler identity formation. *Young Children, 51,* 58–67.

LEAF, M. (1975). Baking and roasting. In J. P. Spradley & M. A. Rynkiewich (Eds.), *The nacirema: Readings on American culture* (pp. 19–20). Boston: Little, Brown.

LEE, R. E. (1998). The marital and family therapy examination program: A survey of participants. *Journal of Marital and Family Therapy, 24,* 127–134.

LYNCH, E. W., & HANSON, M. (1992). *Developing cross cultural competence: A guide for working with young children and families.* Baltimore: Paul H. Brookes Publishing.

MACINTOSH, P. (1988). *White privilege and male privilege: A personal account of coming to see correspondences through work in women's studies.* Working paper No. 189. Wellesley, MA: Center for Research on Women, Wellesley College.

MENA, J. G. (1994). Learning to see across a cultural gap. *Child care information exchange, 5,* 65–68.

NASH, M. (1989). *The cauldron of ethnicity in the modern world.* Chicago: University of Chicago Press.

NIETO, S. (1992). *Affirming diversity: The sociopolitical context of multicultural education.* New York: Longman.

O'CONNOR, S. (1993). *Multiculturalism and disability: A collection of resources.* Syracuse, NY: Center on Human Policy, Syracuse University.

PHINNEY, J. S., & ROTHERMAN, M. J. (1987). *Children's ethnic socialization: Pluralism and development.* Newbury Park, CA: Sage Publications.

ROBLES DE MELENDEZ, W., & OSTERAG, V. (1997). *Teaching young children in multicultural classrooms: Issues, concepts and strategies.* Albany, NY: Delmar.

SHAFFER, D. R. (1994). *Social and personality development.* Pacific Grove, CA: Brooks/Cole Publishing.

SPRADLEY, J. P., & RYNKIEWICH, M. A. (1975). *The nacirema: Readings on American culture.* Boston: Little, Brown.

WEISS, C. I., & MINSKY, S. (1996). *Program self-assessment survey for cultural competence.* Trenton, NJ: New Jersey Division of Mental Health Services.

CHAPTER 14

Integrating Gender into the Practice of Supervising Marriage and Family Therapists

MARSHA T. CAROLAN

Despite the inclusion of gender as a requirement for all training programs accredited by the Commission on Accreditation for Marriage and Family Therapy Education, beginning marriage and family therapists may continue to practice in gender-biased ways (Leslie & Clossick, 1996). It appears that simply acquiring knowledge about gender is not as important as how it is taught. Evidence indicates that coursework taught from an informed feminist perspective is a more effective means of combating gender stereotypes and gendered thinking (Leslie & Clossick, 1996). Likewise, supervision must do more than acknowledge gender. Supervision must incorporate gender into all aspects of the process (Wheeler, Avis, Miller, & Chaney, 1989).

During the last decades, feminist scholars have taught us that gender is far more than something that "affects" families. Gender constructs and determines couple and family life (Goldner, 1988). Gender acts as a guiding principle around which all other aspects of family life are organized (Luepnitz, 1988). A contemporary vision of family life attends to individual and family diversity in terms of equity issues along dimensions of gender, age, class, race, and sexual orientation (Allen, 1988; Hardy & Laszloffy, 1995).

UNDERSTANDING GENDER: ECOLOGICAL ISSUES

Understanding gender requires a knowledge of how gender is socially constructed both within and without the therapeutic session. This requires an understanding of gender as more than an individual property, and requires a conceptualization of the process of family therapy as gendered.

The Social Construction of Gender

Conceptualizing gender as an individual property and articulating differences between men and women were ideas that came early and became important contributions to our understanding of gender. Broadening the conceptualization to include contextual and process factors was the next step necessary to a fuller comprehension of gender-related substantive issues (Hare-Mustin, 1989, 1991). Rather than using gender differences to explain or justify oppression, gender differences and contextual factors could be used to more fully understand how the process of gender is created and re-created by the social and interactional factors that surround us.

It is necessary that both therapists and supervisors of marriage and family therapy understand the concept of gender as a social construction and the subtleties of an ecology in which gender is created and re-created through interactions of the individual with the environment (Ferree, 1990; Thompson, 1993). Historical, cultural, and social factors contribute to the perpetuation of male and female behaviors that are observed as inherent properties rather than consequent or interactive behaviors (West & Zimmerman, 1987).

It also is essential that therapists and supervisors understand the subtleties of power from the metalevel of social analysis to the microlevel of couple interaction. Without a thorough understanding of power, gender can be neither recognized nor understood. The real and sometimes invisible powers of an entrenched patriarchy exists, in spite of the good intentions of clients, therapists and supervisors. Ethical guidelines designed by feminist practitioners (Rave & Larsen, 1995) reflect this awareness of power by stressing the necessity to "acknowledge the inherent power differential between client and therapist" (p. 40). It likewise is essential to acknowledge the inherent power differential between therapist and supervisor (see Emerson, Chapter 2).

Viewing Family Therapy Through the Lens of Gender

Approaching therapy and supervision with an awareness of gender begins with a knowledge of family therapy models. Gender training recognizes the hidden gender dimensions in reified models of family therapy (Walsh & Scheinkman, 1989). It acknowledges the explicit conceptualization of power in contemporary models of therapy such as the narrative model (White, 1993) and models of feminist family therapy (Luepnitz, 1988; Walters, Carter, Papp, & Silverstein, 1988).

Recognizing that gender is the "wellspring of all behavior," the Women's Project in Family Therapy (Walters et al., 1988) has established interventions that identify and work with gendered messages and behaviors to mobilize the family toward wellness. Both men and women can be disadvantaged by the gendered assumptions that direct how they should think, feel, and behave. For example, family of origin or sociocultural messages to females can promote sacrificing and silencing of their inner needs and desire for separateness (Lerner, 1990). Family of origin or sociocultural messages to males can promote silencing their emotions (with the exception of anger, which is often permitted) and suppressing feelings of sadness, helplessness, and dependence.

Rather than viewing gender differences as inevitable, this approach helps us to comprehend the daily and ongoing factors that contribute to gender and allows for the adoption of a more conscious agenda for change. It is not helpful to the process of therapy to maintain an exaggerated position on gender by either focusing on the differences or ignoring the differences that have been created by social interaction (Hare-Mustin & Marecek, 1990).

Family therapists observe that couples negotiate impasses that result in gendered divisions of labor (Hochschild, 1989; Zvonkovic, Greaves, Schmiege, & Hall, 1996) and make decisions that result in what Knudson-Martin & Mahoney (1996) refer to as the "myth of equality." Conscious attempts to illuminate these belief systems can free individuals and couples to make choices and decisions in different ways (Goodrich, 1991). Family therapy can implement a process in which outcomes evolve that are "equally serving the needs and well-being of both partners" (Knudson-Martin & Mahoney, 1996).

The Influence of Gender on Therapeutic Process

A small body of research exists that looks at the influence of gender of the therapist on the process of family therapy, and at the influence of the intersection of gender and race of the therapist and clients on the process of family therapy. Research by Alexander and his colleagues (Warburton, Newberry, & Alexander, 1989) concluded that the task of female therapists is more challenging than that of male therapists. Female therapists tend to encounter more defensiveness, are expected to produce more supportive behaviors, and tend to underestimate their outcomes as compared to male therapists. Similar results were documented by more recent studies (Gregory & Leslie, 1996; Shields & McDaniel, 1992; Stabb, Cox, & Harber, 1997).

It is clear that gender influences all levels of the ecological framework, from the macroconstructions of gender to the microconstructions of gender within individual couples and families. Gender affects the interaction of couples and families with their therapists, and affects the interaction of therapists with supervisors in the supervisory relationship.

UNDERSTANDING GENDER: SELF ISSUES

A personal understanding of gender—as it applies to the self of the therapist and the self of the supervisor—is necessary as a complement to theoretical and substantive knowledge of it. It also is imperative to look at the interaction of gender between therapist and client, and therapist and supervisor.

Gender and the Self of the Therapist

It is necessary for each of us, first as therapists and then as supervisors, to be able to understand gender through self-knowledge (Aponte & Winter, 1987) and knowledge of others in relation to the self. This may begin with the study of family of origin issues and how gendered messages were communicated, understood, and implemented in the family. A useful tool for beginning therapists is the gendergram, developed by White and Tyson-Rawson (1995) for use in couple assessment. I use it to sensitize students and therapists under supervision to the gender influences in childhood, adolescence, and adulthood. The gendergram assists the developing therapist in bringing gendered ideology into clear and concrete awareness by asking us to consider who were the important same and other sex influences during development, what were the messages attached to each person and gender, and so on.

Gender ideology is partly biographically derived, with some idiosyncratic propensities, and partly socially derived, as a response to social opportunities. In essence, individuals construct personal ideologies based on a complex interaction of factors, which are then acted upon and become part of the individual's public and private self.

Each of us sits as a gendered person in the room with our clients, despite our attempts at neutrality. If we make a conscious effort to work toward clarity regarding our gendered biases and ways of knowing about men and women, we will develop stronger skills as therapists. As we differentiate from our families and gain insight into the social and familial influences on us, we can also fine-tune our awareness of the gendered influences nested within the social framework of family and others. Examining our personal assumptions and ingrained notions about the way men and women are, or should be, or shouldn't be, will inform our work with individuals, couples, and families.

To function most effectively as clinicians, most of us really need a broad range of skills and aptitudes. Understanding our gendered development and ideology can assist us in broadening our ability to act in ways that embrace both agency and communion, or our ability to choose from a repertoire of executive and relational skills. In addition, if we can become comfortable with our own socially proscribed masculine and feminine behaviors, we can help our clients to become more comfortable. If we can understand the subtleties of power that have influenced us in relation to gender, we also can help move our clients to more equitable positioning.

Gender and the Self of the Supervisor

The same notions about understanding self must apply to supervisors. Before supervising others around gender issues and gender dynamics, it is imperative that supervisors first educate themselves. Education should include basic training in theoretical and substantive issues of gender. More importantly, it should ideally include being supervised by someone who has been sensitized to gender issues and is willing to make explicit the inherent power issues in supervision. Training with a supervisor who has a feminist understanding of gender will help to assure that the supervisor is especially attuned to the power and control dynamics that can quietly hide within the supervisor-supervisee relationship.

Gender and the Supervisor-Therapist Relationship

Supervisors can help break down some of the hidden dynamics of supervision by putting gendered interactions on the table, as it were, making the process transparent between supervisors and therapists. The supervisory relationship can be conceptualized as one which is inherently hierarchical, regardless of gender dynamics. Acknowledging the hierarchies and working to make them transparent and available for discussion can be a transforming experience.

For example, operating on what we know about the way men and women are socialized to behave with one another, here are a few of the available gendered scenarios to which we can be alert in the supervisory relationship. Female supervisees with female supervisors may be vulnerable to subtle power issues around mother or sister approval, rather than the more coercive aspects of power. Female supervisees with male supervisors may be vulnerable to explicit and implicit issues around traditional male authority and power. Male supervisees with female supervisors may be vulnerable to issues around mother approval. They also may be more apt to consciously or unconsciously dismiss or discount female supervisory input. Male supervisees with male supervisors may be vulnerable to issues around male authority or may be drawn into competitive or co-optive stances.

Rather than taking supervisory sessions at face value, supervisors can reflect on how gender is influencing their supervisory relationship on a day-to-day basis. Supervisors can ask themselves if they are interacting differently with different supervised therapists and if so, if this is due to gender. Supervisors can observe if supervised therapists act differently around them as compared to other supervisors and other therapists and if this is due to gender. Supervisors can discuss self-of-the-therapist issues focused on gender, when appropriate to the case discussion or therapist growth. Supervisors can ask their supervisees to talk to one another about power issues within the supervisory relationship and to present their issues and concerns with one anonymous voice. Supervisors can encourage their supervisees to openly discuss their observations and concerns about power and gender in all types of relationships and make it clear that these are appropriate and not inconsequential concerns for discussion. Supervisors can discuss with colleagues, supervisors, or consultants their own concerns, reflections, and observations about their performance around gender and power issues.

The following case studies were designed to implement the discussion of gender as an integrated issue in supervision. All supervisors and therapists must negotiate their theoretical or conceptual approaches to cases, and these cases obviously represent those of the therapists and supervisors presented. However, issues of gender should ideally transcend any conceptual approach to working with individuals, couples, and families.

CASE STUDY 1

A male therapist sought supervision from a female supervisor on a case involving a married heterosexual couple. The couple presented with complaints of low sexual desire on the part of the wife, and high levels of marital conflict in the relationship. The male therapist had made gradual but steady progress addressing the marital conflict. Both members of the couple reported satisfaction with increased levels of communication and a generally more harmonious interaction. However, the husband expressed dissatisfaction with the infrequency of sexual activity in their marriage. The wife was not dissatisfied with the infrequency of sexual activity and wished that the issue of sex would just go away. Despite the use of sensate focus exercises, the level of sexual activity continued to be problematic for both of them.

The male therapist was questioned about issues of power in the couple relationship. He perceived that the wife had a great deal of power in the relationship. For example, he felt that the wife determined the amount of sex that occurred in the marriage. The female supervisor inquired about the history of both individuals and was told that the wife had experienced the divorce of her parents at a young age, and many years of single parenting by her mother. In late adolescence, she established a good relationship with her stepfather. In young adulthood, she was caught up in an explosive relationship with a man she had fallen in love with before her husband. The husband had come from an intact family in which there was not a lot of closeness or communication and in which there was a moderate amount of physical abuse and alcoholism. During adolescence, he had experimented with drugs and alcohol, then rallied himself and joined the military. During subsequent years the husband had little experience with women, with one exception, a short affair before marrying his present wife.

To supervise this case in a way that was sensitive to multiple levels of gender issues, at least three things were required: awareness of gender issues within the attendant therapist, gender issues between the therapist and clients, and gender issues between the therapist and supervisor. The male therapist was most able to relate to the husband's frustration around sexuality and perceived this to be a deprivation issue regarding the husband's need for sex. He felt that the wife was often unemotional in their sessions and not as engaged as her husband. He believed that the wife was holding most of the power in the marital dyad.

Therapist Issues

The supervisor first explored the self-of-the-therapist issues. How were his beliefs about gender related to his work with these clients? Inquiry unearthed gendered beliefs that reflected the therapist's own life experiences with women in which he often ended up in one-down positions. The therapist also saw deprivation from sex as a power-laden issue for men, as it had been in his family of origin. Finally, the therapist was asked to reflect on how his own beliefs about women, sex, and power might be influencing his work with this couple. He observed that he might be biased in that he clearly identified more with the husband and therefore could not clearly see the dilemmas that the wife might be facing.

The supervisor then suggested that the therapist undertake a thorough exploration designed to separate his own issues from those of his clients. The supervisor invited the therapist to find out more about the wife, to see if he could get a sense of what her salient issues might be, especially ones that might be affecting the power and control issues in their marriage. For example, what was the wife's history with men and intimacy, and how did she perceive the day-to-day realities of the couple's working relationship (e.g., how they managed child care and housework)? Additionally, how might the gendered histories of each partner and daily experiences as working parents be related to their sexual relationship? Similarly, the therapist was urged to ask the husband about his experiences with women and intimacy, and about the daily realities of his life.

Client Issues

Several sessions later, the therapist reported that the wife had revealed a consistent history of abandonment and abuse by a number of men whom she had loved during childhood, adolescence, and young adulthood. He also discovered that the wife worked at a physically strenuous job, returned home to care for two young children by herself, and then was expected to be interested in sex when her husband returned from his late work shift around midnight. Given the opportunity, the wife revealed her frustrations about feeling responsible for the bulk of child care and household tasks. Accordingly, she felt protective about the end of the day when she would reenergize for the morrow by either gaining much needed rest or reading until she fell asleep. Added to the day-to-day realities was her own resistance to closeness with her husband based on past experiences with males.

The husband in turn, revealed that his history with women began with playing a parentified role with his mother as the oldest son of an alcoholic. He finally escaped this role by abusing drugs and alcohol. His history relationally with women was brief so that sexual rejection from his wife felt monumental. He talked about sex as being his primary means of feeling close to his wife. Because he worked a late shift, he often slept during most of the day, and was out when his children returned from school and day care and for most of the evening. However, in the workplace he was primarily with male colleagues. Because he saw himself as a caring father, he was unaware of and surprised by the role that exhaustion and inequity along division of household tasks played in his wife's responses to him.

With this new information, and insight into his own gendered beliefs, the male therapist was able to redirect the intervention with a more politicized and working awareness of individual and dyadic issues of gender and power.

Supervisor and Therapist Issues

It is important that the supervisory relationship be open and flexible enough to allow for the direction of self-of-the-therapist issues in a nonthreatening and collaborative manner. Teachable moments around gender arise frequently in supervision but should be chosen with respect for the therapist and recognition of the power differential between supervisor and therapist. In this case study, the female supervisor looked for a teachable moment when recognition of self-of-the-therapist gender issues in combination with gendered issues in the client relationship would be most useful.

As the case began to change, the male therapist was able to talk about his initial feelings of resentment toward the female supervisor for directing the case toward a gender orientation with which he was not comfortable.

Additionally, he questioned the value of self-of-the-therapist issues until he had experienced changes in his cases, and in himself, as a result of his increasing understanding. Female supervisors working with male therapists should be attuned to male biases and assumptions about women and the natural tendency to more easily identify with the same gender. It also might be true that male therapists might need more encouragement to explore self-of-the-therapist issues with regard to gender.

CASE STUDY 2

A female therapist sought supervision from a male supervisor on a case that involved a couple that was considering marriage. The woman in the couple had made attempts to withdraw from the relationship and was very uncertain about her desire to marry the man, which prompted a mutual agreement to attend therapy. The man, who was quite a bit older than the woman, was eager to marry and did not understand her uncertainties. The young woman had experienced the death of her biological father during her adolescence but had a fairly uneventful history thereafter. She had a close relationship with her widowed mother and casual dating relationships with peers during high school and early college.

The man had experienced a more complex history of neglect and estrangement from his family during his younger years. His adulthood in turn was marked by failed relationships with women, in which he described himself as active pursuer. This included several relationships in which he casually reported receiving physical and verbal abuse from his female partner, sometimes as attempts to deter his pursuit of them. As in the first case, multiple levels of gender issues had to be addressed: awareness of gender issues within the attendant therapist, gender issues between the therapist and clients, and gender issues between the therapist and supervisor.

The female therapist was most able to relate to the woman's concerns about committing to a man who seemed so desperate to be loved. In contrast, she was keenly frustrated with the male client's refusal to express himself emotionally and to acknowledge the female therapist in the session in a respectful way. At this point, the therapist was having difficulty even tolerating this man and felt much more connected with the female client in the dyad.

Therapist Issues

Again, the supervision began with a focus on self-of-the-therapist issues. How were this female therapist's beliefs about gender related to her work with these clients? Inquiry generated gendered beliefs that reflected her own experiences with men in which she often felt dismissed and power-less. In her family of origin, women claimed power by leaving relation-ships but often were unable to exert power within relationships with men. The therapist was feeling so powerless with this male client that she now was seeking permission to terminate and transfer the case. Asked about her reasons for transferring, the therapist described her feelings of invisi-bility in regard to the male client. She described how she felt that she was working very hard to like this man and be helpful to him, despite her sense of being dismissed and not well regarded by him.

The supervisor asked the female therapist to reflect on how her client's response to her might be related to her biases about men as powerful, and how it might be a familiar solution for her to "leave" as a way to maintain her own power as a woman and therapist. He suggested that she consider seeing these clients individually for a few sessions, as a way to perhaps en-gage a connection with the male client. He also suggested that she consider talking to her male client about her feelings of disconnection with him and how this might be representative of other relationships with women in his life. He recommended that she meet with the female client and find out how it was that she moved from wanting to marry this man to her present state, and how her client's gendered beliefs and expectations were operat-ing at this juncture in their dating relationship.

Client Issues

Several sessions later, the therapist reported that she had met with each client individually. She had discovered that her male client was unaware of his externalized presence to others. In fact, he saw himself as much less powerful than women, including the therapist. He was intimidated by the power that she had as a therapist to influence the course of his relationship with this woman and felt immobilized by this anxiety. The therapist was able to deconstruct with him some of his desperation around being in love and in a relationship and how it was related to his earlier history. The ther-apist also discovered that her female client was struggling with wanting to love this man and feeling disrespect for him. In the beginning, she had been attracted to him because he was older, and she assumed, wiser in the ways of the world. As their relationship evolved and he revealed himself as vulnerable, and even at times as fragile, she was unable to maintain her respect for him. She was operating on gendered assumptions that men must be powerful and strong at all times.

With this new information, the therapist brought her clients together in a couple's session. She asked her clients, among other things, to share with one another their insights and responses to their individual sessions. She then was able to move the intervention to a more genuine level of in-teraction in which she as a therapist was no longer feeling disempowered.

Supervisor and Therapist Issues

To reiterate, the supervisory relationship must be open and flexible enough to allow for the direction of self-of-the-therapist issues in a non-threatening and collaborative manner. Interestingly, in this case study, the supervised therapist eventually revealed that she had wanted to see these clients individually but was afraid to challenge her supervisor, whom she understood was diametrically opposed to individual treatment when couples presented. She and her supervisor were able to talk about how her fears around challenging her supervisor were similar to her frustrations with her male client. Male supervisors with female therapists should be attuned to female biases about men, and especially to power issues between female therapists and male clients and female therapists and male supervisors. Female therapists may feel intimidated by male supervisors and not allow themselves to act on their own feelings of competence and authority, which might need to be more proactively encouraged by male supervisors.

CONCLUSION

These cases provide a snapshot of how gender might be integrated into the supervisory process. Supervision provides a continual array of opportunities in which gender can be discussed, in terms of the therapist's self, the therapeutic alliance, and the supervisory alliance. Supervision that integrates gender appropriately begins with the awareness of gender as a central organizing principle of family life. It is up to the supervisor to see that supervised therapists understand the applicability of gendered knowledge to therapy and incorporate them consistently in their therapeutic and supervisory relationships.

REFERENCES

ALLEN, K. R. (1988). Integrating a feminist perspective into family studies courses. *Family Relations, 37,* 29–35.

APONTE, H., & WINTER, J. E. (1987). The person and practice of the therapist: Treatment and training. In M. Baldwin & V. Satir (Eds.), *The use of self in therapy* (pp. 84–98). New York: Haworth.

FERREE, M. M. (1990). Beyond separate spheres: Feminism and family research. *Journal of Marriage and the Family, 52,* 866–884.

GOLDNER, V. (1988). Generation and gender: Normative and covert hierarchies. *Family Process, 27,* 17–31.

GOODRICH, T. J. (1991). *Women and power: Perspectives for family therapy.* New York: Norton.

GREGORY, M. A., & LESLIE, L. A. (1996). Different lenses: Variations in clients' perception of family therapy by race and gender. *Journal of Marital and Family Therapy, 22*, 239–251.

HARDY, K. V., & LASZLOFFY, T. A. (1995). The cultural genogram: Key to training culturally competent family therapists. *Journal of Marital and Family Therapy, 21*, 227–237.

HARE-MUSTIN, R. (1989). The problem of gender in family therapy theory. In M. McGoldrick, C. M. Anderson, & F. Walsh (Eds.), *Women in families: A framework for family therapy* (pp. 61–77). New York: Norton.

HARE-MUSTIN, R. (1991). Sex, lies and headaches: The problem is power. In T. Goodrich (Ed.), *Women and power: Perspectives for family therapy* (pp. 63–85). New York: Norton.

HARE-MUSTIN, R., & MARECEK, J. (1990). The meaning of difference: Gender theory, postmodernism and psychology. *American Psychologist, 43*, 455–464.

HOCHSCHILD, A. (1989). *The second shift*. New York: Viking Press.

KNUDSON-MARTIN, C., & MAHONEY, A. R. (1996). Gender dilemmas and myth in the construction of marital bargains: Issues for marital therapy. *Family Process, 35*, 137–153.

LERNER, H. G. (1990). *The dance of intimacy: A woman's guide to courageous acts of change in key relationships*. New York: Harper & Row.

LESLIE, L. A., & CLOSSICK, M. L. (1996). Sexism in family therapy: Does training in gender make a difference? *Journal of Marital and Family Therapy, 22*, 253–269.

LUEPNITZ, D. (1988). *The family interpreted*. New York: Basic Books.

RAVE, E. J., & LARSEN, C. C. (1995). *Ethical decision making in therapy: Feminist perspectives*. New York: Guilford Press.

SHIELDS, C. G., & MCDANIEL, S. H. (1992). Process differences between male and female therapists in a first family interview. *Journal of Marital and Family Therapy, 18*, 143–151.

STABB, S. D., COX, D. L., & HARBER, J. L. (1997). Gender-related therapist attributions in couples therapy: A preliminary multiple case study investigation. *Journal of Marital and Family Therapy, 23*, 335–346.

THOMPSON, L. (1993). Conceptualizing gender in marriage: The case of marital care. *Journal of Marriage and the Family, 55*, 557–569.

WALSH, F., & SCHEINKMAN, M. (1989). The hidden gender dimension in models of family therapy. In M. McGoldrick, C. M. Anderson, & F. Walsh (Eds.), *Women in families: A framework for family therapy* (pp. 16–41). New York: Norton.

WALTERS, M., CARTER, B., PAPP, P., & SILVERSTEIN, O. (1988). *The invisible web: Gender patterns in family relationships*. New York: Guilford Press.

WARBURTON, J., NEWBERRY, A., & ALEXANDER, J. (1989). Women as therapists, trainees, and supervisors. In M. McGoldrick, C. M. Anderson, & F. Walsh (Eds.), *Women in families: A framework for family therapy* (pp. 152–168). New York: Norton.

WEST, C., & ZIMMERMAN, D. (1987). Doing gender. *Gender & Society, 1*, 125–151.

WHEELER, D., AVIS, J. M., MILLER, L. A., & CHANEY, S. (1989). Rethinking family therapy training and supervision: A feminist model. In M. McGoldrick, C. M. Anderson, & F. Walsh (Eds.), *Women in families: A framework for family therapy* (pp. 135–151). New York: Norton.

WHITE, M. (1993). Deconstruction and therapy. In S. Gilligan and R. Price (Eds.), *Therapeutic conversations* (pp. 22–61). New York: Norton.

WHITE, M. B., & TYSON-RAWSON, K. J. (1995). Assessing the dynamics of gender in couples and families: The gendergram. *Family Relations, 44,* 253–260

ZVONKOVIC, A. M., GREAVES, K. M., SCHMIEGE, C. J., & HALL, L. D. (1996). The marital construction of gender through work and family decisions: A qualitative analysis. *Journal of Marriage and the Family, 58,* 91–100.

CHAPTER 15

Supervision and Sexual Orientation

Supervisors, Supervisees, and Clients Can Sure Fill a Closet Fast

Timothy R. Waskerwitz

Late one evening, two young family therapists had just finished sessions with a series of couples and families. As they entered the room where their supervisor had been anxiously waiting for them, they plopped into chairs and each let out heavy sighs.

"It's been one hell of a night," one said.

The other looked off into space and sighed again. The supervisor began the session with the cursory "Well, does anyone have anything they want to discuss?" A somewhat muffled voice spoke up.

"Yeah, what the hell is homophobia, and do I have it?" The supervisor and the other therapist looked shocked and began to stare nervously at the confused therapist. "My new client just told me that, after meeting me tonight for the first time, he was glad to find I wasn't gay. He said he expected I would be because all male therapists must be. First of all, how does he know I'm not, and second, why did that make me feel so uncomfortable?"

The room had suddenly become very warm and the supervisor cleared his throat, turned, and said, "I don't really know why your client said that, but at some point in the future it may be important. How did the rest of your session go?"

The subject was never brought up again.

Supervision is the process of understanding what therapy is and how it works. It evolves, and it is a product of the particular perspectives and theories of change that supervisors and supervisees bring to the table. A supervisor's goal should be to affirm the uniqueness of perspectives, personal history, culture, and developing philosophy of supervisees and clients. Many times this is a tall order for the supervisor, especially when dealing with complex and little understood issues such as sexual orientation. Individual comfort levels and expertise vary greatly and can have major impact on the outcome of therapy when working with gay, lesbian, and bisexual (GLB) clients and therapists. As Markowitz (1991) indicated, despite the fact that many lesbians, gay men, and bisexuals have come out of the closet, many practitioners in the field of marriage and family therapy have not yet come out of the dark.

It wasn't until 1991 that the American Association for Marriage and Family Therapy (AAMFT) included "sexual orientation" in its code of ethics, and only in 1997 that the Commission on Accreditation for Marriage and Family Therapy Education (COAMFTE) included sexual orientation in its antidiscrimination clause. In their recent review of the literature, Clark and Serovich (1997) point out that from 1975 through 1995, of 13,217 articles reviewed in 17 journals, only 77 (.006%) focused on gay, lesbian, and bisexual issues or used sexual orientation as a variable. This suggests that as a field, we may be slow in recognizing the needs of GLB clients and therapists (Clark & Serovich, 1997).

This chapter will attempt to raise some of the salient issues we will face when working with gay, lesbian, and bisexual clients and supervisees. It also will address the perspectives of GLB supervisors.

Most family therapists will encounter GLB clients at some point in their careers (Green, 1996). In a survey of AAMFT clinical members, 72% reported that about 10% of their practice involved gay men, lesbian women, and bisexuals (Green & Bobele, 1994). However, as few as 50% of the respondents in another survey indicated that they felt competent to treat this population (Clark & Serovich, 1997). That suggests that many practitioners and supervisors need to improve their competency in working with GLB clients. But what happens if we continue to remain uneducated or we practice without fully understanding what and who we are treating? This lack of information and training, as well as avoidance of self-examination of issues involving sexual orientation, could be harmful. Many professionals today are practicing with a number of misperceptions and "guesses" about sexual orientation. These unexamined biases or perceptions about GLB individuals are based most often on stereotypes and may be detrimental to clients in the same way that racism may negatively impact ethnic minority clients (Greene, 1994).

WHO ARE WE TALKING ABOUT?

The literature on sexual orientation indicates that GLB clients are a diverse population. Gay men are not the same as lesbians, and homosexuals are not the same as bisexuals. The differences between homosexuality and bisexuality are not well discussed in the literature (Laird & Green, 1996), and often only as an addendum to discussions about gay and lesbian issues. Even less discussed are issues involving transgendered persons.

In fact, there may exist more differences among GLB individuals than similarities. The diversity between and within the various GLB distinctions must be kept in mind when exploring supervision involving GLB clientele.

GLB CLIENTS

Many times therapists are confronted with a host of issues that involve more than just sex when clients bring up sexual orientation. This is when things may become difficult as some therapists confuse sexual identity with sexual orientation. It is this confusion that brings about stereotypes and misperceptions. Three distinct aspects of sexual identity were identified by Money and Erhardt (1972): gender identity (how people identify themselves as male or female); sexual orientation (choice of sexual or affectual partners); and sex role behavior—the extent to which one's activities are regarded as masculine, feminine, or both (Patterson, 1994). Further, many of the theories and research perspectives about the development of sexual orientation have been developed through the lenses of people from predominantly heterosexual society and culture (D'Augelli, 1994).

> Deprived of convention, we gays and lesbians create our own road maps to navigate the obstacles and challenges placed before us by a hostile society. In doing so, without encouragement from role models and families, we repeatedly invent original solutions to life's dilemmas. (Siegel & Walker, 1996, p. 43)

Therapists unfamiliar with the literature therefore may mislabel some behaviors of GLB clients as pathological because they do not fit the heterosexual framework. For example, relational patterns that actually serve to protect the relationship of same-sex couples typically are considered as dysfunctional in heterosexual relationships (Markowitz, 1991).

When asked what they felt therapists should know when working with same-sex couples, gay men and lesbians in relationships responded with the following (Long, 1996). Therapists should understand the impact of the "invisibility" of same-sex relationships, and they should have some knowledge about the coming out process and how it is different when experienced with families and at work. They also should have some idea about the history of and struggle for gay rights, an awareness of what social battles gays and lesbians currently may face, and the effect homophobia has on individuals and couples. Therapists also should understand that despite certain specific differences, GLB families function somewhat similarly to heterosexual families. For example, studies consistently show that children raised by same-sex parents have normal psychosocial development (Patterson, 1994).

HOMOPHOBIA

Homophobia has become a common term used to describe prejudice against GLB persons. It technically means "fear of sameness," but implies a fear and avoidance of homosexuals. The term was originally used by Weinberg in 1972 to describe heterosexuals' "dread of being in close quarters with homosexuals" (Shidlo, 1994), and it includes those people who not only fear homosexuals, but who also seek out and assault them (Herek 1984; Kite, 1994). Weinberg also included the "self-loathing" homosexual people felt toward themselves.

The internalization of homophobia is a developmental event experienced by all gay men and lesbians raised in a heterosexist and anti-gay society and may be the cause of psychological distress (Shidlo, 1994). Internalized homophobia may be defined as a set of negative attitudes and affects toward homosexuality in other persons and toward homosexual features in oneself (Shidlo, 1994). Therapists therefore may need to help GLB clients reduce the amount of homophobia they feel or that they internalize.

Therapists and supervisors may fear that any lack of understanding or experience with GLB issues, or any previous attempts at avoidance may imply some form of homophobia. In fact, "internalized oppression is one of the most salient factors in the therapist's resistance to raising the issue of sexual orientation in supervision" (Russell & Greenhouse, 1997, p. 33). What is most encouraging is that homophobia decreases with personal contact with gay men, lesbians, and bisexuals (Green & Bobele, 1994).

HETEROSEXIST BIAS AND HETEROSEXISM

Heterosexist bias is defined as the conceptualization of human experience in strictly heterosexual terms that ignore, invalidate, or derogate any other form of sexual orientation, behavior, or relationship (Herek, Kimmel, Amaro, & Melton, 1991). Heterosexist bias in research often assumes that GLB individuals constitute homogenous groups, and this leads researchers to overlook important mediating factors of culture, resources, and history. Despite increased attention to sexual orientation issues, reviews of current literature indicate that this bias still exists (Clark & Serovich, 1997).

Part of the bias is evident when family therapists mistakenly believe they can apply theory and technique, which apply to straight couples, to gay and lesbian couples. For example, many people who are unfamiliar with the variation in nonheterosexual relationships assume that one person in every relationship must play the part of the male and the other the female (Markowitz, 1991). This assumption is further evidence of a confusion between sexual and gender orientation. Therapists need to help families understand that heterosexism and society's prejudice are responsible for the stress they experience when a family member comes out (Dahlheimer & Feigal, 1991). Heterosexism and homophobia together are referred to as "homonegativity" (Russell & Greenhouse, 1997; Shidlo, 1994).

LANGUAGE AND SEXUAL ORIENTATION

Formal training programs in family therapy and other mental health professions rarely examine the role of heterosexual bias in their curriculum and their use of heterosexist language. However, the American Psychological Association's Committee on Lesbian and Gay Concerns in 1991 set guidelines for avoiding heterosexual bias in language. For example, clinicians are alerted to questions in standard interviews that are heterosexually biased: "At what age did you first have intercourse?" "Are you married?" Language also can be a problem because of the unique meaning GLB individuals may give to common words. For example, the term "family" may refer to a network of close friends, or the entire realm of the gay community (Long, 1996).

THE GLB THERAPIST-SUPERVISEE

Although it is not known how many GLB therapists there are, it is known that gay, lesbian, and bisexual therapists are often isolated from each other. They tend to have few support systems especially established for their specific professional interests (Clark & Serovich, 1997). In addition, GLB clinicians also may be set apart from their heterosexual colleagues in a variety of ways. Gay therapists who choose to identify themselves as gay, lesbian, or bisexual often run the risk of being labeled as a "GLB therapist" and then are held responsible for handling all the GLB cases in the agencies and programs in which they work. Many feel that if they choose to avoid discussion about sexual orientation or choose not to disclose their orientation, they may be labeled homophobic, which augments existing worries about internalized homophobia. They also may worry that the GLB label will negatively influence future job prospects. Many GLB therapists feel they may have a "lowered status" in their programs and agencies due to the stigma attached to their sexual orientation (Long, 1996). Finally, GLB clinicians often carry the standard for work on sexual orientation issues and often are a majority of participants in workshops, seminars, and courses dealing with sexual orientation. They also are the authors of most of the relevant body of literature (Markowitz, 1991).

Most gay communities are small and have limited venues for social interactions. About half (46%) of all GLB therapists responding to a survey expressed concern about boundaries and social encounters (Gartrell, 1994). Often therapists experience greater likelihood of possible dual role relationships because of this. Gartrell (1994) discusses some of the difficulties lesbian therapists experience in maintaining boundaries with lesbian clients who live in the same community. Moreover, 13% of the reports of therapist sexual abuse involve lesbian therapists and female clients. Clearly, peer consultation and supervision are crucial to minimize the impact of dual roles.

One of the most common questions GLB therapists ask is how and when they should disclose their sexual orientation. Self-disclosure in any form is important to the therapeutic process. Disclosure about sexual orientation issues can be particularly beneficial especially when it enables the client the opportunity to explore his or her own identity (Gartrell, 1994). The ability to use personal experience in discussing long-term relationships can be critical, and many GLB therapists have much personal experience to offer clients of any orientation. Therapists' self-disclosure also can help create an atmosphere of safety for clients to explore their own feelings. At minimum, all therapists—GLB or not—must be able to normalize how confusing coming out is, and be able to use personal stories to point out the insidious effects of stereotyping that impact our reactions to homosexuality (Dahlheimer & Feigal, 1991).

However, careful consideration should be given to how a client could benefit from the therapist's disclosure of his or her own sexual orientation and experiences. Such sharing must not be for the therapist's own self-interest. In addition, by determining in advance when to disclose, the therapist can be free of worry about when and how it might come up (Gartrell, 1994; Siegel & Walker, 1996).

GLB SUPERVISION

GLB supervisors can be very helpful to GLB supervisees: They already are familiar with what it is like to be a GLB therapist. However, all supervisors—GLB or not—have the responsibility to monitor the presence of homonegativity in therapy and supervision. In a landmark article on GLB supervision, Long (1996) points out that supervisors must engage in some form of self-examination about their own heterosexism before working with supervisees on the issues. In addition, supervisors should carefully scrutinize the educational environment they create for students and supervisees to disclose and explore sexual orientation issues. Stereotypes can be present in therapy, class discussions, and supervision. Accordingly, instructors and supervisors are encouraged to monitor their use of stereotypic terms or references in these settings. Long suggests the use of video-tapes, role plays, and panels of GLB therapists to help educate students and supervisees.

Is there one model of supervision that would be more beneficial in working with GLB supervisees or in exploring sexual orientation? Probably not. As Haley points out, "A supervisor who uses a single method of teaching for all trainees will produce therapists who follow a method with all clients and do not adapt therapy to each one" (Haley, 1988, p. 362). The issues of differentiation and isomorphism are what are important.

Differentiation

When ambiguity about sexuality is exposed, it is typically ignored or denied because of the discomfort involved. A discussion about sexual orientation represents a potential threat to the certainty about orientation that most heterosexuals (and some homosexuals) find comforting and secure (Russell & Greenhouse, 1997). Discussion of sexual orientation issues requires not only a certain level of comfort with the issue but a more highly differentiated sense of self to understand it.

The supervisor always must be aware of the significant role differentiation plays in supervision and therapy. The process of differentiation is continual. One never stops learning about oneself, and we continually learn from others. It is helpful to keep in mind that the instructor has as much to learn as the learner (Papero, 1988). When the supervisor is less differentiated than the therapist, or the therapist less differentiated than the client, with regard to sexual orientation, difficulties arise and the progress of therapy is limited. When homonegativity is not specifically addressed in clinical relationships, it operates as a "covert process" and has various negative impacts at multiple levels (Russell & Greenhouse, 1997). Of course supervisors can't force someone to learn something he or she is not ready to learn or understand. The supervisor must be able to understand and assess "readiness" in supervisees to learn (Liddle, 1988).

Isomorphism

The concept of isomorphism comes from general systems theory. Although White and Russell (1997) distinguish four facets to the use of this term, two are very pertinent to GLB supervision. Isomorphism may refer to a "parallel process" wherein patterns that occur in the therapeutic relationship occur in the supervisory relationship and vice versa. Isomorphism can be used to intervene. Supervisors should pay close attention to the role isomorphism plays because they "are not passive observers of pattern replication, but intervenors and intentional shapers of the misdirected sequences they perceive, participate in and co-create" (Liddle, 1988,

p. 155). When homonegativity exists at any level of the therapeutic system, it may be replicated at other levels. When it is attended to at one level of the system, it will be attended to at other levels. It is important to understand the impact which the mode of therapy, the supervisory and educational settings, and the various resources available to therapists have on clients. Not only the theoretical orientations of therapists but also the policies and beliefs of staff and administrators can play a role in this process (White & Russell, 1997).

HOW TO BE HELPFUL WITHOUT BEING GLB

In addition to being supportive and affirming, heterosexual therapists and supervisors can offer insight into sexual orientation from their own perspective. Unfortunately, some straight therapists often tread lightly around gay issues in order to avoid being wrong or accused of being homophobic (Markowitz, 1991). GLB therapists have had to confront their own fears and stereotypes in the coming out process. It may be helpful for straight therapists to do the same kind of self-examination to help them understand their own sexual orientation while exploring homonegativity. Because the exploration of sexual orientation can be threatening, and some GLB issues may be unfamiliar to straight therapists, straight therapists may consider doing co-therapy with a GLB therapist. They also may consider obtaining consultation or supervision by a GLB supervisor or colleague. All therapists are encouraged to read continually—the professional literature, to be sure, but also popular gay literature that portrays GLB people (Dahlheimer & Feigal, 1991). In addition, any person, gay or straight, can benefit from participating in an affirmative activity such as a gay pride parade or rally.

CONCLUSION

Supervisors are ultimately responsible for facilitating the development of a safe and affirming environment in which supervisees can explore critical issues that impact their work with clients (see Emerson, Chapter 1). In this safe setting, the supervisor needs to help all supervisees understand their own sexual orientations and challenge any homonegativity. It is particularly important, though, for GLB supervisees to be able to integrate their gay, lesbian, or bisexual selves with their professional identities (Russell & Greenhouse, 1997). Moreover, if supervisors want their supervisees to exhibit confidence and competence when working with GLB individuals, they must model healthy respect, acceptance, and genuine interest in understanding this unique population.

Developing research and curriculum on gay, lesbian, and bisexual issues cannot remain the responsibility of GLB persons. It should be the responsibility of everyone involved in family therapy and the mental health field (Herek et al., 1991). The academic community must make concerted efforts to include information about gay, lesbian, and bisexual perspectives in coursework and in text materials. Instructors should actively seek texts that present affirmative views of this population and acknowledge publishers who produce them (Herek et al., 1991). As far as "don't ask, don't tell," we should be concerned about what the greater message may be: What we are saying by focusing on what is not being said by omission, neglect, or neutrality (Green, 1996).

REFERENCES

CLARK, W. M., & SEROVICH, J. M. (1997). Twenty years and still in the dark? Content analysis of articles pertaining to gay, lesbian, and bisexual issues in marriage and family therapy journals. *Journal of Marital and Family Therapy, 23,* 239–253.

DAHLHEIMER, D., & FEIGAL, J. (1991). Bridging the gap. *Family Therapy Networker, 15,* 44–53.

D'AUGELLI, A. R. (1994). Lesbian and gay male development: Steps toward an analysis of lesbians' and gay men's lives. In B. Greene & G. M. Herek (Eds.), *Lesbian and gay psychology: Theory, research, and clinical applications* (Vol.1) (pp. 118–132). Thousand Oaks, CA: Sage Publications.

GARTRELL, N. K. (1994). Boundaries in lesbian therapist-client relationships. In B. Greene & G. M. Herek (Eds.), *Lesbian and gay psychology: Theory, research, and clinical applications* (Vol. 1) (pp. 98–117). Thousand Oaks, CA: Sage Publications.

GREEN, R. J. (1996). Why ask, why tell? Teaching and learning about lesbians and gays in family therapy. *Family Process, 35,* 389–400.

GREEN, S. K., & BOBELE, M. (1994). Family therapists' response to AIDS: An examination of attitudes, knowledge, and contact. *Journal of Marital and Family Therapy, 20,* 349–367.

GREENE, B. (1994). Lesbian and gay sexual orientations: Implications for clinical training, practice, and research. In B. Greene & G. M. Herek (Eds.), *Lesbian and gay psychology: Theory, research, and clinical applications* (Vol. 1) (pp. 1–24). Thousand Oaks, CA: Sage Publications.

HALEY, J. (1988). Reflections on supervision. In H. A. Liddle, D. C. Breunlin, & R. C. Schwartz (Eds.), *Handbook of family therapy training and supervision* (pp. 358–367). New York: Guilford Press.

HEREK, G. M. (1984). Beyond "homophobia": A social psychological perspective on attitudes toward lesbians and gay men. *Journal of Homosexuality, 10,* 1–21.

HEREK, G. M. (1994). Assessing heterosexuals' attitudes toward lesbians and gay men. In B. Greene & G. M. Herek (Eds.), *Lesbian and gay psychology: Theory, research, and clinical applications* (Vol. 1) (pp. 206–228). Thousand Oaks, CA: Sage Publications.

HEREK, G. M., KIMMEL, D. C., AMARO, H., & MELTON, G. B. (1991). Avoiding heterosexist bias in psychological research. *American Psychologist, 46,* 957–963.

KITE, M. E. (1994). When perceptions meet reality: Individual differences in reactions to lesbians and gay men. In B. Greene & G. M. Herek (Eds.), *Lesbian and gay psychology: Theory, research, and clinical applications* (Vol. 1) (pp. 25–53). Thousand Oaks, CA: Sage Publications.

LAIRD, J., & GREEN, R. J. (1996). Lesbians and gays in couples and families Introduction. In J. Laird and R. J. Green (Eds.), *Lesbians and gays in couples and families: A handbook for therapists* (pp. 1–12). San Francisco: Jossey-Bass.

LIDDLE, H. A. (1988). Systemic supervision: Conceptual overlays and pragmatic guidelines. In H. A. Liddle, D. C. Breunlin, & R. C. Schwartz (Eds.), *Handbook of family therapy training and supervision* (pp. 153–171). New York: Guilford Press.

LONG, J. K. (1996). Working with lesbians, gays, and bisexuals: Addressing heterosexism in supervision. *Family Process, 35,* 377–388.

MARKOWITZ, L. M. (1991). Homosexuality: Are we still in the dark? *The Family Therapy Networker, 15* (1), 26–35.

MONEY, J., & ERHARDT, A. (1972). *Man and woman, boy and girl: Differentiation and dimorphism of gender identity from conception to maturity.* Baltimore: Johns Hopkins University Press.

PAPERO, D. V. (1988). Training in Bowen theory. In H. A. Liddle, D. C. Breunlin, & R. C. Schwartz (Eds.), *Handbook of family therapy training and supervision* (pp. 62–77). New York: Guilford Press.

PATTERSON, J. (1994). Children of the lesbian baby boom: Behavioral adjustment, self-concepts, and sex role identity. In B. Greene & G. M. Herek (Eds.), *Lesbian and gay psychology: Theory, research, and clinical applications* (Vol. 1) (pp. 156–175). Thousand Oaks, CA: Sage Publications.

RUSSELL, G. M., & GREENHOUSE, E. M. (1997). Homophobia in the supervisory relationship: An invisible intruder. *Psychoanalytic Review, 84,* 27–42.

SHIDLO, A. (1994). Internalized homophobia: Conceptual and empirical issues in measurement. In B. Greene & G. M. Herek (Eds.), *Lesbian and gay psychology: Theory, research, and clinical applications* (Vol. 1) (pp. 176–205). Thousand Oaks, CA: Sage Publications.

SIEGEL, S., & WALKER, G. (1996). Connections: Conversations between a gay therapist and a straight therapist. In J. Laird and R. J. Green (Eds.), *Lesbians and gays in couples and families: A handbook for therapists* (pp. 28–68). San Francisco: Jossey-Bass.

WHITE, M. B., & RUSSELL, C. S. (1997). Examining the multifaceted notion of isomorphism in marriage and family therapy supervision: A quest for conceptual clarity. *Journal of Marital and Family Therapy, 23,* 315–333.

CHAPTER 16

A Lesson in Healing
A Broken Femur and
Negative Stereotyping

ESTHER E. ONAGA

Research in social psychology shows that a person's physical appearance influences a viewer's perception about the individual. This story is an example of how erroneous initial perceptions led to a parent's distress and gives implications for educational programs that are dedicated to teaching professionals in human services. It is also a story about the roles of professionals and friends in the healing processes from two injuries—a broken femur and negative stereotyping.

It started as a rather ordinary bleak winter day, with the temperature in the high 20s. The ground was snow covered with patches of ice. My four-year-old son, Scott, dressed in snow pants and a coat, was playing on the swing set—his favorite pastime. Scott's facial expression while he swung was that of pure ecstasy. He seemed to be in a world of his own, taking a break from a world in which he was a bit different. He has autism.

I was taking a reading break after dinner when two neighborhood youths came to the door to report that Scott was crying. He was not able to stand so I carried him into the house trailed by the neighborhood boys and my daughter. I asked them to get Linda, a pediatrics nurse, living two doors down the street.

Scott had limited language and could not explain what had happened. Moreover, I could not get his attention to respond to me as his crying continued. However, I knew that he must be in great pain for he was not a child who easily complained of pain. I recall once when he came back from the schoolyard with his foot bleeding from stepping on a piece of glass. His reaction was one of an observer. He reported to me that his foot was bleeding with no tears or expression of pain. It was as if he was looking at someone else's injury. He did not seem to connect the injury to himself. Therefore, because his current behavior was such a contrast to what I was used to, I became more distressed about what could be causing this reaction. His cries were not his common exclamations of frustration, disappointment, or anger. He was inconsolable, his lips had turned black, and his leg was limp. Moving him caused him to scream louder.

Linda, the pediatrics nurse, and I hypothesized that Scott had broken his leg. We took him to the hospital, where Linda quickly escorted us into the emergency room. The pediatrician on call immediately sent us down to the X-ray division where we learned that our hunches were correct. Scott indeed had fractured his left femur, the large leg or thigh bone which, ironically, is one of the hardest bones to break. The break was a bad one; the break was angled and the bones were crossed. It was clear that they needed to straighten the broken bone into a straight line as part of the healing process.

I asked Linda who was the best orthopedic surgeon in town. She gave me two names. I knew that Scott's father would want the best as he had an unfortunate experience with a misdiagnosis that led to his having a permanent condition requiring multiple treatments for his hip. By a stroke of luck, one of the surgeons she recommended was in the hospital at the time. They paged him, and he soon appeared and introduced himself. A pleasant man of casual demeanor, he tried to start a conversation with Scott. Anyone who did not know of Scott's condition would assume that he was a child without disabilities. He is quite a handsome boy who at the initial interaction would appear to be aware of his surroundings. Thus it was not a surprise that the doctor approached him as if Scott were a typical four-year-old. I shared that Scott had a language delay and probably could not respond to his questions. He responded, "I know all about that." "Sure," I thought, "another smug, arrogant surgeon who knows everything." He then went further and shared that he had a son, older than Scott, with a similar condition. This man had a kind and gentle manner with Scott and I was reassured that he had the sensitivity to deal with him. Besides, from Linda's description of his reputation among the health professionals, this surgeon was one of the best that we could have to help Scott. He explained that this injury would not have long-term effects on Scott's mobility. The bad news, however, was that he needed to be in traction and in the hospital for 3 weeks. After having a minor surgery to insert pins into his left knee, Scott's leg would be weighted. By the pulling of the weights, his fractured femur would be straightened. Intermittently, the radiologist would be taking X rays to monitor the healing process. As there was no alternative, I accepted it. However, I was worried about how Scott would handle 3 weeks of hospitalization!

Transitions into new situations were difficult for Scott and fear was his common reaction to new events. I would use the words "OK" or "safe" to reassure him that he would be fine. Many times these words helped calm him. Other times, he wanted to be squeezed or held tightly. He would say "hug." I suppose this is no different from children without disabilities. Scott seemed to feel comfort and a sense of safety with my physical presence and my talking to him. I could not hug him in his condition so I held his hand and squeezed it. In any case, I knew that I would be needed to stay with Scott to help him make the transition into this new, strange environment. Linda arranged for a babysitter to take care of my daughter, and I called Scott's father.

Scott wanted me close to him so I moved a chair next to his hospital bed. Of course, he wanted me to be on the bed with him, but the rules were that the hospital bed's rails needed to be raised. He looked like a caged, frightened boy. Fortunately, Scott was able to sleep after a while and I managed to get some sleep on a reclining chair.

Hospitals are the last places for anyone who wants to rest. Shift changes, monitoring of vital signs, lights turning on and off, and buzzers going off do not create a restful environment. The next morning was time for the surgery to insert the pins.

All went well. I decided to wait around just in case I was needed. I got some coffee and tried to meditate. Caffeine and meditation do not go together but, here in the pediatrics wing, that was about all I could do. Scott returned from surgery in a bed equipped for traction with weights. He was a bit groggy but he seemed all right. A nurse gave me instructions on how to clean the area around the newly inserted pins on his knee. This procedure was to be done several times a day to ensure cleanliness. I was prepared to have him throw an outrageous fit, but he did not. Rather, he simply said, "Cover." He wanted his injured leg to be covered. I could not fault him for that. The traction equipment looked like some medieval contraption for torture. His leg hung in midair with ropes linked to weights. He looked anything but normal. We devised a support for a blanket to cover his injured leg. This seemed to calm him.

After having some rest and checking in at the office, I headed back to the hospital to do the night coverage. I realized that the reclining chair would become a very familiar bed for the next 3 weeks. Toward midnight, my neighbor, a resident at the hospital came over to greet us and announced that she was the resident in charge. What a pleasant surprise! She knew Scott and knew about his language delay. She gave me more information about broken femurs and the need for traction, again reassuring me that this injury would not have a long-term effect on Scott's mobility. Although she was busy, she managed to check in with us a few times when she was there. I looked forward to her brief visits.

Word went out that Scott had a broken femur. Neighbors, friends, and his teachers came to see him. Some brought him candy, others brought toys. Nevertheless, it was clear that Scott needed 24-hour supervision in the hospital. This need became even clearer when a nurse grabbed a little cup of orange liquid set on his hospital tray and tried to give it to him as medicine. It was shampoo. Scott needed another adult staying with him not just for a few days but throughout his hospital stay. This meant having a schedule of coverage 24 hours a day. Fortunately, we received help from friends, neighbors, and colleagues. Our babysitter and her family came at various times to relieve me during the day. The young boys in the neighborhood came to help. I appreciated having people extend their support to us when we were in need.

In spite of all the help, I began experiencing that phenomena common among new parents—sleep deprivation. My work at the office needed attention. Although colleagues at work understood my dilemma, it still was difficult to drop all of the responsibilities. I managed to catch up on sleep whenever I had someone to cover for me at the hospital. Since Scott's dad is a pilot, he was able to help when he was not flying, but often he was gone. Moreover, night coverage was hard for him because a bad back was exacerbated by the hospital sleeping conditions. After a week of running back and forth from hospital to home and work, I just wanted to stop the world and take a long nap. Couldn't there be a pause button to temporarily suspend all activities in the world?

Unlike me, Scott appeared to have adapted to this new setting. Aside from not liking hospital food and having the tissue around the pins in his knee cleaned, Scott was fine. His father and I helped him adapt to the strange environment of the hospital by bringing food from home for him. Scott liked tacos without any lettuce and rice balls wrapped in nori, a type of seaweed that is used to make sushi. He didn't seem to mind missing his routine of riding the bus to his preprimary program and being away from home. He seemed fairly content with having the television for his cartoons and a Magna Doodle for his drawing. Two play therapists took him into the playroom for an hour each day for activities such as making bubbles, dropping marbles, moving beads on a stand, and reading to him. They even made a cast around the leg of his sister's Ken doll to show him how a leg injury would be treated. They let him watch how the cast was put on and gave him the doll. I am not sure how much he understood that soon he too would be in a similar cast.

Suddenly this relatively agreeable scene shattered. I was having my 3-hour morning nap when the phone rang. My babysitter had been filling in for me at the hospital and she was greatly agitated. There had been a new resident assigned to my son's case and he had had a lot to say to my babysitter. First, the resident said that I was to stop bringing brown rice wrapped in seaweed because my son was not getting much nutrition from that food. He likened such a diet to feeding him sweet rolls. He also said that all the candy on his bed table should be removed. He surmised that Scott was having too much candy and that was what led to his not wanting hospital food. He noticed that Scott had a problem with speech so he had put in a request for a speech therapist to do an evaluation on him. He also wanted a nutritionist to meet with me to educate me about nutrition. Being half awake, I was not sure I was hearing correctly. By the time she repeated all of the instructions again, I was fully awake, enraged, and distraught. I asked her why he was telling her all of this and not me. Her response was, "I think he thinks you do not speak English well because he asked that I pass his concerns and information to you."

I could not go back to my nap so I decided to call on Scott's pediatrician for assistance. I was able to leave a message for him to call, and remarkably, I got a quick response. I shared what the babysitter had said and asked if he could have the resident removed as Scott's doctor. If that were not possible, my plans were to have Scott removed from the hospital in his traction bed. The pediatrician took notes and asked me to let him investigate.

Retrospectively, I guess I was being a bit unreasonable without having talked to the resident. However, I realized that I was in a land where I was a minority and where brown rice and seaweed were not common food items on dinner tables. "This would never have happened in Hawaii," I thought to myself. "But isn't this 1984? And isn't this a sophisticated town? After all, we have two medical schools!" I had a lot of questions, and a lot of anger about why this even happened.

I was too agitated to sleep so I decided to catch up with work at the office. I was too shocked at the ignorance of the resident to fully concentrate on my work. All I could think about was how stupid, how arrogant, and how disrespectful he was, and how he did not talk with me about his concerns. Obviously the resident had been making mental notes about Scott and me for a while. It was not a single incident that led him to give my babysitter this message to pass on to me. He must have been observing and judging for a while before sharing his thoughts. I was taking all of this quite personally, and I became preoccupied with this incident.

The pediatrician spent time the next day talking with the nursing staff and the resident. He instructed me to talk with the resident because there obviously was a misunderstanding. When I did talk with the resident he explained that he only wanted to help Scott. He did not know that I realized that Scott had a disability. Moreover, he wanted to make sure that Scott had good nutrition. Therefore he had asked the dietitian to come to see me about food that could be adapted to meet Scott's preferences. He also asked the hospital staff to monitor all of the food that Scott ate over the course of a week. He was going to make sure that Scott ate nutritious hospital food. When I told him that I would continue to bring food to Scott—such as tacos and brown rice balls—he did not like that because he thought that such food would decrease Scott's appetite for the "more nutritious" hospital food.

Unhappily, what the resident did not know is that one of the characteristics of people with autism is their sensitivity to and extraordinary need for routine and familiar food. For example, I knew that tacos of any type would not do. Scott would tell me if there was even a speck of lettuce in his taco. Accordingly, up to this point my approach had been to simply acknowledge his discovery of the speck of lettuce, remove the offending particle, and hand him back the taco. If I were to say, "You must eat the taco with the lettuce," Scott would dig in his heels and begin his loud protest about eating the speck of lettuce. These protests then would escalate into a scene I would not wish anyone to experience. Knowing Scott's typical reaction to change, I knew that however well intentioned this resident was, he did not have a clue about Scott and autism. I was rather amazed at how fervently he approached this situation as the expert. His need to have control over the food now seemed to me almost an obsession.

I realized how I, too, had become obsessed with making my point about the brown rice and seaweed. I assured him that having a nutritionist come to see me about nutritious food was unnecessary as I fully understood the different food groups and the necessity for having balanced foods in one's diet. I also wanted him to know that although brown rice and seaweed were not common to mid-America, they too had nutritional qualities and value beyond the "sweet rolls" to which he had likened them. I told him that brown rice was a major part of the macrobiotic diet that has been recommended for people with a variety of ailments such as heart disorder. (Macrobiotics is a diet involving balancing the yin and yang of foods to improve physical, mental, and emotional health.) I also informed him that the bran coating on this whole grain rice is a weapon against cholesterol. Brown rice, unlike white rice, has more protein, phosphorus, riboflavin, vitamin E and calcium. (I wish we had known a little more about antioxidants at that time because I could have added that also in praise of brown rice!)

Wisely, the resident let me talk, so I went on to explain the value of nori. "Now seaweed, although a strange food for most midwesterners, should be respected for its nutritional qualities." I shared that besides being fat-free, seaweed is one of the richest sources for essential minerals. Nori has calcium and phosphorous, and is especially high in iron, iodine and magnesium. I suggested that he try some. I think I said that more in the spirit of an "I dare you to do it" attitude than one of sincerely trying to expand his level of awareness. In return, I was rather amazed at his tenacity.

Although he acknowledged that these foods might have nutritional qualities, he still wanted to see Scott's intake of food from the records kept by the dietitian on what was eaten at each meal. He said I could continue to bring in these foods, but he would be monitoring the progress of Scott's eating. If he did not have a balanced diet, then he would have to ask me to stop. I was getting annoyed at this level of discussion and just wanted it ended. After all, we were not even dealing with a child who had a condition where strict dietary requirements would be necessary for recovery. I resigned myself to accept his final statement. I thought that, maybe, we would be out of the hospital before I had to deal with this man again.

True to the resident's wishes the dietitian reliably recorded what was eaten and what was left on the tray. I continued to bring in food. The candy disappeared but Scott did not mind. It was his regular visitors who snacked on the candy, who wondered what had happened to it. I just told them, "Whatever makes the resident happy. He thinks Scott is a candy addict." (This is far from the truth.) I thought it was simplest to take the candy away so the resident would feel I was respecting his wishes. But I contemplated how unfortunate it was that people had to "play the game" with the powers of medical authority, and what a shame it was to pay them handsomely for their idiocy.

One of the concerns that I began to have was that the nursing staff, although polite and good to Scott and me, might be equally uninformed about the nutritional qualities of the food that I had been having Scott eat. I thought I would make some mini rice balls for them to try and have some of them wrapped with nori. (I know that for the unaccustomed consumer, nori may taste a bit fishy.) I made a platter and passed it among the nursing staff. Some of them were adventurous and tried the nori. I was pleased that they were open to the experience. However, I noticed that one of the shift supervisors was very distant with me and also noticed how protective she was of the resident. I gathered that she may have informed him of her concerns about my behavior and Scott's diet.

I guess I'll never know what precipitated such an outrageous conclusion about who I was or how Scott's nutrition was in jeopardy. I only hope that the next time the resident sees an Asian face he will not assume that English would not be spoken or understood or that she or he is uninformed about nutrition.

This incident triggered memories of other incidents in Michigan. As an American citizen living in Hawaii throughout my elementary and secondary school years, I was accustomed to being among a large number of Asians. Arriving in a midwestern town of few Asian Americans was a new experience. First of all, I did not realize people would think of me as a foreigner. Comments such as "You speak good English" too often were directed to me. I also remember arguing with a postal worker that Hawaii was a state and that the postage rate should not be an overseas rate. How odd that a United States postal service person would not recognize Hawaii as a part of the United States! Having biracial children also has been an experience. On one or two occasions I was mistaken as their babysitter and not their mother. Both children have light skin and have Caucasian features. I, on the other hand, have a darker complexion and Asian and Pacific Islander features.

Given these prior experiences, I should not have been so outraged by the resident's conclusions. We live in two worlds: one world based on the individual's perception of self, and the other world based on others' perceptions of who you are. When there are wide differences in perceptions between these two worlds, conflict and injury can result. How then can these two worlds become closer to one world as people learn to be open and not quick to make judgments about others who are different? Or how can we better work through these differences?

WHAT COULD WE HAVE DONE?

Thinking back on how things could have been done differently, I have constructed a number of scenarios that might have resulted in a better solution. First of all, I could have been proactive and made a point of introducing myself to the new resident. Certainly, after having one conversation with me he would have known that I could speak English. Second, the resident could have talked to me about his concern over Scott's language delay. I was not aware that the hospital records did not show that he had problems with both receptive and expressive communication. If this had occurred, the referral to a speech therapist would not have been necessary. However, the biggest challenge was the issue of food. I am not sure what would have convinced the resident that the candy on the bed table was there for days, not because I was replenishing the larder, but because Scott was not eating it. Perhaps we could have done a little study, counting the number of pieces and documenting who consumed them. But that seems more appropriate for a field research study than for developing a treatment environment supportive of healing the femur of a child. Candy aside, a conversation could have taken place to discuss how Scott could be provided the best foods. From such a discussion, I, as a parent would learn that hospital dietitians are able and willing to accommodate a patient's food choices and needs. I also would feel that the resident was more of an ally and not an adversary. This type of approach would have helped me be less resentful about documenting Scott's eating habits. As always, in hindsight, many other approaches could have been taken to avoid this unfortunate situation.

The last week of Scott's stay in the hospital was rather uneventful. Prior to leaving, Scott was given a full body cast. He did remarkably well in adapting to his new armor. We managed to keep on an even keel with the resident. He seemed to be satisfied that Scott was having a balanced diet. I was not too motivated to speak with him as I felt that little would be accomplished by continued dialogue. The nursing staff was helpful, and the school had made accommodations for Scott to return to the classroom in his body cast and wheelchair. The physical therapist paid a visit to teach us how to care for him. Being at home again was divine. Neighbors came to visit, and by then, it was early spring and we could take Scott on neighborhood outings in his wheelchair. Even with his body cast, Scott began to move himself around the house. He was eager to be mobile again.

POSTSCRIPT

Eight years later, Scott is in middle school. He is a lean, tall boy who continues to be blessed with good looks. His left leg remains healed. The only physical reminder of the injury is two dimples on his left knee where the pins were inserted for the traction. Although Scott does not suffer any physical effects from the injury, he continues to have bad memories about the incident. A few years ago we were viewing old videos and came across the tape covering different times during his recovery. Some of the footage on the video shows the neighborhood kids taking him for a ride around the block on his wheelchair. His body cast left him sitting in an awkward position, but the footage shows him gleefully playing with them. When shown the video, Scott demanded that it be stopped. He did not want to watch it. He repeated over and over again, "Don't you ever show me this again. Is that clear?" Today that videotape is marked "Dangerous, Do Not Show It to Scott."

Scott's attractiveness continues to be an asset for him as people generally seem to feel he is quite approachable. A few years ago his sister routinely walked him home from his elementary school. One day, she reported "Mom, do you know he is popular?" I gathered that the students in his school were fond of him, but I was less prepared to hear his sister make such a statement. His language has improved, but his speech is still much like that of a five- or six-year-old. His body is that of a budding teen, and he is showing innocent expressions of interest in girls. He is joyous and appreciates living in the moment. How I envy him for being able to enjoy the moment and seeing basic truths of life so clearly! Many peers, teachers, and friends say, "He is so funny!" That funny part of him is his ability to blurt out basic truths that none of us would dare speak. I think it reminds us about how we too once were innocent and how socialization and education have transformed that innocence into politically correct and socially correct language and behavior.

Currently, I am able to use the experience to teach students across the disciplines about diversity. For students majoring in the helping professions, I have included learning activities to help them not to judge others too quickly, learn respectful behaviors when working with others who are different, and learn that individuals and families have strengths that can be used to create solutions to challenges they are facing. Students who are not focused on the helping professions also need to learn about individual differences and the need to avoid drawing conclusions about people without knowing them. I challenge students to think critically, develop observational skills, and develop skills to obtain information to answer questions they may have. For all students, I continue to look for methods to increase self-awareness in the arena of diversity, to provide skills on how to work with people who are different from you, and how to communicate. I teach the fallacy of making assumptions about people based on their physical characteristics.

My anger, shock, and outrage over the incident eight years ago has been replaced with thoughts about how to use this experience in a more constructive manner. Fortunately, I have the opportunity to contribute to the education of young professionals in human services through my teaching. I have also had time to reflect on how differences can be approached. For instance, it is so easy to take the stance that you are right, and the other person needs to be the one who changes. I believe that the resident and I both were of that opinion. In such a situation, success in learning on either side is diminished. On thinking about the resident's attitude, my offer to him to have some rice and seaweed was probably an ineffective approach as I believe he may have felt that I was challenging his authority rather than increasing his awareness. Scott's health was not jeopardized by the resident's mistaken perceptions. Rather this incident was a lesson for me about the need to educate professionals about not jumping to conclusions too quickly.

CHAPTER 17

Training in Context
An Ecosystemic Model

JULIE BROWNELL
DEBORAH KLOOSTERMAN
PATRICIA B. KOCHKA
JUDITH VANDERWAL

This chapter presents a model of supervision based on an integrative ecosystemic theoretical approach. Integrative therapy is defined as tailoring therapeutic content through the use of more than one approach to meet the needs of the client system. Literature linking an integrative theory of family change to a supervisory model is needed (Pitta, 1996). We believe the ecosystemic framework supports such a linkage between supervision and family change. An understanding of the ecosystemic framework is vital to comprehension of this supervisory model. This framework has served the social sciences well by providing a foundation for studying family systems holistically. Its basic tenets may be familiar to students, clinicians, and researchers who have been trained in family systems. We also believe that parallel process, or isomorphism, operates throughout all the levels of the supervisory system.

THE MODEL

The integrative ecosystemic model is depicted graphically in Figure 1. The model assumes the following:

- A foundation in the culture of therapy.
- Knowledge of human ecosystems (Bronfenbrenner, 1979; Bubolz & Sontag, 1993). An orientation toward identifying and adapting resources to promote intrasystem growth through differentiation (Papero, 1988), behavior change, and insight.
- Responsibilities in diverse roles at all levels of the supervisory system.
- The dynamic and multidirectional nature of growth facilitated by family therapy and supervision.

INTEGRATIVE ECOSYSTEMIC SUPERVISORY SYSTEM
. Isomorphic . Resource Based . Solution Centered .

FIGURE 1. The integrative ecosystemic model

The ecosystemic view is one in which human development is seen as a function of both biological and contextual processes. Outcomes are generated over time through the interactions of biology and environment (Bronfenbrenner, 1979; Ford & Lerner, 1992). Ecosystemic therapists attend to both the environmental (contextual) and biological aspects of human development. Our model encompasses the intrapsychic as well as the physical and physiological components that influence individuals to choose different life paths. In the integrative ecosystemic perspective, the therapist conceptualizes the dynamic process of change as impacting several environmental levels. Recursive and reciprocal effects are expected at other levels. This circular interactional view gives the therapist a broader base for strategizing and intervening at any level of the system.

An ecosystemic framework depicts change at one level effecting change at other levels. It incorporates the following:

- A holistic framework that views the relationship between problems at one level and the constraints operating at another level.

- The view that people are resourceful and can solve problems, but constraints existing at various levels may prevent them from doing so.
- Interventions with only one source of influence (unilevel interventions) are likely to provide short-lived benefits and little change.
- How people organize and communicate and the complementarity of organizational and communicative processes.
- The roles of individuals as they interact across multiple levels, and the circular and reciprocal effect of such interactions.
- A transgenerational view that problems occurring at one level of a system may involve developmental roots extending beyond the current relationship and into previous generations.

THE INTEGRATIVE ECOSYSTEMIC THERAPIST

The ecosystemic framework provides the integrative therapist with an opportunity for creating a holistic treatment plan. The marriage and family therapy program at Michigan State University acquaints beginning therapists with diverse models, providing opportunities to build individualized theoretical foundations. Some therapists focus on one or two models, recognizing a fit that meshes with their personality, experience, and worldview. Others want more diversity and flexibility, viewing change as possible through a number of effective channels: educating, altering perceptions, responding to the change of others, developing insight, releasing constricting emotions, confiding in others, socializing painful experiences, clarifying communications, exercising one's will, lowering anxiety, and resolving grief (Nichols, 1988). There is room for diverse techniques and styles. In our model, therapists embracing this holistic view are defined as integrative ecosystemic therapists.

The integrative ecosystemic therapist must be able to articulate the rationale underlying each of the various interventions or approaches to therapy. Because the danger is always present that therapy may be ineffective because of insufficient knowledge and training in different theoretical approaches, the integrative therapist must be able to defend the relationship between theory and practice. The integrative therapist is both advantaged and disadvantaged by multifarious choice.

THE INTEGRATIVE ECOSYSTEMIC SUPERVISORY SYSTEM

The ecosystemic approach relates not only to therapy, but also to the transactional patterns between individuals in all levels of the supervisory system. Just as the therapist examines multiple levels in relation to his or her client, the supervisory system must also consider multiple levels of inter-action. Effective and appropriate supervision and therapy are rooted in common ground.

The supervisory system is composed of three major subsystems: (1) the supervisor-of-supervision and the supervisor-trainee, (2) the supervisor-trainee and the therapist, and (3) the therapist and the client system. Our model assumes that a goal of supervision is to broaden supervisor-trainees' and therapists' understanding of the relationships between theory and practice.

From an integrative ecosystemic perspective, the supervisory system is dynamic, context specific, and unique (Liddle, 1988). The supervisory system is representative of the culture of therapy. The supervisory system takes a unique form. It is environmentally dependent on factors such as the program, department, college, university, region of the country, season and traditions, as well as the persons of the therapist, clients, supervisor-trainees, and the supervisor-of-supervision. The stage of professional de-velopment of both the therapist and supervisor-trainee will impact the supervisory system (Breunlin, Liddle, & Schwartz, 1988; Liddle, 1988; Taibbi, 1993; Tomm, 1993).

The supervisory system focuses on process and increases awareness of the effects of interpersonal interactions throughout the system. Effective supervision utilizes the same skills as those needed for therapy (Breunlin, Liddle, & Schwartz 1988; Liddle 1988). Joining, active listening, interper-sonal skills, competent interview techniques, and theory-driven interven-tions are as important to effective supervision as they are to therapy (Lid-dle, 1988). Insight into process is also important. Content is adjusted to reflect the changing needs of each level of the supervisory system. Move-ment is made toward growth in the form of differentiation, behavior change, and insight within each subsystem (Storm, 1991).

Isomorphism

Ongoing identification and monitoring of isomorphism is essential to an effective supervisory system (Liddle 1988; Schwartz, Liddle, & Breunlin 1988). Isomorphism affects every level of the supervisory system and has the potential to both support and to undermine all aspects of interpersonal processes. The interconnectedness of these systems facilitates parallel processes. Interactional patterns replicate themselves at every level of the system. These processes serve to underscore the bidirectional nature of su-pervision where interactional information may be experienced from the client level up or the metasupervision level down. When identified, the isomorphic process can serve not only as a diagnostic tool, but also as a means of intervention at all levels of the overlapping hierarchy of systems.

Contextual Interpretations

Each supervisory system and subsystem has factors different from and in common with other supervisory systems. Factors perceived, named, and evaluated within a particular system are determined by contextual interpretations (Falicov 1988; Quinn 1996). For example, the manner in which specific supervisory events and practices are punctuated reflects and affects not only the particular supervisory system, but also the institutional setting in which that system is embedded (Breunlin, Liddle, & Schwartz, 1988). Therefore, contextual interpretations shape the culture of therapy.

The late twentieth century may be characterized as a time of loosening boundaries. It is a time of confusion and controversy regarding the appropriateness of rigidity versus flexibility in particular situations. It is important that, within the legal and ethical constraints of our culture and our professional organizations, we respect the rights of others to believe, behave, and choose for themselves. This is a delicate issue that requires attention in every interpersonal relationship. Sociocultural awareness must be a constant factor in our ongoing professional development if we are to be effective in our roles as professionals (Falicov, 1988). Respect for the uniqueness of perspectives, culture, and personal history of each member of the supervisory system is important (Falicov, 1988).

Supervisor and supervisee bring different experiences, strengths, limitations, perceptions, and beliefs to the relationship (Falicov, 1995). The twentieth century has challenged us with a new awareness of the multiplicity of human viewpoints and behaviors. Each of us has the challenge to behaviorally integrate respect for differences. This is especially important when confronting a strongly held difference of opinion with a peer, a supervisor, a trainee, or a client.

Diversity of Roles

Role diversity is another ecosystemic aspect of the integrative supervisory system. Supervision involves a dialogue through which concepts of therapy and supervision are explored, mediated, tested, and developed within a unique relational context. The primary task of the supervisory system is to facilitate the growth of the family members, the therapist, and the supervisor-in-training, while simultaneously shaping the growth of the profession. Flexibility and diversity are supported in a hierarchical manner within the system. The ability to reflect on one's diverse roles within the system is an advantage for all participants.

The supervisor-of-supervision and supervisor-in-training roles include that of coach, educator, provider of resources, safety net, support person, stimulator, modeler of communication and systemic thinking, assessor, and contractor between all system levels. The dynamic and isomorphic patterns within levels of the supervisory system are so powerful that they often are mirrored between the supervisor-in-training, the therapist, and the clients. Thus the supervisor-of-supervision, supervisor-in-training, therapist, and clients become recipients, in some manner, of the modeling and education that takes place at any level of the system, though it may originate at the upper hierarchical levels. If we approach supervision with the desire simply to impart information to our supervisor-in-training, we are missing an important element, the recursive effect of gaining more knowledge in our own diverse roles. The growth process is indeed a circular one.

Hierarchy within Systems

Supervisory systems must be hierarchical to be effective, but the interactions can be isomorphic. Some aspects of therapy may be perceived as "doing supervision" with clients (Friedman, 1991, p. 1). Processes are similar at each level of the system (Breunlin, Liddle, & Schwartz, 1988) and, at the same time, each subsystem has its own well-defined boundaries. For example, the therapist (not the supervisor-in-training, or supervisor-of-supervision) treats the client. "To guard against boundary violations, communication should follow levels of the training system; the supervisor-of-supervision communicating with the supervisor-in-training, the supervisor-in-training with the therapist, and the therapist with the family" (Schwartz, Liddle, & Breunlin, 1988, p. 219).

A major focus of supervision is on the supervisor-in-training's professional development. "The supervisory experience is one that enables a supervisee to explore his or her treatment processes, recognize and deal with personal limitations, and expand strengths and understandings of individual and family interactions" (Pitta, 1996, p. 19). Boundaries between personal and professional issues in supervision are somewhat blurred in the sense that personalities and values influence and interact with professional choices and actions (Aponte, 1994; Papero, 1988; Storm, 1991; Taibbi, 1993; Tomm, 1993).

Power is inherent in hierarchical relationships. Clients may see their therapists as experts, and a supervisor-in-training may see the supervisor-of-supervision as an expert. This belief that the therapist or the supervisor possesses high levels of competency and knowledge gives the therapist or supervisor power in the relationship. With this power comes responsibility. As therapists and as supervisors of therapists, we have the responsibility to be personally healthy, knowledgeable, and ethical. We must ensure that our powerful positions do not result in harm or perversion in the therapeutic relationship. In a well-functioning supervisory relationship, both therapist and supervisor feel safe, valued, respected, and challenged to grow professionally and personally (Liddle, 1988; Roberts, 1992). Such a relationship is strength-based. Supervisory structure and dialogue are contextually relevant, systems-oriented, and congruent with meeting the needs of the supervisee, the client system treated by the supervisee, and the professional obligations of the supervisory role (White & Russell, 1995). Mutually accepted supervisory goals are chosen and their achievement is facilitated.

Responsibilities within Roles

It is important for all members of the supervisory system to be informed of their role responsibilities. Therefore, open communication between all levels is necessary for optimal functioning within this system. The role of supervisor-of-supervision includes carrying out the administrative responsibilities (Nichols, 1988). The structure of supervision is hierarchical in areas in which ethical, institutional, or legal requirements have precedence (Breunlin, Liddle, & Schwartz, 1988). Formal (contractual) patterns of interaction between supervisor-of-supervision and supervisor-in-training include time, length, and frequency of meeting, persons present, the completion of paperwork requirements, goal-setting, and evaluative procedures. Goals and objectives for supervision are set early in the supervisory relationship, during the joining process, and are reviewed periodically. Sequencing of supervisory content is congruent to theory, perceived needs and developmental stage of the supervisee, relatively flexible, and evolved within an emotionally and intellectually supportive context (Liddle, 1988; Taibbi, 1993). A task of supervision is to assess the therapist's strengths and limitations, as well as the needs and resources of the therapist-client subsystems.

Regardless of the developmental level of the supervisee or the supervisor, clinical supervision demands four things of the supervisor: consistency, accessibility, flexibility, and accountability. Consistency demands that the supervisee be met with regularly, and that the supervisor be prepared to listen, question, and console if necessary. Accessibility means that the supervisor is available to intervene, advise with "risky" clients, and identify potential ethical issues. Flexibility indicates responsiveness to changing needs and perceptions within the supervisory system. Accountability involves the willingness to follow-through on assurances that have been made to the supervisee. The accountable supervisor stays alert, respects trainee confidentiality, maintains his or her own learning and development, models professional behavior and, as a gatekeeper for the profession, evaluates professional competence.

CONCLUSION

The integrative ecosystemic supervisory model links an integrative theory of family change to a supervisory model. Our model incorporates the many factors, directions, and dynamics characteristic of family systems. It allows consideration of the complexity of the contexts in which we practice. It keeps us focused and thereby expands our vision to a holistic view of the supervisory system.

REFERENCES

APONTE, H. J. (1994). How personal can training get? *Journal of Marital and Family Therapy, 20,* 3–15.

BREUNLIN, D., LIDDLE, H. A., & SCHWARTZ, R. (1988). Concurrent training of supervisors and therapists. In H. A. Liddle, D. C. Breunlin, & R. C. Schwartz (Eds.), *Handbook of family therapy training and supervision* (pp. 207–224). New York: Guilford Press.

BREUNLIN, D. C., KARRER, B., McGUIRE, E., & CIMMARUSTI, R. (1988). Cybernetics of videotape supervision. In H. A. Liddle, D. C. Breunlin, & R. C. Schwartz (Eds.), *Handbook of family therapy training and supervision* (pp. 194–206). New York: Guilford Press.

BRONFENBRENNER, U. (1979). *The ecology of human development.* Cambridge, MA: Harvard University Press.

BRONFENBRENNER, U., & CECI, S. (1994). Nature-nurture reconceptualized in developmental perspective: A bioecological model. *Psychological Review, 101,* 568–586.

BUBOLZ, M. M., & SONTAG, S. M. (1993). Human ecology theory. In Boss, P. G., Doherty, W. J., La Rossa, R., Schumm, W. R., & Steinmeiz, S. K. (Eds.), *Sourcebook of family theories and methods: A contextual approach* (pp. 419–450). New York: Plenum.

FALICOV, C. (1988). Learning to think culturally. In H. A. Liddle, D. C. Breunlin, & R. C. Schwartz (Eds.), *Handbook of family therapy training and supervision* (pp. 335–357). New York: Guilford Press.

FALICOV, C. (1995). Training to think culturally: A multidimensional comparative framework. *Family Process, 34,* 373–388.

FORD, D., & LERNER, R. (1992). *Developmental systems theory: An integrative approach.* Newbury Park, CA: Sage Publications.

FRIEDMAN, S. (1991). *The new language of change.* New York: Guilford Press.

LIDDLE, H. A. (1988). Systemic supervision: Conceptual overlays and pragmatic guidelines. In H. A. Liddle, D. C. Breunlin, & R. C. Schwartz (Eds.), *Handbook of family therapy training and supervision* (pp. 153–171). New York: Guilford Press.

NICHOLS, W. C. (1988). An integrative psychodynamic and systems approach. In H. A. Liddle, D. C. Breunlin, & R. C. Schwartz (Eds.), *Handbook of family therapy training and supervision* (pp. 110–127). New York: Guilford Press.

PAPERO, D. (1988). Training in Bowen therapy. In H. A. Liddle, D. C. Breunlin, & R. C. Schwartz (Eds.), *Handbook of family therapy training and supervision* (pp. 62–77). New York: Guilford Press.

PITTA, P. (1996, Winter). An integrated supervisory model. *The Family Psychologist,* 16–18.

QUINN, W. (1996). The client speaks out: Three domains of meaning. *Journal of Family Psychotherapy, 7*(2), 71–83.

ROBERTS, H. (1992). Contextual supervision. *The Supervision Bulletin, V*(3), 1–2.

SCHWARTZ, R. C., LIDDLE, H. A., & BREUNLIN, D. C. (1988). Muddles in live supervision. In H. A. Liddle, D. C. Breunlin, & R. C. Schwartz (Eds.), *Handbook of family therapy training and supervision* (pp. 183–189). New York: Guilford Press.

STORM, C. (1991). Changing the line: An interview with Edwin Friedman. *The Supervision Bulletin, IV*(3), 1–2.

TAIBBI, R. (1993). The way of the supervisor: Facing fear, rigidity, power, and death. *Family Therapy Networker, 17*(3), 50–55.

TOMM, K. (1993). Defining supervision and therapy: A fuzzy boundary? *The Supervision Bulletin, VI*(1), 2.

WHITE, S., & RUSSELL, C. (1995). The essential elements of supervisory systems: A modified delphi study. *Journal of Marriage and Family Therapy, 21*, 33–53.

Index